THE SONG OF SONGS
The Soul and the Divine Beloved

Born in 1944, John Davidson has had a lifelong interest in mysticism. Graduating in 1966 from Cambridge University with an honours degree in natural sciences, he worked for seventeen years at the University's Department of Applied Mathematics and Theoretical Physics.

In 1984, he left the University to pursue independent interests, and since then has written a number of books, including a series on science and mysticism. The present book is the fifth in a series on Christian origins, following on from his ground-breaking work, *The Gospel of Jesus: In Search of His Original Teachings.*

BY THE SAME AUTHOR

On Science and Mysticism

Subtle Energy (1987)
The Web of Life (1988)
The Secret of the Creative Vacuum (1989)
Natural Creation and the Formative Mind (1991)
Natural Creation or Natural Selection? (1992)

On Christian Origins

The Robe of Glory (1992)
The Gospel of Jesus (1995, revised 2004)
The Prodigal Soul (2004)
The Divine Romance (2004)
The Odes of Solomon (2004)

THE SONG OF SONGS

The Soul and the Divine Beloved

John Davidson

cb

CLEAR BOOKS

First published in Great Britain in 2004 by
Clear Press Limited,
Unit 136, 3 Edgar Buildings
George Street, Bath BA1 2FJ
www.clearpress.co.uk

Designed by Rick Fry and John Davidson
Typeset by John Davidson
Cover design by Jerry Goldie
Printed in India by Ajanta Offset

British Library Cataloguing in
Publication data available

Library of Congress Cataloging in
Publication data available

ISBN 1–904555–10–1

DEDICATION

To the Divine Beloved

My Beloved went down to his garden,
To the beds of spices,
To pasture his flock in the gardens
And gather lilies.

My Beloved is mine and I am his.
He pastures his flock among the lilies.
Song of Songs *6:2–3, JB*

You who dwell in the gardens,
The companions listen for your voice;
Deign to let me hear it.
Song of Songs *8:13, JB*

ACKNOWLEDGEMENTS

This work would not have been possible without the prior work of many scholars.

Biblical passages are drawn mostly from the *Authorized King James Version* and *The Jerusalem Bible*. Extracts from *The Jerusalem Bible*, published and copyright © 1966, 1967 and 1968 by Doubleday (USA & Canada), a division of Random House Inc., and by Darton, Longman & Todd (rest of the world) are reprinted by permission of the publishers.

Passages from Origen's commentary on the *Song of Songs* are from *Origen: The Song of Songs, Commentary and Homilies,* Ancient Christian Writers, no. 26, tr. and annotated R.P. Lawson, copyright © 1957, published by Newman Press, Westminster, Maryland / Mahwah, New Jersey, 1957, and are used by permission of the Paulist Press (www.paulistpress.com).

Excerpts from *The Guide of the Perplexed* by Moses Maimonides are from the translation of Shlomo Pines (*The Guide of the Perplexed*, Chicago, 1963), and are reproduced by permission of University of Chicago Press.

Extracts from:

The Love of God by St Francis de Sales are from the translation by Vincent Kerns (*The Love of God: A Treatise by Saint Francis de Sales;* Burns and Oates, London, 1962).

Spiritual Canticle, The Ascent of Mount Carmel and *The Living Flame of Love* by St John of the Cross are from the translation of E.A. Peers (*Complete Works of St John of the Cross;* Burns and Oates, London, 1964, first published 1935).

On Canticles by Gregory of Nyssa were translated by H. Musurillo (*From Glory to Glory: Texts From Gregory of Nyssa's Mystical Writings;* Charles Scribners' Sons, New York, 1961; John Murray, London, 1962).

The Odes of Solomon are from *The Odes of Solomon: Mystical Songs from the Time of Jesus* (Clear Books, Bath, 2004) by John Davidson.

The Treatise of the Pool by 'Obadyah Maimonides are drawn from the translation of P. Fenton (*The Treatise of the Pool;* Octagon, London, 1981).

Bernard of Clairvaux's *On the Song of Songs* are from the translation of K. Walsh and I.M. Edmonds (*The Works of Bernard of Clairvaux, On the Song of Songs,* 4 vols.; vol. 1: Irish University Press, Shannon, 1971; vols. 2–4: Cistercian Publications, Kalamazoo, Michigan, 1976, 1979, 1980).

The Ladder of Perfection by Walter Hilton are from the translation by L. Sherley-Price (*The Ladder of Perfection,* Penguin, London, 1988).

The *Zohar* are drawn from the translations of D. Goldstein, F. Lachower and Isaiah Tishby (*The Wisdom of the Zohar,* Oxford University Press, Oxford, 1989) and Gershom Scholem (*The Zohar: The Book of Splendour;* Rider, 1977, first published 1949).

The Manichaean Psalm Book and the Mandaean Prayer Book are modernized adaptations of the original translations, respectively, of C.R.C. Allberry (*A Manichaean Psalm-Book,* Part II; Kohlhammer, Stuttgart, 1938) and E.S. Drower (*The Canonical Prayerbook of the Mandaeans;* E.J. Brill Academic Publishers, Leiden, The Netherlands, 1959).

The Nag Hammadi Codices are drawn from *Nag Hammadi Studies* XI: *Nag Hammadi Codices V,2–5 and VI,* ed. Douglas M. Parrott, 1979; *Nag Hammadi Studies* XX: *Nag Hammadi Codex II,2–7,* vol. 1, ed. Bentley Layton, 1989; *Nag Hammadi Studies* XXI: *Nag Hammadi Codex II,2–7,* vol. 2, ed. Bentley Layton, 1989; and *Nag Hammadi Studies* XXX: *Nag Hammadi Codex VII, XIII,* ed. Birger A. Pearson, 1996, all published by E.J. Brill Academic Publishers, Leiden, The Netherlands.

The *Acts of Thomas* are modernizations and collations of the translations of M.R. James (in *The Apocryphal New Testament;* Oxford University Press, Oxford, 1989 [1924]) and W.R. Wright (in *The Apocryphal Acts of the Apostles;* Williams and Norgate, Edinburgh, 1871).

The precise sources of these and other excerpts are provided in the relevant notes and references.

We have done our best to track down all the relevant copyright holders or administrators for all material for which it appeared copyright permission would be required. In the event of any errors or omissions, please advise us so that matters may be rectified.

I am also grateful to a number of friends who have been through the manuscript making various valuable suggestions, in particular, Miriam Caravella, Mousson Finnigan, Judith Handelsman, Geoff Wade, and Elwanda Whitten.

CONTENTS

Acknowledgements   vii

Introduction   1

PART I – ORIGINS AND BACKGROUND

1. The Setting of the *Song*   7

   A Most Obscure Book   7
   Dates, Authors and Authenticity   11
   The *Song of Songs* and the Ancient Wisdom   14
   The Soul, the Saviour and the Universal Mystic Teachings   19
   The Saviour and the Creative Word   23
   The Lover and the Beloved – the Disciple and the Master   25
   The Bride and the Bridegroom   30

2. The Symbolism of the *Song*   34

   A Rosetta Stone to Mystic Symbolism   34
   Mystic Symbols in the *Song of Songs*   36
   A Veiled but Universal Language   43
   Two Kinds of Parable   48
   Jewish and Hebrew Symbolism   51
   Early Echoes of the *Song*   52
   Four Levels of Meaning   56
   The Content of the *Song of Songs*   69

PART II – THE SONG

Title and Prologue:
    Your Love is more Delightful than Wine   79

    The Song of Solomon   80
    The Kisses of his Mouth   81
    More Delightful than Wine   83
    The Fragrance of your Perfume   84
    Your Name is an Oil   85
    In your Footsteps   88
    Into your Chambers   90
    How Right it is to Love you   91

First Poem: I am Black but Lovely   93

    Take no Notice of my Swarthiness   96
    My Mother's Sons   98
    Where will you Lead your Flock?   100
    Like a Vagabond   103
    The Tracks of the Flock   104
    Your Cheeks show Fair   105
    A Sachet of Myrrh   107
    Your Eyes are Doves   109
    All Green is our Bed   111
    Beams of Cedar   112
    The Rose of Sharon   114
    A Lily among Thistles   114
    His Longed-for Shade   115
    In his Banquet Hall   118
    His Right Arm Embraces me   121
    Until it Please to Awake   122

Second Poem: I Hear my Beloved   125

  See how he Comes   128
  Come then, my Love   130
  Show me your Face   135
  Catch the Little Foxes   136
  He Pastures his Flock   137
  On the Spicy Mountains   138
  On my Bed at Night   139
  I Will Seek Him   142
  I Found him whom my Heart Loves   143
  Until It Please to Awake   145

Third Poem: Who is this Coming Up from the Desert?   149

  Like a Column of Smoke   154
  Veterans of Battle   156
  A Throne of Wood from Lebanon   158
  Crowned with a Diadem   160
  How Beautiful you are   162
  Wholly Beautiful   163
  To the Mountain of Myrrh   166
  The Haunt of Lions   167
  What Spells Lie in your Love   170
  How Delicious is your Love   171
  She is a Garden Enclosed   174
  Fountain that Makes the Gardens Fertile   176
  Let my Beloved Come into his Garden   178
  Eat, Friends, and Drink   180

Fourth Poem: I Sleep, but my Heart is Awake   183

    My Heart is Awake   186
    I Hear my Beloved Knocking   188
    My Head is Covered with Dew   189
    I have Taken off my Tunic   191
    The Hole in the Door   194
    The Watchmen Came upon me   197
    Sick with Love   199
    What makes your Beloved better?   200
    His Appearance as Lebanon   201
    Altogether Lovable   205
    Where did your Beloved go?   207
    Among the Lilies   207

Fifth Poem: I Went Down to the Nut Orchard   211

    Fair as Jerusalem   216
    Your Eyes Hold me Captive   217
    Countless Maidens   218
    My Dove is Unique   219
    I went Down to the Nut Orchard   220
    If the Vines were Budding   222
    As their Prince   223
    A Dance of Two Camps   224
    O Prince's Daughter   225
    The Work of a Master Hand   226
    A Heap of Wheat   227
    An Ivory Tower   228
    The Pools of Heshbon   229
    The Tower of Lebanon   229

A King is Held Captive   230
In Stature like the Palm Tree   231
Your Breath Sweet-Scented as Apples   232
Wine Flowing Straight to my Beloved   234
I am my Beloved's   235
Let us Go to the Fields   236
We will Go to the Vineyards   236
The Gift of My Love   238
Why are you not my Brother?   239
Into my Mother's House   240
His Right Arm Embraces me   241
Until it Please to Awake   242

Finale: Who is this Coming Up from the Desert?   243

Leaning on her Beloved   244
Under the Apple Tree   244
Like a Seal on your Heart   245
Love is Strong as Death   247
Love no Flood can Quench   248

Epilogue: You who Dwell in the Gardens   251

Deign to let me Hear It   252

Notes and References   255

Abbreviations   265

Bibliography   269

INTRODUCTION

The *Song of Songs* is the third in a series of three books concerned with the interpretation of ancient parables and allegories from biblical and early Christian times. Following on from *The Prodigal Soul* and *The Divine Romance,* it consists of an introduction to and an allegorical, mystical interpretation of the biblical *Song of Songs,* a suite of interlinking poems also called *Canticles* or the *Song of Solomon.*

The *Song of Songs* is characterized by its colourful and ample imagery. However it is interpreted, no one denies that this is so. In fact, the meaning given to the *Song* as a whole is determined by the interpretation of its many metaphors and allusions. But such imagery can be understood in many ways. It seems appropriate therefore, to provide some support for the mystical interpretation suggested.

Help is certainly at hand, for the metaphors found in the *Song* have been used extensively in the mystic literature of the ancient Middle East, where their meaning is often more explicit. There are also a great many references to and a number of full-scale commentaries on the *Song of Songs* by Jewish and Christian mystics. All these greatly aid our understanding and reinforce the mystical point of view. But how to convey this information in a concise and digestible fashion, so as to impart confidence that the interpretation has a secure foundation?

My primary aim is to bring out the spiritual meaning of this suite of poems for the ordinary reader, and to convey something of its beauty. Bearing this in mind, I have kept the commentary as simple as possible, interweaving it with supporting passages from other sources. Many of these quotations are simply too beautiful or too pertinent to omit. Two introductory chapters are also provided to help set the scene.

Those wanting an even more complete picture of ancient mystic metaphor could refer to my more extensive, *The Gospel of Jesus: In Search of His Original Teachings,* along with two books on ancient parables and allegories *(The Prodigal Soul* and *The Divine Romance),* and another containing the collection of early Christian mystical poems known as *The Odes of Solomon.* Numerous examples are given in these books that further illuminate the meaning of the metaphorical language of mysticism in the ancient Middle East. Anyone wanting to delve even more extensively into the mystical terminology of the world's spiritual and religious traditions, could try the multivolume, *A Treasury of Mystic Terms.*

An interpretation of poetry and an attempt to uncover its meaning is not an exact science. Science attempts to define meaning; poetry suggests or conveys meaning, often at a variety of 'levels', simultaneously. In the case of the *Song,* this meaning is rich and abundant. This is the power of metaphor and imagery over rational and philosophical exposition. But it makes the task of the commentator more challenging. For when one meaning is given, it can appear to exclude others, while if an attempt is made to express something of all the meanings, the commentary becomes in danger of taking on the character of an unintelligible bramble bush.

In the interests of readability, I have tried to pursue a middle course, but I do not suggest that the whole of the meaning is conveyed by my commentary. Actually, the meaning lies in the original Hebrew poetry, not in any interpretation or translation, however accurate. In fact, the real meaning lay in the mind and experience of the unknown poet who wrote so long ago. That being so, any commentary can only be considered as a personal interpretation and a guide for readers. If someone has alternative suggestions, then that is to be expected. Among the numerous extant commentaries, there are many variant viewpoints.

Regarding the supplementary quotations used and their translations, there are occasions when the intended mystic meaning seems clear, but it has not been adequately conveyed. Sometimes, the simple capitalization of a word makes all the difference. God, for example, could not be expected to have manifested the creation with a human 'word'. But if we write 'Word' – meaning his creative Power or Emanation – we have a statement with which many mystics throughout the ages would agree.

In instances of this sort, and where supported by the full context, I have taken the liberty of either very lightly editing the text, or of adding explanatory words in parentheses. I have also tended to modernize old-fashioned English.

In a very few cases, where a number of scholarly translations are available of some particular text, I have combined them, indicating this by a reference to the various sources consulted. Also, because of the variety of typographic styles found in the many quotations, I have standardized the layout, as well as the spelling and punctuation. The aim has always been to help convey meaning with clarity, lucidity and simplicity.

Any significant clarifications or additions to a translation offered by myself or the original translator have been placed in round brackets, while significant conjectured words or phrases, usually provided by the original translator to fill gaps in an original, defective manuscript, appear in square brackets ([ ]). Where translations used have been edited for any of the above reasons, this is indicated by the use of *cf.* in the source reference.

The translation used for the *Song of Songs* is that of the *Jerusalem Bible*. To my mind, this is the most lyrical of all the English versions. I have also consulted many other references, translations, commentaries and studies of the *Song of Songs* – some ancient, some modern, some Christian, some Jewish, some interesting, some bizarre, some mystical, some profane. Many of these are listed in the Bibliography. Should the reader feel so inclined, he could therefore pursue his own line of research.

The *Song of Songs* is set as a dialogue between a Lover and her Beloved, with further additions from a 'chorus' of devotees, as well as from the poet him or herself. Few renderings, however, offer any help as to which character is speaking, something which does not always become clear even from a careful study of both the context as well as the original language.[1] Together with the poem's symbolism, this can sometimes combine to make translated texts more or less impenetrable.

The original Hebrew is more helpful since the speaker can often (but not always) be ascertained from the gender of various words. But even then, as becomes clear from a brief discussion of the problem in the Jewish *Mishnah*,[2] dating from the late second century AD, there was doubt even two thousand years ago as to who was speaking, for a 'he' can easily become a 'she' in transcription or oral transmission.

It is not surprising, then, that the various translations and commentaries sometimes differ as to who is speaking, and there is ample precedent for the few instances where I have differed with the translators of the *Jerusalem Bible*.

In the *Jerusalem Bible,* as a help to the reader, the translators have added the subheadings 'The Bride', 'The Bridegroom' and 'The Chorus'. However, they could equally well have used 'The Lover' and 'The Beloved', as in the *New Jerusalem Bible* and the *New English Bible*. Being marginally more modern in character, the latter designations have been adopted here. Either way, the metaphors of the Bride or Lover and the Bridegroom or Beloved have been used by mystics of all nationalities and ages to symbolize the love of the soul for the divine Beloved, and any combination would have served the purpose just as well.

Human work is rarely perfect. In this instance, the opportunity for error is magnified by the variants and uncertainties of some parts of the Hebrew text, obscurities in both the literal as well as metaphorical meaning of the original language, and the many possibilities suggested to the interpreter by the generous imagery of the *Song*.

Indeed, there can be no other biblical book which has generated such a wide variety of interpretations and studies. In the last century alone, scholars have produced a wealth of diverse studies, commentaries and translations. During this period, in keeping with modern attitudes concerning the relationship of man and woman, the weight of scholarly opinion has swung away from the allegorical and mystical interpretation. With the exception of some traditional Christian and Jewish interpreters, the *Song* is now generally seen as a eulogy of human love at a purely physical level.

Personally, I think that this is a step in the wrong direction, but it is not my intention to argue the mystical point of view in a philosophical manner. Spirituality is not so much a matter for debate, as for experience and practice. All the same, I have read through a great deal of the scholarly literature, where numerous interesting and illuminating points are raised. Even so, I remain unconvinced by many of the overall conclusions concerning the primary meaning of the *Song*.

But I have no personal axe to grind, either way. There is no particular underlying reason why I should defend the spiritual character of the *Song of Songs*. If the *Song* had struck me as a collection of ancient love lyrics or as a drama of competing human lovers, I would not have written this book. But when I read the *Song,* its mystical meaning seems to jump out of the pages. Therefore, I have tried to share something of the beauty and the spiritual meaning that I find in it. I will be happy if some of my readers are similarly inspired.

PART I

Origins and Background

ONE

The Setting of the Song

A Most Obscure Book

Few people would deny that many biblical books, especially those of the Old Testament, are at best difficult to understand and at worst downright unintelligible. Spanning a period of nearly one thousand years, biblical texts contain examples of literature written in many different styles. Some are allegorical or mythological, some seemingly historical or legendary, some purport to be prophetic, others are more instructive and discursive. In many of these writings, especially those of the earliest period, God seems to flit in and out of the pages more like an all-powerful and vengeful wizard than a divine and loving power. It has to be admitted, therefore, that much of the Bible – supposedly the basis of both Jewish and Christian faith – is very difficult for anybody in modern times to truly comprehend.

So much depends upon individual or particular religious interpretation – on the tinted glasses of belief and dogma through which we view these texts. Nevertheless, some biblical books have always posed greater difficulties than others. Among these is the *Song of Songs*.

Sometimes dubbed the most obscure book in the Bible, mystics and the spiritually minded – for more than two millennia – have expressed their belief that the *Song of Songs* is a mystic dialogue between a Lover and her divine Beloved. Many of the Jewish Rabbis of old – in both early Christian as well as medieval, Kabbalistic times – have endorsed this view. They have pointed out that its correct interpretation is allegorical and that its meaning is entirely mystical in character. Many Christian writers, too, including both the early fathers as well as later mystics, have also reached the same conclusion. It is for this reason that the *Song of Songs* is an accepted part of both Jewish and Christian sacred literature. Yet, its exact and complete interpretation has always remained something of a mystery and a matter of debate. There is not even complete agreement as to who is represented by the Lover and the Beloved.

It is certain that whatever interpretation is given to the *Song,* there will always be passages which remain of doubtful or multiple meaning. When interpreted literally, it is well nigh impossible to make a coherent story out of it. When understood metaphorically or allegorically, there are a number of possible meanings that can be given. Perhaps this was the intention of the unknown author, and the various levels of meaning within the *Song* are presently discussed. There is, however, another fundamental reason why not only the *Song,* but so much of the sacred and mystic literature of the world, is sometimes so difficult to understand.

In general, mystic literature is not a presentation of an intellectual, theological or theosophical system. It is a description of a living experience gained by persistent effort at spiritual practice, also called contemplation, recollection, interior or mystic prayer and by many other names. But unless a reader has some personal understanding or feeling for this kind of experience, the literature describing it will seem obscure. As many mystics have recognized, the *Song of Songs* describes mystical experience. It is not surprising, therefore, that it is those of a devotional and mystic trend of mind who have generally found the greatest inspiration in it. They have understood something of the experience, while those of a more scholarly or theological bent of mind have been baffled by it.

Mystical experience, however, can be of many kinds, and a close study has led me to the conclusion that the experiences, feelings, allusions and general tone of the *Song of Songs* can best be understood as the intensely personal relationship that develops between a devoted soul and a living spiritual teacher or mystic of the highest order – a living Master or Saviour.

There are many cases on record of this high degree of pure and mystic love. We find it in the expressions of love between Jesus and his disciples, between the third-century Iranian mystic Mani and his disciples, in stories of the saintly Rabbis and their followers, between the later Sufi mystics like Rumi and Hafiz and their own spiritual Masters, and there are many other instances too. But unless a person has some inkling of the mystic nature and spiritual intensity of this kind of love, it is unlikely that they will realize that this is what is being described. Other interpretations – relating to the reader's own personal experience and thinking – will therefore be put forward in its place. A number of scholars, for example, when analysing the writings, sayings and love poetry of mystics, Jesus included, have even suggested that these mystics have advocated various perverse or licentious practices. Yet little could be further from the truth.

One of the purposes of this chapter, therefore, is to sketch something of the character of this mystic and transcendent love. For without some understanding of it, I do not think that the *Song of Songs* can ever be fully comprehended. There is no doubt about the existence of a love such as this. It is witnessed by the writings of a great many mystics. The only question is whether or not this is what the *Song* is all about.

Dates, Authors and Authenticity

A precise dating of the *Song of Songs* is difficult. It is a part of the *Septuagint,* the Greek translation of the Bible made in the third century BC. Josephus, the great Jewish historian of the first century AD, speaks of it,[1] and it is mentioned by some of the early Christian fathers who clearly regarded it as an established text. This indicates that the latest date of authorship would have been in the third century BC. But the earliest date remains a matter of dispute.

Bearing in mind its possible historic allusions, the *Song* is generally dated some time after the return of the Israelites from Babylonian exile late in the sixth century BC, some 2500 years ago. The presence of two Persian loan-words in the *Song* probably indicates that it was written after the founding and expansion of the Persian empire in the sixth century BC. Scholars have varied in their opinions, however. While some have dated the *Song* as late as the third century BC, others have claimed that at least parts of it were written as early as the ninth.

The geographical references and place names in the *Song* largely reflect a background of the Northern Kingdom of Israel before its destruction by the Assyrians in 721 BC. This could indicate an early date. The southern kingdom of Judah is represented only by the "daughters of Zion",[2] the "daughters of Jerusalem",[3] and by the mention of Engedi which lies on the borders of the Dead Sea.[4] There are also some linguistic features of the *Song* which suggest an early date. But conclusions based on this kind of evidence are unreliable. For purely literary reasons, the poet could have adopted a linguistic style and a historical setting prior to his own time. Furthermore, poetic language is often archaic, as well as unusual, in character.

The truth is that so little is known of the social history of ancient Israel, and the extant evidence is so slight and open to interpretation, that no certain conclusions can be drawn concerning an exact dating of the *Song*. Nevertheless, the general consensus places it between the fifth and third centuries BC.

The matter is made more complex by a lively debate as to whether the *Song* was all written at the same time, by the same author. Although some scholars have argued against this, there is considerable evidence that it was. The writer has a unique and recognizable style that is present throughout. The refrains that recur in different parts of the *Song*, the consistent but idiosyncratic use of similar or identical metaphors, the characteristic and identifiable wordplay, assonance, rhythm and similar poetic devices — all these point to one author. Moreover, the *Song* has one underlying theme and meaning. In fact, an unfolding and development of this theme can be discerned, as we will see. All this points to a unity of composition and authorship.

In common with many other biblical documents, however, there is no reliable historical information as to who wrote the *Song*. It is not even clear whether it was written by a man or a woman. In fact, though traditionally attributed to Solomon, who the author was remains a complete mystery. Nobody actually has the slightest idea at all.

Like all ancient documents, the text of the *Song of Songs* has undergone a history of copying and recopying by a variety of scribes – some professional, some amateur, some careless, some tired, some who understood it, some who did not – and all liable to human error. It may have had additions made and parts removed or repositioned, according to the inclinations and beliefs of these copyists. Some scribes, themselves with literary aspirations, may have attempted to 'improve' the text or to recast it according to their own beliefs. Some may have attempted to undo the assumed 'errors' of previous copyists. This has been the fate of the Hebrew and Greek texts, as we now have them. Consequently, there are some significant differences of detail between the Hebrew, in which the *Song* was originally composed, and the Greek of the *Septuagint*. Which is the more correct is often difficult to determine because the oldest Greek and Hebrew texts we have today are both dated so many centuries after their originals were written.

It is possible, therefore, that some of the text has been altered or obscured. There are certainly places where the details of the original text are unsure. However, almost miraculously, the meaning can usually be determined – at least in general terms, and usually in particulars. Poetry probably fares better than prose over the course of time since well-loved poetry becomes familiar to large numbers of people, and attempted tamperings with the text are more readily observed and remedied. Moreover, the *Song*'s distinctive style is such that it would have been difficult to edit or add portions without it being immediately noticeable. Allegorical texts are also generally simpler and easier to translate meaningfully than philosophical or mystical treatises.

The Song of Songs and the Ancient Wisdom

Although an accepted part of the canon in both Jewish and Christian Bibles, it is a strange fact that nowhere does the *Song of Songs* refer explicitly to God or even to mystical or spiritual matters. In fact, in a number of places, the poet quite intentionally mimics the style of ancient Egyptian and Semitic love lyrics. Only on a few occasions is a term (soul) used that can be understood as spiritual or mystical. The Lover speaks of "he whom my soul loves", for instance. But even this is translated as "he whom my heart loves" in the *Jerusalem Bible,* although the actual Hebrew word *(nefesh)* is more accurately rendered as 'soul' or 'being'.[5] Even so – by tradition – the *Song* has always been placed along with a body of mystical, spiritual and moral writings known collectively as Wisdom literature. This includes *Proverbs, Ecclesiastes,* the *Psalms, Job,* the *Wisdom of Solomon* and the *Wisdom of Jesus Ben Sirach (Ecclesiasticus).*[6]

Wisdom literature, comprised of sayings, axioms, pithy observations on life, fables, parables and anecdotes has been produced in all Middle Eastern and neighbouring countries for as long as records exist, for human beings have always needed and appreciated guidance on how to live. Egypt, Greece, Palestine, Syria, Mesopotamia, Iran and other countries have all contributed, and some texts can be dated as far back as the third millennium BC. Some of this is less mystical than others, of course, but much of that found in the Bible gives expression to the highest mystical truths.

The word 'Wisdom' is translated from the Greek, *Sophia,* and the Hebrew, *Hokhmah.* Reading through the biblical Wisdom literature, it becomes clear that the term has two meanings. Firstly, it refers to the spiritual wisdom or teachings, the esoteric description of the inner path and its practice, as well as the best advice on leading a spiritual life in this world while seeking God within oneself.

Secondly, Wisdom is the creative Power of God. Here it is identical with the *Logos* or Creative Word of God, the Power by which mystics say that God has created and continually sustains the creation. This understanding is borne out by the more detailed research of many scholars, both Christian and Jewish, but one has only to read certain passages from the Wisdom literature for the matter to become clear. In *Proverbs,* for instance, in a passage probably stemming from around the fifth century BC – following a literary custom of the times – Wisdom speaks directly:

> Yahweh created me when his purpose first unfolded,
>   before the oldest of his works.
> From everlasting I was firmly set,
>   from the beginning, before the earth came into being.
>
> The deep was not, when I was born,
>   there were no springs to gush with water.
> Before the mountains were settled,
>   before the hills, I came to birth;
> Before he made the earth, the countryside,
>   or the first grains of the world's dust.
> When he fixed the heavens firm, I was there,
>   when he drew a ring on the surface of the deep,
>   when he thickened the clouds above,
>   when he fixed fast the springs of the deep,
>   when he assigned the sea its boundaries, …
>   when he laid down the foundations of the earth –
> I was by his side, a master craftsman,
>   delighting him day after day,
>   ever at play in his presence,
>   at play everywhere in his world,
>   delighting to be with the sons of men.
>
> *Proverbs 8:22–31, JB*

Here it is clear that Wisdom is God's creative Power. Expanding upon the theme, in the *Wisdom of Solomon,* a Greek composition probably dating from the first century BC, there are some beautiful passages concerning the nature of Wisdom. Being a

feminine noun in both Greek and Hebrew, Wisdom is referred
to here as "she":

> For she is within herself a spirit intelligent, holy,
>> unique, manifold, subtle,
>> active, incisive, unsullied,
>> lucid, invulnerable, benevolent, sharp,
>> irresistible, beneficent, loving to man,
>> steadfast, dependable, unperturbed,
>> almighty, all-surveying,
>> penetrating all, intelligent,
>> pure and most subtle spirits;
> For Wisdom is quicker to move than any motion;
> She is so pure she pervades and permeates all things.
>
> She is a breath of the Power of God,
>> pure emanation of the glory of the Almighty;
> Hence nothing impure can find a way into her.
> She is a reflection of the eternal Light,
>> untarnished mirror of God's active Power,
>> image of his goodness.
>
> Although alone, she can do all;
> Herself unchanging, she makes all things new.
> In each generation she passes into holy souls,
>> she makes them Friends of God and prophets;
> For God loves only the man who lives with Wisdom.
>
> She is indeed more splendid than the sun,
>> she outshines all the constellations;
> Compared with light she takes first place,
>> for light must yield to night;
> But over Wisdom, evil can never triumph.
> She deploys her strength
> from one end of the earth to the other,
>> ordering all things for good.
>
> *Wisdom of Solomon 7:22–30, 8:1, JB*

The "Friends of God and prophets" are truly "holy souls", says the writer. Wisdom has made them into Masters or Saviours, the real Messengers and Prophets of the Divine. The reference to mystics as the "Friends of God" has been a common metaphor in the Middle East in both ancient and more recent times.

It is clear from these two passages alone that Wisdom is far more than the heights of human understanding. The one stems from the other, no doubt, but the former is the primal emanation of God, the latter arises from an awareness of its indwelling presence. Wisdom is the essence of Truth, Beauty, Reality and Being – all meant in a mystic sense – while true human wisdom is the reflection of these qualities at the human level.

The traditional inclusion of the *Song of Songs* among literature which is explicitly mystical in content is an indication of its hidden meaning, and the way it was understood in ancient times. Additionally, the *Song* is credited to the pen of Solomon, the archetypal wise king of Jewish history, who probably lived during the tenth century BC, and was held to have been Israel's greatest sage. Solomon is also one of the characters who appears in the *Song of Songs*, cast in the role of the divine Beloved. Over a period spanning more than a millennium, many mystic writings were ascribed to him, not as forgeries, but simply to inform the reader of their content and the ancient mystical tradition to which they belonged. Two major portions of *Proverbs*, together with *Ecclesiastes* and the *Wisdom of Solomon* are attributed to Solomon, for instance, though *Ecclesiastes* was written in Hebrew sometime between the fifth and third centuries BC, and the *Wisdom of Solomon* was written in Greek during the first century BC. Even as late as early Christian times, an unknown hand penned the deeply devotional and mystic poems called the *Odes of Solomon*. No one suggests that they were written by Solomon himself, nor did the writer intend anyone to believe this. It was simply a way of indicating that the contents were of a mystic nature.

Solomon's legendary wisdom is described in *1 Kings:*

Yahweh gave Solomon immense wisdom and understanding,
  and a heart as vast as the sand on the seashore.
The wisdom of Solomon surpassed the wisdom
  of the sons of the East, and all the wisdom of Egypt.
He was wiser than any other, ...
  he composed three thousand proverbs,
  and his songs numbered a thousand and five....
Men from all nations came to hear Solomon's wisdom.

1 Kings 5:9–14, JB

Solomon's understanding is compared to the wisdom of Egypt, traditionally regarded as the ancient repository of mystic lore. The identification of wisdom with mystic insight is thus underlined. It is noteworthy, too, how such wisdom overcomes all human barriers: "Men from all nations came to hear Solomon's wisdom." Truly wise men can be – indeed are and have been – from every race and culture. Transcending all human limitations, they are the ones who have experienced the universal mystic Reality within themselves. From them, all superficiality, pretension or artifice is absent. What they have to offer is fundamental to humanity. It is basic to our inner human constitution. It lies beyond all narrow boundaries of country, race or religion.

Solomon's wisdom is similarly described in the *Wisdom of Jesus Ben Sirach*. Addressing Solomon, the writer says:

How wise you were in your youth,
  brimming over with understanding like a river!
Your mind ranged the earth,
  you filled it with mysterious sayings.
Your name reached the distant islands,
  and you were loved for your peace.
Your songs, your proverbs, your sayings
  and your retorts made you the wonder of the world.

Wisdom of Jesus Ben Sirach 47:14–18, JB

The Soul, the Saviour and the Universal Mystic Teachings

It is, then, in the tradition of the Wisdom literature that the *Song of Songs* has been composed. It is a dialogue, as we have said, between the Lover and her Beloved. In the interpretation of the present commentary, the Lover is the soul and her divine Beloved is the Lord, the Master or Saviour.

In the mystic literature of the Middle East, there are many references – in many different ancient languages – to the Saviour. He is called the Redeemer, the Helper, the Brother, the Messenger, the true Apostle of God, the divine Man, the Son of God, and so on. Alluding to the many parables and examples used by mystics, he is also known as the Shepherd, the Protector, the Helmsman, the Gardener, the Fisherman, the Sower of the Seed, the Treasurer, the King, the Standing (Existing) One, the Living One, and by many other names. In modern times, in the English language, such a Son of God has been called a living Master or a perfect Master, and the same age-old mystic teachings are still being taught and practised.

Christians tend to believe that only Jesus is credited with having been a Saviour. This, however, is incorrect, as even a brief study of the ancient literature will demonstrate. Jesus was neither the first, the last, nor the only Saviour. He was one in a long line of divine Redeemers, each held by their followers to have been as great as every other. The advocates of the various religions tend to believe that only the Saviour or Saviours to whom they give their allegiance were divinely appointed Saviours of humanity. But this is a very narrow outlook. Why should God be so merciful and loving to just one generation, in one part of the world, from one tiny slice of history, ignoring all other people? It makes little sense. It seems altogether out of character with the actions one would expect of an all-loving and all-powerful, universal supreme Being, and more in keeping with the narrow-mindedness and partisan beliefs of sectarian and divisive human beings!

It is necessary for an understanding of the commentary which

follows that the role and basic teachings ascribed to these
Saviours – whether one believes in them or not – are understood.
All these great mystics, ancient or modern, have said that God
and his creation lie within. They have taught that the soul is a
particle of God, a drop of his ocean, a flame of his fire, a ray of
his sun. They have all said, in one way or another, that the soul
is a child of divine origin who once lived in conscious union
with God, but who has been sent out into the creation by him.
Descending through a hierarchy of heavenly regions of decreas-
ing spirituality, she ultimately reaches the material realm. Once
here, she becomes absorbed in the play of life and forgets her
divine heritage. Content to struggle unhappily, she ekes out a
selfish existence amid the darkness, the struggle and the hell of
materiality.

There is a reason for the soul's unhappy state – while here, she
has become a victim of her own actions and mental processes.
All actions, thoughts and desires – good or bad – leave an
impression on the mind. After death, although the physical body
disintegrates and returns to dust, the subtle impressions on the
mind continue to accompany the soul – and to demand fulfilment. The soul is therefore forced to take another birth in the
physical arena, where the process is repeated. The soul thus
revolves in a seemingly endless fashion in a cycle of birth, death
and rebirth. Under the influence of the mind, deeds are com-
mitted, the results of which have to be accounted for in future
lives. The deeds and desires of one life determine the fabric of
the next.

These actions and their resulting impressions on the mind
may be called the 'sins' of the individual, but the term is being
used in a 'technical', mystic sense, with a far wider spread of
meaning than its common usage in religion. To begin with, it
does not carry the moralistic overtones of the latter. To the
mystic, morality and a spiritual way of life are both essential and
natural, but they are not ends in themselves; nor are they a
platform from which to condemn others or feel superior to

them. The leading of what is generally termed a good life is personal, and is the natural outcome of the quest for God within.

Now, according to these mystics, the 'sins' that lead to rebirth are the result of both good *and* bad actions and thoughts. Good 'sins' bear good fruit in future lives, while bad 'sins' bring misery in their wake. But, good or bad, it is these sins which keep a soul separate from God. Sin may therefore be defined as that which keeps a soul away from God. In the mystic context, sin is thus equivalent to karma, which simply means 'action' – good or bad. The law of karma is the natural law of justice – cause and effect – by which souls receive their just deserts and are led from birth to birth.

The devil, incidentally – who figures so prominently in Judaism, Christianity and Islam – is essentially the force of negativity within our own minds. 'He' is also the administrator of sin, the force that balances the equations of karma, ensuring that everything is accounted for in the greater scheme of things.

In this analysis, a human being is considered as consisting of the divine spark of the soul, the intermediate agency of the mind, and the physical covering of the body. Though people may seek their identity in their body or mind, mystics say that the real self is the soul. The soul, then, becomes entangled with the mind and the senses, and is held captive in the physical body under the law of karma or sin, reaping in one life what she sowed in the past. This is the true nature of God's justice. It is also the mystic meaning of the Lord's 'anger' or 'wrath'.

The Lord, however, has not forgotten the soul and, from the sublime heights of eternity, a divine Messenger or Saviour is sent to rescue her and bring her back to her eternal home, once more to be united consciously with him. This is the role of the Saviour and, from a mystical viewpoint, this is the real meaning of salvation or redemption. It is a state of being or consciousness attainable even during this life. As St Gregory the Great (*c.*540– 604) says:

> The saints enter eternity even in this life,
>   beholding the eternity of God.
>
>   *St Gregory the Great, Morals 8, in CWJC1 p.117*

Incidentally, there is considerable evidence that reincarnation was a part of the mysteries or secret teachings in many of the mystic schools of the ancient Jewish, Roman and Hellenistic world. There is a well-known comment in the *Wisdom of Solomon* that suggests that the writer of this text held a belief in reincarnation about which he otherwise kept silent:

> I was a boy of happy disposition,
>   I had received a good soul as my lot,
>   or rather, being good, I had entered an undefiled body.
>
>   *Wisdom of Solomon 8:19–20, JB*

There are also possible allusions to reincarnation in the psalms attributed to the Teacher of Righteousness, found among the Dead Sea Scrolls.[7] Evidence also exists that the Pharisees in the time of Jesus gave some credence to the belief,[8] and it is well known that many of the gnostics of early Christianity firmly believed that Jesus had taught reincarnation.[9]

So although the *Song of Songs* does not allude to reincarnation, and a belief in it or otherwise makes little difference to the interpretation of the *Song*, there is no doubt that its writer would have been familiar with the idea and could easily have subscribed to it. The belief was widespread in Egypt and in the ancient Middle East and, indeed, in the Celtic and Druidic religious milieu of ancient Europe. It is mentioned here because the role ascribed to the Saviours cannot be fully appreciated without an understanding of this age-old doctrine.

Now it is a fact that this simple mystic teaching is universal. It is found among all races and cultures, of all epochs and eras, as only a little research in comparative religion will verify. There is a God, say the mystics – a universal mystic Reality. And there is a universal mystic teaching which describes this Reality and how to attain it.

There are many finer points and aspects to this mystic path that have often remained secret, known only to initiates, especially in the past. Moreover, the language and manner by which this teaching is expressed varies from time to time, from place to place, and from culture to culture, but not its essence. What we are identifying as the soul, for example, has sometimes been qualified as the 'immortal soul' or spirit, in contrast to the 'lower soul' or 'carnal soul' that we are calling the mind. Both the 'immortal soul' and the 'lower soul' have also been called the 'heart' of man. But these are only differences of nomenclature, and a study of the ancient literature reveals that the general and fundamental teachings have always remained the same.

When the mystics who give these teachings depart, then the real meaning gets lost, confused and diluted. In some instances, the teachings are synthesized with extant cultural and religious beliefs and customs, and a new sect emerges, as did Christianity as an off-shoot of Judaism. The human mind then comes into play and the reality is increasingly forgotten. By degrees, the inner spirituality evaporates, leaving only the outer shell of organization, ritual and dogma. The new sect may die out slowly or rapidly – or it may flourish. It depends upon the circumstances, the social and religious climate of the times and the character of the individuals involved, especially in the early stages. But whatever happens, it is never the purpose of the highest mystics to create sects, divisions and religions. This is the work of those who follow after.

The Saviour and the Creative Word

It is a characteristic of this universal mystic teaching, both of the past as well as present times, that the Messenger or Saviour sent from God to rescue the soul imprisoned in the physical realm is understood to be a personification or incarnation of the Creative Word or Wisdom of God. As many mystics have pointed out, the Lord has created the creation by means of his Word. This is the primal Power in creation, the "pure emanation of the glory of the Almighty".[10] It is the cosmic motor or primal vibration underlying all other movement and existence.

This Power has been given many names over the course of time, according to its characteristics. As regards the individual, perhaps the most significant of these characteristics is that it may be seen inwardly in mystic transport or meditation as divine light, and heard inwardly as divine sound or music. Consequently, the Word of God has been called the Voice of God or the Call of God. But the term has nothing to do with stentorian voices emanating from behind dark clouds or burning bushes! These are human literalizations of mystic teachings.

It is the practice of meditation upon this Power that lies at the heart of the teachings of a true Saviour. This primal Power, say the mystics, is one with God. The Saviour, Redeemer or perfect Master is also one with this creative Power, and hence with God. Indeed, the real Saviour or divine Beloved is not the physical, human form of a Master, but this creative Power itself, and it is through union with this Power that the soul can find her way back to God. But union, essentially, means love, and this divine love affair begins with the love of a human being for the Creative Word, humanly incarnate as a Master.

According to the *Wisdom of Solomon,* where Wisdom is synonymous with the Creative Word, there is always at least one such mystic somewhere in the world. We have already encountered this passage:

> In each generation she (Wisdom) passes into holy souls,
>   she makes them friends of God and prophets;
> For God loves only the man who lives with Wisdom.
>
> *Wisdom of Solomon 7:27–28, JB*

A Saviour, then, comes to this world as a personification of the Word of God. While here, he is the "light of the world"[11] for his disciples. And since God is an ocean of light and love, a living Master is also an ocean of light and love. It can perhaps be imagined, therefore, how a disciple might come to feel towards his or her Master. As Jesus Ben Sirach writes:

> If you see a man of understanding, visit him early,
>   let your feet wear out his doorstep.
>
> *Wisdom of Jesus Ben Sirach 6:36, JB*

A sincere disciple will always long to be with his Master, to see him and to hear him speak. It is this love that is so vividly portrayed in the *Song of Songs*.

The Lover and the Beloved – the Disciple and the Master

In world religions, the Saviour or Saviours being venerated have generally become so stylized and placed upon such a high pedestal that people have forgotten that their original disciples generally lived nearby and had close personal contact with them. They could listen to their words of wisdom, and be taught the techniques of spiritual practice and how to follow the mystic path. They could talk to them, laugh with them, and be inspired by them.

In this world, everyone expresses the content of their inner mind and being through their words, their tone of voice and their actions. Everything about a person reflects what they are within themselves. We are also surrounded by a subtle atmosphere that reflects our inner make-up. The same is true of a living Master. And when one considers that a Master has tapped right into the source of divine love, then it can be understood that the love pouring out of him is beyond description. For those who are receptive to this love, words can do no justice to the experience. The presence of this divine love, overflowing from such a God-intoxicated soul, fills the minds and souls of his disciples with an overwhelming bliss and an overpowering sense of love and gratitude for the great gift they have been given.

This outward contact might in itself be sufficient to awaken an intense feeling of love in a soul for the Master, but there is far more to the relationship of Master and disciple. When a Master initiates or baptizes a disciple, he comes to dwell within that disciple in a spiritual, radiant and subtle form. This is something quite technical, so to speak, and since it is referred to specifically in the *Song of Songs,* it needs to be adequately considered.

Part of the esoteric teachings of the Masters, largely kept secret in previous times or described only in metaphors, is that the seat of the mind and soul in the human form is at the single eye[12] or eye centre. This centre is located between the eyebrows. But it is a subtle, mental centre: there is nothing physical about it. In ancient Jewish, Christian and allied literature, it is generally referred to as a "door" or a "gate" leading from the body to the heavenly realms within.[13] It has been called the "narrow door", the "gates of life", the "gates of righteousness",[14] the "gates of the light",[15] and by many other names. It is the "door" at which Jesus advised:

> Knock, and it shall be opened unto you.
> *Matthew 7:7*

It is through this door that the writer of the *Book of Revelation* claims to have left his body and "was in the Spirit":

> After this I looked,
>   and, behold, a door was opened in heaven:
> And the first Voice which I heard
>   was, as it were, of a trumpet talking with me;
>   which said, "Come up here,
>   and I will show you things that must be hereafter."
> And immediately I was in the Spirit.
> *Book of Revelation 4:1–2; cf. KJV*

It is hence the door by which the soul can "escape from the body", either at the time of death or before:

The soul … when she desires to depart from the body, opens
a door for herself to escape from the body and goes forth like
a dove.

Mandaean Text, Thousand and Twelve Questions I:282; cf. TTQ p.189

It is the entrance to the inner worlds where the Creative Word,
the "Word of Truth" is contacted:

> Come inside, my brethren, by the narrow door,
>   and let us comfort one another with the Word of Truth.
>
> *Manichaean Psalm Book, MPB p.156*

Thus, as the early Christian *Clementine Homilies* says, it is

> … the gate of life, through which alone is the entrance to
> eternal life.
>
> *Clementine Homilies III:18, CH p.64*

At his initiation, a disciple is given a simple method of spiritual
practice or mental prayer which enables him to concentrate all
his thoughts and attention at this subtle door or centre. From
there, the attention is taken further in, and – on the threshold of
the inner, heavenly realms – he meets with the spiritual, astral or
light form of his Master.

No meeting can be filled with more love and sweetness than
this mystic encounter. The disciple will have felt the close, inner
presence of his Master for some time. He will have received
guidance, love, inspiration, uplift and much more from him. His
spiritual practice will have come to be inspired and motivated by
the single thought of meeting with the radiant or spiritual form
of his divine Beloved inside. Now that longing has been satisfied.

Meeting a Master in the physical world is always fulfilling in
the deepest possible manner. Through the powerful atmosphere
created by a Master's presence, the soul is lifted up to a state of
consciousness, love and bliss that is ordinarily very hard to
achieve and maintain. It can be readily imagined, therefore, how

intoxicating the meeting with the inner Master will be, and how much a loving disciple will come to long for this encounter.

No one stands higher in a devotee's estimation than his or her Master, for the power and love of the perfect Master is the power and love of God in human form. The devotee knows that without the Master, nothing mystical would have been achieved, and that with him, everything can be achieved. But although people may read every day of such a love, as between Jesus and his disciples, it is still almost impossible to imagine or to comprehend without personal experience. In the realm of love, experience is the only true guide to understanding. And how many people have had the opportunity to meet, let alone to love, a perfect, living Master?

It is this meeting with the spiritual form of the Master which is described in John's gospel, and which is commonly misconstrued as a description of a physical 'second coming'.[16] The meaning of the various passages is very clear. Jesus says that his second coming, in the form of the "Spirit of Truth" – the Word – will be *within* his disciples. "He dwells with you, and will be *in* you," he says:

> And I will pray the Father,
> > and he will give you another Comforter,
> > that he may abide with you forever;
> Even the Spirit of Truth, whom the world cannot receive,
> > because it sees him not,
> > neither does it know him.
> But you know him,
> > for he dwells with you, and will be in you.
> I will not leave you comfortless: I will come to you.
>
> *John 14:16–18; cf. KJV*

This inner, spiritual meeting is, he says, the fruit of a high, divine love. "I ... will manifest myself to him," he continues. "I" and "my Father will ... make our abode with him." All this happens inside:

He that loves me shall be loved of my Father,
    and I will love him, and will manifest myself to him....
If a man loves me, he will keep my words:
    and my Father will love him, and we will come to him,
    and make our abode with him.

John 14:21, 23; cf. KJV

Again, speaking of his physical death and subsequent appearance within his disciples, he reiterates that he will appear "in you", *within* them:

Yet a little while, and the world will see me no more;
    but you will see me: because I live, you will live also.
On that day, you will know that I am in my Father,
    and you in me, and I in you.

John 14:19–20; cf. KJV

The yearning for this meeting with the inner form is described in a number of early Christian texts,[17] also receiving considerable attention in the Manichaean psalms. Among other terms, the radiant form is known as the *Eikon*, the Image or the Likeness of the Saviour:

Jesus, the light of the faithful, I beseech you,
    do not forsake me.
Your beautiful Image, my Father,
    reveal it to me and your unsullied brightness....
Let it arise and come to me quickly.

Manichaean Psalm Book CCLII; cf. MPB p.61

It is also called the "Familiar", seen with the inner or spiritual faculty of sight – "my eyes of light":

I was gazing at my Familiar with my eyes of light,
    beholding my glorious Father,
    him who waits for me ever,
    opening before me the gate to the Height.

> I spread out my hands, praying to him;
> I bent my knees, worshipping him also,
>   that I might divest myself
>   of the image of the flesh
>   and put off the vesture of manhood (the body).
>
> *Manichaean Psalm Book CCXXVI; cf. MPB p.19*

It is this kind of high, spiritual love between Master and disciple that is described in the *Song of Songs*. It is a love quite distinct from anything associated with the "image of the flesh" or the "vesture of manhood". But unless a person has some inkling of the nature of this love and the means of attaining it, many of the specific allusions in the *Song of Songs* will not be understood.

The Bride and the Bridegroom

It is clear from a study of early Christian literature that many of the early Christians realized that Jesus was speaking of this spiritual form in some of his parables. The Shepherd of John's gospel who waits by the door of the sheepfold,[18] permitting his disciples to "go in and out and find pasture" (in the heavenly realms) is this inner form.[19]

So, too, is the Bridegroom who comes at midnight taking the wise virgins with him into the "bride chambers" (the heavenly realms). Meanwhile, the foolish ones are trying in vain, at the last minute, to put the oil of spiritual practice into their lamps – to bring light to their souls.[20] As one of the Manichaean psalmists writes:

> Let me be worthy of your bride chambers
>   [that are full of] light.
> Jesus Christ, receive me
>   into your bride chambers, [you my] Saviour....
> I am a maiden (devotee) unspotted and holy.

Let me see your Image, my holy Father,
    which I saw before the world was created....
Purify me, my Bridegroom, O Saviour,
    with your Waters ... that are full of grace....

My lamp (my soul) shines like the sun;
I have lit it, O Bridegroom,
    with the excellent oil of purity.
Christ, take me into your bride chambers....
Let me rejoice in all the bride chambers,
    and give me the crown of the Holy Ones.

Manichaean Psalm Book CCLXIII; cf. MPB pp.79–80

Another of these psalms speaks of the spiritual fulfilment of this inner meeting, when the soul is taken to the eternal or immortal realm:

Christ, my Bridegroom, has taken me to his bride chamber,
    I have rested with him in the land of the immortal.

Manichaean Psalm Book CCLIII, MPB p.63

The imagery of the soul as the Bride or the Lover and the spiritual form of the Saviour as the Beloved or the Bridegroom was not invented by Jesus. It was already well known in Jewish literature from writings such as the *Song of Songs*. There is no doubt, however, that Jesus' use of the metaphor in his simple parables caught the people's imagination, for it occurs again and again in the literature of early Christianity. In the apocryphal *Acts of John*, the intensity of love experienced in this spiritual union can be glimpsed when the apostle John says:

Join yourselves together in an inseparable marriage,
    holy and true, waiting for the one true
    incomparable Bridegroom from heaven,
    even Christ, the everlasting Bridegroom.

Acts of John (fragment), ANT p.266

And from an early Christian Nestorian hymn, it is again clear
that this "Bridegroom" is spiritual, not physical:

> The Bridegroom in his chamber
>> is like the sun that rises in the East,
>> whose rays pervade the firmament,
>> and whose light gives joy to the creation.
>
> The Bridegroom in his chamber
>> is like the Tree of Life in the Church,
>> whose fruits are good for food,
>> and whose leaves for medicine.
>
> The Bridegroom in his chamber
>> is like the spring that runs through Eden,
>> of which the wise have drunk,
>> and by which (even) the foolish have obtained knowledge.
>
> The Bridegroom in his chamber
>> is like an unblemished pearl,
>> which the chief merchants bought,
>> and through which they were enriched and ennobled.
>
> *Nestorian Hymn; cf. NR2 p.275, in MEM p.118, SPZ p.732*

There is no doubt, here, that the "Bridegroom in his chamber"
is not only the spiritual form of the Master encountered in the
spiritual realms, he is also the focus of the devotee's spiritual
worship and love. Such love creates an eternal bond between the
soul and the Beloved. Thus, in the *Odes of Solomon*, probably
dating from the first century AD, the poet, writing in the name
of the Saviour, likens the nature of this bond to that between the
"Bride" and the "Bridegroom":

> I laid upon them the yoke of my love:
> But as the arm of the bridegroom upon the bride,
>> so is my yoke upon those who know me.
> And as the bed that is spread in the bridal chamber,
>> so is my love for those who believe in me.
>
> *Odes of Solomon 42:7–9, OSD p.176*

The love of the disciple for the Master is deep and strong. It is "laid upon" disciples like the yoke that binds oxen to each other and to the plough. They have no option but to follow where they are led. It is like the strong hand of the Bridegroom claiming his Bride. It is full of feeling and spiritual emotion, like the "bridal chamber". But the bond is always one of love; no force is applied.

Note, too, how the odist also speaks of the "*bed* that is spread in the bridal chamber". Like many good metaphors or analogies, the "Bride" and the "Beloved" belong to a family of metaphors, in this case centred on the theme of marriage and worldly love. The writer of the *Song of Songs* exploits many of these allied metaphors. The Lover speaks of "kisses", "lips", "chambers" and her "bed", for instance. There are also long passages where both the Lover and the Beloved extol each other's spiritual beauty using the images of physical loveliness. These metaphors all have a mystic meaning, as we will see.

TWO

The Symbolism of the Song

A Rosetta Stone to Mystic Symbolism

The *Song* is both simple and complex. Understood in its simplest mystical form, its essential theme – that of the divine love and the intense longing of the soul to meet the mystic Beloved in the heavenly regions – is inherently simple. Such love simplifies by burning up and replacing all lower yearnings and complexities of the mind. But the use of metaphor and allegory can make the interpretation of the poems appear complex, especially after the lapse of about two and a half thousand years. Moreover, the Middle Eastern origin of the Bible must be recalled, and the undoubted fact that the average Western mind of modern times has little natural affinity with the lyrical symbolism of ancient Oriental poetry.

Mystical realities are, by their nature, altogether transcendent. Even when trying to describe some powerful emotion or experience of this world, we often say, "I cannot adequately convey what I felt or what I saw." How much more then does the mystic poet encounter difficulties when attempting to describe the sublime reality of higher worlds or higher states of consciousness? Yet there is no inspiration more in touch with the divine Source than mystic inspiration, and many of the world's greatest works of literature – those which still retain their appeal even after the lapse of thousands of years – are almost entirely mystical in nature. Even if the message is little understood, the language archaic, and the meaning surrounded and clouded by the sanctimony, hyperbole and dogma of external religion, the words of spiritual teachers can nevertheless touch a chord of truth deep in our human hearts. The result is that to those of a mystic or spiritual disposition, such writings – though written long ago – can become a source of inspiration in daily, modern life.

As an example of mystic poetry, the *Song of Songs* is remarkable. Its vivid metaphors and powerful images fall one upon the other in a profusion of colourful symbols, as the poet skilfully and tenaciously pursues his or her theme:

> The *Song of Songs* embodies a surplus of meaning in its artistic unfolding of lyrics that portray a poetic genius and emotional warmth of universal impact and appeal.
>
> *James Reese, Oxford Companion to the Bible, OCB p.709*

But its poetry is no gush of uncontrolled words. Its masterly feeling for language, its careful use of imagery, its brilliant rhythms and assonances all demonstrate the steadiness, conviction and control of mind of one who is both a master of his craft and has experienced his subject. Indeed, the abundance of symbols is so great that the *Song of Songs* can almost be taken as a Rosetta Stone to the interpretation of ancient mystic poetry, especially of the Middle East. It provides a key: an understanding of the *Song* opens the door to understanding the symbolism and imagery of many other mystical writings.

It could not be expected that such an imaginative and creative writer would have remained entirely within the confines of any established framework, and there is little doubt that a number of the images used are entirely of the poet's own devising. In fact, the unusual vocabulary of the *Song* contains around fifty words found nowhere else. The majority of its images, however, are detail and embellishment to families of metaphors that commonly occur elsewhere in a more general form, and their meaning usually becomes clear from a study of the context and the nature of the metaphor.

The *Song of Songs* employs several hundred metaphors and

allusions of various kinds. Yet all are woven into a composite whole with a natural ease, and without any feeling that they have been forced in for the sake of the exercise. There is little that can be compared to it in character and quality. Thus, while other writers are content with "wild beasts" as images of human imperfections, our poet identifies them as "lions" and "leopards". And while other authors speak of the divine creative Power as the Tree of Life, perhaps never indicating any particular species, the originator of the *Song* speaks of no less than eight varieties of trees or shrubs, individually identified by name.

Again, while others mention unspecified fragrances, our author comes forward with a list of herbs, ointments and spices – myrrh, aloes, frankincense and so on – that are used even in present times for their healing powers or other properties. Similarly, while many other writers have spoken of the Shepherd and his flock, also alluding to the pastures of the soul, for our poet, the Shepherd "pastures his flock amongst the lilies"[1] – a most evocative expression, not encountered elsewhere. By being more detailed, the poet thus adds both colour and meaning to his or her theme.

Understandably, a few of the metaphors remain difficult to interpret with confidence after the lapse of considerably more than two millennia. We can only assume, therefore, that the poet and his or her associates knew what was meant, even if we fail to do so today.

One is also left to wonder about the further output of such a skilled writer, access to which would undoubtedly clear up many of the remaining obscurities in the text. It is unlikely that a poet such as this wrote just one masterpiece and left it at that. But sadly, nothing remains which could conceivably be credited to the same pen.

Mystic Symbols in the Song of Songs

The Bride, the Bridegroom, the Beloved and other images of love represent only one family among many of the metaphors, symbols and similes used in the *Song of Songs.* In this, the writer was not alone. The shepherd, the king, living water, fountains, gardens, and many other such images are part of a rich language of mystical expression that has been used by Middle Eastern writers for five or six millennia.

As a prelude to the *Song of Songs,* therefore, it is worth exploring some of the foundations to this ancient language, considering its metaphors as falling into a number of groups or families. We have already encountered the imagery associated with the love of man and woman. Bride, bridegroom, lover, beloved, marriage, kisses, wedding garments, beds, bridal chambers and more have all been used to describe the interplay of love between the soul and God. The stories in the second book in this series, *The Divine Romance,* are founded upon this family of metaphors.

Almost everyone has an interest in worldly love and romance -- hence the use of such symbols. Mystics choose their language not so much for the sake of poetic lyricism as for its ability to communicate to ordinary people. They take examples, parables and metaphors from everyday life. In fact, from ancient Mesopotamian texts predating the Bible to the extensive writings of the Sufis of Islam, several millennia later, mystics of the Middle East have been remarkably consistent in their choice of metaphors. Similar images appear again and again. Variations on and embellishments to the theme are always present, but the essential images have remained very much the same. Indeed, the parallels between the *Song* and lyrics of some of the Sufi poets such as Hafiz and Rumi are sometimes extraordinary. In his *Divan,* Hafiz in particular speaks throughout of intoxication with the wine of divine love, and the inner tavern or wine house where the spiritual form of the Beloved is encountered, together with a wealth of images concerning the Beloved's face, cheek, lips, hair, and so on, all of which appear in the *Song.*

In ancient times, farming was a prominent aspect of everyday life. Consequently, God and the Saviour were cast as the shepherd, with the devotees as the sheep or the goats. The divine Shepherd keeps his flock or community of followers safe from the ravages of wild beasts and thieves, which symbolize human imperfections in many of the ancient texts. So far as a sheep or goat is concerned, the wolf and the lion are the epitome of dangerous animals, beasts that were hence used as terms for the devil. The fold into which this Shepherd brings his sheep is the fold of love, the fold of his grace or the fold of the creative Power. He collects his sheep, who have become spiritually lost and injured in the confusing wilderness of the material world, and keeps them spiritually safe. The oriental shepherd also *leads* his sheep or goats, unlike his occidental counterpart who generally follows behind with a dog. This is again an image used metaphorically, as in the twenty-third psalm: "He leads me."[2] The divine Shepherd leads his sheep into the meadows of the heavenly regions, into the quiet and peaceful pastures of refuge and safety. There, spiritual 'food' and 'water' – divine love and bliss – are plentiful and sweet. There, the soul is protected from the hot noonday sun of physical existence.

To desert people, or to any who live in arid areas, the availability of water, springs and fountains is vital to existence. Hence, the Creative Word, as the divine Source of Life, was described as the eternal Well or Fountain, the Spring of Immortality, and the Living Water. In this family of metaphors, the Lord or Saviour is the gardener who plants his plants, his vines or his trees – he initiates his souls into the mystic path. He waters them from the divine Spring of Living Water. He is also an experienced gardener: he has planted many trees before and knows how to make them thrive throughout all the seasons of life – the coolness or hardship of winter, the heat of summer, the growing season of spring, and the decline of autumn. In a similar parallel, the gardener is also the sower who sows the seed of the Word, watching over it as it germinates and grows, as in the well-known parables of Jesus.[3]

The gardens and fields in which this divine gardener or farmer plants his souls are the heavenly realms of creation, like the 'garden planted in Eden'.[4] In fact, the word for paradise in Greek is the same as that for garden. In the garden of creation are found both the Tree of Life, as the creative Power, as well as the Tree of Knowledge of Good and Evil, representing the regions of the negative power or devil – the Serpent or snake who also lives in the garden.

If the higher realms are gardens, then this world is a spiritual desert. It is also portrayed as a valley, the "valley of the shadow of death",[5] the heavenly regions being depicted as the mountains and hills. A number of early mystics even used geographical place names to represent the regions of creation, as in the allegorical gnostic poem, the *Robe of Glory*.[6]

Because the soul inhabits the body and gives it life, so the body was known as the house, the cottage or the dwelling place of the soul. Since the soul is a nomad and a wanderer in the desert of this world, having no fixed or permanent abode, the body was also described as a tent. Likewise, if – in religion – man worships God in a temple, then the true temple where God is to be found and worshipped spiritually is the temple of the human form. Similarly, the human body was also called a tabernacle – a temporary and movable tent used as a place of worship in ancient Judaism.

Food and drink are close to everybody's heart – or stomach. They are a constant source of pleasure and, without them, we rapidly die. Drawing once again on the mundane, mystics have hence described the divine grace of the creative Power as the sweetest and most nutritious food and drink. It is milk, sometimes described as flowing from the breasts of the Lord. It is sweeter than honey from the comb and more sustaining than bread. It is the staff of life, the true "manna" supporting the children of God as they cross the spiritual desert.[7] It is also fragrant and sweet wine, bringing a divine intoxication far superior and more enjoyable than all intoxications this world has to offer.

The divine table is sometimes depicted as a banquet presided over by the king – another symbol for the Lord and Saviour. Here, the disciples are the servants or subjects of the king, whether faithful or disobedient, as in the parables of Jesus,[8] as well as in the *Psalms*[9] and elsewhere. In ancient times, at his coronation, a king was also anointed with oil. Taken metaphorically, this implied the spiritual king, the Messiah or Christ – which both mean the 'Anointed One'. A Saviour is anointed with the oil of the mystic Name or Word of God.

Likewise, a king had a personal seal with which he marked his orders and correspondence. It was the insignia of his office and the stamp of his personal authority. The Creative Word hence became known as the seal or sign of the mystics, while mystic baptism was known as being sealed.

Sometimes a king would lead his people into war. Mystically, a spiritual or holy war is waged by every aspirant against the enemies of the human passions and imperfections. The banner or standard that is raised over them as they fight is that of love, and the sword that their divine leader gives them is the creative Power. An ancient army would also have its champion. This too was used to represent the Master who leads his spiritual warriors to victory in the holy war, taking them back to God.

The Command or Law of the divine King was naturally the creative Power – the Order or Will of God manifested in creation. It was also called the Voice or Word of God – his emanation by which everything comes into being. Hence, the Word was portrayed as his Breath coming from his Mouth. It was also the divine Wind or Fragrance, since terms for breath, wind and fragrance were commonly the same in Greek and Semitic languages, providing the opportunity for a natural word-play. Associated with the divine Voice and Breath is music. Hence, glad songs, hymns of praise and other similar metaphors all served to symbolize the sound of the heavenly music of the Word when heard within in mystic transport.

Again, family and social relationships are an important part of every person's life. God was thus depicted as the Father, with Wisdom or the Holy Spirit as the Mother. The soul is naturally the son or daughter of the Divine, protected by him as a father protects his child. Fellow human beings are hence brothers and sisters – children of the same divine Father.

The Saviour is also the divine Friend, just as Abraham was always known as the Friend of God. Mystics were the "Friends of God and prophets".[10] In this context, disciples are the companions or the maidens who crowd around the Friend.

Mystics have also used man's fondness for business metaphorically. They have described the spiritual goal as a pearl or a diadem, which all souls – as merchants – seek.[11] The chief merchants, those who have the wealth to purchase and distribute such pearls as they please, are the Masters or Saviours.

One of the most confusing families of metaphors used by these ancient writers was the allegorization of Jewish history as the story of the soul. As is commonly known, around 600 BC, large numbers of Israelites were enslaved by military conquerors, and were taken to live in exile in Babylon, the chief city of ancient Mesopotamia, for a period covering several generations. In addition, the origins of the children of Israel, according to a historical interpretation of *Genesis, Exodus* and so on, are also to be traced to their enslavement in Egypt during the time of the Pharaohs. From there, under the guidance and leadership of Moses, they were freed and led to the promised land of Canaan, the area lying between the River Jordan and the Mediterranean, approximating roughly to the country now known as Israel.

Under these circumstances, the lost and longed for homeland became imbued, in the minds of the slaves and exiles, with an air of sanctity and perfection. It became the Holy Land, a land of fertility, vitality, happiness and abundance, somewhere out of reach but where everything is perfect – a land "flowing with milk and honey".[12]

Jerusalem, too, became the 'holy city', while the first Temple at Jerusalem, said to have been built by Solomon around 1000 BC, became the holiest of shrines, with its own innermost sanctum, the 'holy of holies'. Even in early Christian times, before the Roman destruction of the second Temple in 70 AD, Jews from throughout the 'known world' regularly sent gifts to the Temple, which, understandably, had become fabulously rich.

The coincidence of parallels between the history of the

Israelites and the plight of the soul was too apparent to have been ignored. Mystics have always said that the soul, held captive in the physical world for many births (or 'generations'), is in exile from its true spiritual home with God. Only by meeting a living Saviour can a soul gain release from the otherwise endless procession of birth, death and rebirth.

Middle Eastern mystics have hence compared the children of Israel, enslaved in Egypt or exiled in Babylon, to the soul living in the slavery and forced labour of the physical universe. Only with the coming of the Saviour, Moses, were the Israelites freed from slavery and led back to their true and promised home. Egypt thus became a synonym for the physical universe and the physical body, while the Egyptians were symbolic of people dominated by worldliness. Similarly, Babylon, scene of their later exile, also came to represent the world. In the same way, the promised land, "flowing with milk and honey", became a symbol for the eternal realm or true home of the soul with God. So too did the city of Jerusalem, with its temple and holy of holies.

How much of the Jewish legend is actual history, how much ancient events have been exaggerated and embellished, and how much is a literalization of a story told by Moses and the other prophets as a mystic allegory is no longer possible to determine. Scholars are in general agreement, however, that many biblical narratives have been subject to a great deal of amplification, enhancement and mythologizing. Conflicting versions of the same story commonly occur in the *Pentateuch,* for instance, indicating that these books were put together by combining two or more variant traditional texts.

Though the borderline between history and myth has become blurred, there is no doubt that by the time the *Song of Songs* and other mystic literature was written, the story was well established and was commonly used as a means of explaining the mystic path. Indeed, so much was written about the historical return of the Israelites to their homeland that one of the ways by which the *Song of Songs* gained acceptance and a place for itself in posterity was by skilful allusion to the details of this legend. In later

centuries, metaphors associated with the history of the Israelites
were still in use, as in the *Robe of Glory* and other places.[13]

All these families of metaphors are represented in the *Song of
Songs*. Were there the space, many volumes could be filled with
interesting and inspiring illustrations of their use from the
ancient literature, where they are often used in explicitly mystical
contexts with no doubt as to the author's meaning.[14]

In fact, only two major groups of mystical metaphor are
completely absent from the *Song*. Firstly, there are the maritime
metaphors in which the world is depicted as a stormy ocean,
with the Saviour as the helmsman or pilot who guides or ferries
the soul across. Here, eternity is the harbour of Life, and the
soul on its return to God is sometimes portrayed as voyaging on
a ship of light. These images were common in early Christianity
and even more so in Manichaean times. Understandably, such
metaphors would have had the greatest meaning for those
familiar with the sea. They probably arose in the Mediterranean
regions of Israel and Asia Minor, or perhaps around the Persian
Gulf, or in areas bordering on the Sea of Galilee, or along the
banks of the twin Mesopotamian rivers of the Tigris and
Euphrates.

Secondly, there is the imagery of the Saviour as the divine
Physician who heals his souls from the wounds or diseases of
their sins. This is particularly Christian in character and,
although encountered in *Isaiah* and elsewhere,[15] its populari-
zation is probably due to its use by Jesus. It is undoubtedly the
origin of many of the New Testament miracle stories, as externali-
zations of mystic truth.[16] The later gnostics and Manichaeans
were also fond of this imagery.

A Veiled but Universal Language

It is evident that an appreciation of this language of metaphor is
necessary if these ancient texts are to be understood. To the
mystically minded of those times, this would have been second

nature. They would have automatically enjoyed the imagery, the wordplay and the double or hidden meanings.

But there were more than literary reasons for the use of allegory and metaphor. Mystics have commonly been persecuted by the people of this world. Even in our more tolerant, modern culture, the followers of a mystic are at least considered odd, and may still become the target of social, religious or family prejudice. In the past, both the mystics, and sometimes their followers as well, have been summarily beheaded, crucified, and otherwise executed or generally mistreated; or their writings have been burned and banned. As Jesus describes "Jerusalem", epitomizing the Jewish people:

> O Jerusalem, Jerusalem, you who killed the prophets,
>   and stoned them that were sent to you.
>
> *Matthew 23:37; cf. KJV*

He is referring to the treatment meted out to the mystics and prophets in the period during which the *Song of Songs* was written. Mystics, however, are always full of love. They are neither vengeful nor vindictive. They never hold a grudge or react emotionally. They come to serve the real seekers of truth, and uncomplainingly put up with the mistreatment, abuse and threats of the worldly minded. Without advertising, proselytizing or imposing themselves on others, they use every means at their disposal to communicate their message. Consequently, so that their writings may be preserved for the benefit of future generations, they have often resorted to allegory and parable. They have also employed the same method for teaching their own initiates, for we human beings are fond of stories, and more readily appreciate spiritual truths when they are wrapped up in an entertaining tale.

With the passage of time, future generations then repeat or read these stories and parables, benefiting from a partial understanding of the spiritual meaning, though often remaining unaware of the spiritual height of the message thus preserved.

The preservation of these teachings, however, makes the task of future mystics easier, for they can then demonstrate that they are not inventing new teachings or trying to create a religion. They can confidently point out that what they are teaching is the same as that taught by mystics of the past. For mystics are members of an eternal and universal brotherhood whose wisdom spans vastly more than the time, the space and the cultures of this world.

As we have indicated, these mystic symbols constitute a cross-lingual language of mysticism. Many of the metaphors and allegories used in the Bible and the Wisdom literature are present in the mystic writings of ancient Iran and Mesopotamia. Traces of the same imagery can even be glimpsed in early Babylonian and Sumerian cultures, dating back to the fourth millennium BC. Metaphors like the Tree of Life, the Water of Life, the Shepherd and the priceless pearl of immortality are to be found among the writings inscribed upon the thousands of clay tablets unearthed by archaeologists in Mesopotamia during the nineteenth and twentieth centuries. In fact, despite the supposed early associations with Egypt, Judaism bears far more the imprint of ancient Mesopotamia and the Middle East, than it does of ancient Egypt.

The Iranian mystic, Zarathushtra, dating back perhaps to 1500 BC, as well as later Zoroastrianism, also drew upon this source of ancient imagery. Zarathushtra, for instance, speaks of the creative Power as the Word *(Manthra)*,[17] and describes the Saviour as the Shepherd (*Fshuyant* or *Vastrya*).[18]

The same metaphors are again encountered in the beautiful and devotional psalms found among the Dead Sea Scrolls, discovered during the mid-twentieth century in caves near the ancient settlement of Khirbet Qumran. These pre-Christian texts are commonly attributed to the Essenes, a contemplative and esoteric branch of Judaism at that time. And the psalms themselves are usually attributed to the Essene Saviour, the mysterious Teacher of Righteousness, about whom practically nothing is known.

Perhaps a century and a half later, Jesus also used this language in his sayings and parables. The same imagery is found in the gnostic Mandaean literature of southern Iran and Iraq, and in the writings of the early Christians both in the canonical as well as the gnostic and apocryphal texts. The third-century Iranian mystic, Mani, and his followers also made extensive use of this language. And, in later times, the mystics of Islam – the Sufis – used the same allegories, parables and metaphors to express the same essential spiritual truths.

Neither the Old nor the New Testaments are unique. The books that comprise them are part of a rich heritage reflecting the cultural and religious life of the ancient Middle East. It is true that their manner of expression evolves to some extent with the passage of time. Compare, for instance, the mythological character of *Genesis* with the far simpler language of *Proverbs,* and the even simpler message of Matthew, Mark and Luke. But although the emphasis and idiom may change, the fundamental imagery and themes remain pretty much the same. The perennial message always needs restating and re-presenting in the popular language of the day. And when that becomes archaic, it needs restating once again. It is a continuous and repeating process.

It must be remembered, too, that the national, political and religious map of Eastern Europe, Asia Minor and the Middle East has been drawn and redrawn many times over the last 6000 years. Prior to the advent of Muhammad and Islam, followed by the extensive Arabic conquests in the latter half of the first millennium AD, Mesopotamia, Syria and the surrounding countries were home to a variety of religious traditions, prominent among them being Judaism. Arabic itself is a Semitic language, belonging to the same family of languages as Hebrew, Aramaic, Syriac and more ancient languages of the same area such as Akkadian and Phoenician. Islam also accepts the Bible as sacred literature, the *Qur'an* and Islamic writers making frequent references to the Jewish patriarchs and prophets, as well as Jesus, regarding them all as true Messengers of God.

But while the political, social and religious background evolved and shifted ground, the multilingual, cross-cultural language of mystic metaphor survived and even flourished. Providing some continuity in an ever changing world, it enabled mystics to write and speak of mystical matters to the spiritual seekers of all nations, while the uninitiated or unaware may have thought that they were speaking of mundane or religious affairs. As Jesus is often quoted as saying, "he who has ears to hear, let him hear".[19] He knew that his parables could not be understood by all, for the meaning was hidden behind the veil of metaphor.

Centuries later, in the Middles Ages, the same veiled language of mystic metaphor was used by European groups – the Bogomils, the Troubadours, the Cathars, the Albigensians and others. Even Dante used this imagery in his epic work, *The Divine Comedy*. Many of the Christian mystics understood this language too, at least in part, as is demonstrated by their interpretations of the *Song of Songs*.

The influence of Middle Eastern mystical expression reached Europe not only through Judaism and Christianity, but also through the Sufis who came along with the Moorish occupation of Spain and parts of southern France. In fact, early medieval Spain became a melting pot and a haven of intellectual and spiritual freedom. From within its boundaries, protected from the strong hand of catholic Rome, Sufism, Jewish Kabbalism, Christian mysticism and gnostic understanding in many guises spilled over into the rest of Europe, providing spiritual fuel for early Renaissance thought. It was this hotbed of 'heresy' – as the orthodox perceived it – that prompted the Pope and catholic political powers to instigate the Inquisition in the thirteenth century. First to be eradicated by the sword were the gnostic Albigensians of southern France. Later, encouraged by their 'success', the Inquisition moved on to 'clean up' Spain as Moorish rule declined and fell.

During the recurrent periods when mystics and their disciples were persecuted and executed, this veiled language was necessary, both for the preservation of their lives, as well as their written teachings. The language of metaphor, therefore, has helped to carry the torch of universal mysticism through the long dark

ages of persecution and suppression. The light has never been
extinguished. The inner path and proper guidance for the
journey have always been there for those who have sought to
find it.

Two Kinds of Parable

Over the centuries, many Jewish writers have pointed out that
large sections of the Bible are more easily understood if interpreted allegorically. Among these was the Arabic-speaking Jew,
Moses Maimonides (1155–1204), a renowned medieval mystic,
philosopher and scholar, as well as a leader of the Jewish
community in Egypt. In *The Guide of the Perplexed,* a volu-
minous and fascinating treatise concerned largely with the
interpretation of Jewish sacred writings, Maimonides points out
that the writings of the mystics – the "prophecies of the
prophets" – are written almost entirely in parables and metaphorical language:

> Undoubtedly, it has become clear and manifest that the
> greater part of the prophecies of the prophets proceeds by
> means of parables.... This figurative use of language is
> exceedingly frequent in the books of prophecy.
>
> *Moses Maimonides, Guide of the Perplexed II:47, GP2 p.407*

Maimonides then refers to descriptions of the *Exodus* story in
which gates are opened in heaven and manna rains down upon
the Israelites,[20] or where the Lord threatens to blot someone out
of his book.[21] Clearly, says Maimonides, there are no gates or
doors in heaven, nor does the Lord really have a book in which
he writes, and from which he blots out.

Maimonides also observes that parables and allegories are
written in one of two ways. Some, he says, are written such that
not only are their words and phrases meant to be specifically and
meaningfully interpreted, but they are also intended as particular

subject areas in themselves. In others, the story is worded in a general fashion, and only its broad outline and essential message are intended to be meaningful. Indeed, the purpose of the verbiage may sometimes be to conceal the mystic meaning, perhaps to avoid suppression in times of persecution. If, therefore, a person were to mistake one sort of parable for the other, then the natural outcome would be confusion:

> Know that the prophetic (mystic) parables are of two kinds. In some of these parables each word has a meaning, while in others the parable as a whole indicates the whole of the intended meaning. In such a parable, very many words are to be found, not every one of which adds something to the intended meaning. They serve rather to embellish the parable and to render it more coherent or to conceal further the intended meaning; hence the speech proceeds in such a way as to accord with the parable's external (overall) meaning. Understand this well.
>
> An example of the first kind of parable is the following text (from *Genesis*):
>
> And behold a ladder set up on earth and the top of it reached to heaven; and behold the angels of God ascending and descending on it. And behold the Lord stood above it.[22]
>
> In this text, the word "ladder" indicates one subject; the words "set up on earth" indicate a second subject; the words "and the top of it reached to heaven" indicate a third subject; and the words "behold the angels of God" indicate a fourth subject; the word "ascending" indicates a fifth subject; the word "descending" indicates a sixth subject; and the words "and behold the Lord stood above it all" indicate a seventh subject. Thus every word occurring in this parable refers to an additional subject in the complex of subjects represented by the parable as a whole.
>
> *Moses Maimonides, Guide of the Perplexed I, GP1 pp. 12–13*

Maimonides goes on to give an example of the second kind of parable concerning the seduction of a young man by a married woman, found in *Proverbs*.[23] Here, he says, the various phrases and descriptive passages in the story carry only a general meaning, and are not to be interpreted as meaningful in themselves in any symbolic or allegorical manner.

The *Song of Songs* is a 'parable' of the first kind, whose metaphorical language has been carefully crafted to convey the particular mystic truths that the writer had in mind. Maimonides indicates, in his various quotations and interpretations of the *Song of Songs,* that this is so. There is, for instance, a passage in the *Song* where the Lover – the soul – says:

> My mother's sons turned their anger on me,
>   they made me look after the vineyards.
> Had I only looked after my own!
>
> *Song of Songs 1:6, JB*

In the commentary following this chapter, it is interpreted to mean that our own real work in life is to build up our own spiritual treasure, to work in our own "vineyard" rather than to labour all our lives toiling for others in the "vineyard" of this world. "My mother's sons turned their anger on me" also has a specific, metaphorical meaning, as we will see.

Maimonides provides a similar interpretation. Calling the *Song of Songs* the "poetical parables that have been coined for these notions", he writes about the very personal nature of the search for human perfection:

> This ultimate perfection, however, pertains to you alone, no one else being associated in it with you in any way.... Therefore you ought to desire to achieve this thing (perfection, spiritual wealth), which will remain permanently with you, and not weary and trouble yourself for the sake of others, O you who neglect your own soul so that its whiteness has turned into blackness through the bodily faculties having

gained dominion over it. As is said in the beginning of the poetical parables that have been coined for these notions: (and here he quotes the above passage from the *Song of Songs*).

Moses Maimonides, *Guide of the Perplexed III:54; cf. GP2 pp.635–36*

There are other passages, too, in *The Guide of the Perplexed* where the *Song* is similarly interpreted.[24] Indeed, much of Maimonides' book is taken up with explaining the real and mystic meaning hidden in the otherwise bizarre stories and writings of the Old Testament. Hence the title of his book.

Jewish and Hebrew Symbolism

Jewish and Hebrew symbolism employs practically every conceivable means of encoding and conveying meaning, including a few methods that are found practically nowhere else. At the simplest level, there are metaphors like 'shepherd' or 'living water'. Frequently, there are *double entendres,* like the use of the one word *(ruach)* for 'wind', 'breath', 'fragrance' and 'spirit'. Then there are words that are used simply because they sound similar to the word that actually conveys the intended meaning. This is like the cockney use of 'trouble and strife' (for the 'wife') or 'apples and pears' (for the 'stairs'). The medieval *Zohar,* for instance, interpreting the line from the *Song of Songs,* "the maidens love you", says: "do not read *alamot* (maidens), but *olamot* (realms, *i.e.* heavens)."[25] Sometimes, the letters of a word are to be re-ordered for the actual word intended to be revealed. In other instances, the numbers assigned to the letters of Hebrew words and sentences are totalled, allowing the author's real meaning to be deciphered, also permitting correspondences between things that are ostensibly unconnected to be disclosed.

There is a famous example of this kind of riddle in the New Testament *Book of Revelation*. The writer has been speaking of the "Beast" without revealing who he means by the epithet. He then speaks of the "name of the Beast" and the "number of his name",[26] adding:

> Here is wisdom. Let him who has understanding count the number of the Beast: for it is the number of a man; and his number is six hundred threescore and six (666).
>
> *Book of Revelation 13:18; cf. KJV*

The problem is that this 'crossword clue' has been so well encrypted that despite many contenders, to this day no one is entirely sure of the answer!

In addition to the general use of metaphor and *double entendre,* it is possible that the *Song of Songs* contains meanings encoded in these ways. Certainly, some of the Jewish, especially Kabbalist, commentators claim to have discovered hidden meanings encoded in this manner. But, except in one instance, I have not tried to get into this kind of symbolic interpretation. To begin with, it demands deep understanding of Hebrew and Jewish religious literature and, in any case, the general meaning is clear enough without getting involved in such details and complexities. But Moses Maimonides describes these kinds of symbolism and encrypted meaning in *The Guide of the Perplexed.*[27]

Early Echoes of the Song

No piece of writing, biblical or otherwise, is uninfluenced by the literary styles of its author's time and place. In the case of the Bible, much of the material has come from a culture so alien to Western thought, past or present, that the texts themselves have become imbued with an aura of sanctity simply by virtue of their obscurity and sense of otherness. But this is due entirely to the gulf between cultures several millennia and many thousands of miles apart. So deep-rooted is this sense of biblical 'untouchability' that it is only in the last hundred and fifty years or so that an open minded scholarly analysis of the various texts, together with archaeological discoveries in the Middle East and Egypt, have revealed antecedents that enable us to see something of the literary history and development of biblical writings. As previously intimated, it has been realized that *Genesis,* for instance, owes much to the mythology of ancient Mesopotamia.

The *Song,* too, has its literary parallels – poetic styles and imagery of ancient times used intentionally and with great skill by its author. In a number of places, for example, in a repetitive refrain, the Beloved refers to the Bride as his "sister":

> You ravish my heart,
>   my sister, my promised Bride.
> You ravish my heart
>   with a single one of your glances,
>   with one single pearl of your necklace.
> What spells lie in your love,
>   my sister, my promised Bride!
> How delicious is your love, more delicious than wine!
>
>   *Song of Songs 4:9–10, JB*

And:

> She is a garden enclosed,
>   my sister, my promised Bride;
> A garden enclosed,
>   a sealed fountain.
>
>   *Song of Songs 4:12, JB*

Similarly, in the last poem, the Bride expresses her wish that her Beloved were her "brother":

> Ah, why are you not my brother,
>   nursed at my mother's breast!
> Then if I met you out of doors, I could kiss you
>   without people thinking ill of me.
>
>   *Song of Songs 8:1, JB*

At first sight, it might seem that the poet is indicating the pure
and spiritual nature of the love he seeks to portray. This may
indeed be so, but it is also true that this form of address is found
in Egyptian love lyrics of an entirely worldly nature. Out of a
sense of respect, husbands also address their wives as "sister" in
the Jewish *Book of Tobit*.[28] It is this kind of literary parallel which
has led twentieth-century scholars to suggest that the *Song* itself
is simply another love song written in an ancient style.

A closer study of these Egyptian love songs, however, reveals
that although many are exactly what they appear, some of them
readily lend themselves to a mystical interpretation, suggesting
that they too contain a veiled mystic meaning. Take, for example,
a song dating from the second millennium BC:

> I have found my brother in his bed,
>   my heart is glad beyond all measure.
> We each say:
>   "I will not tear myself away."
>
> My hand is in his hand,
>   I wander together with him
>   to every beautiful place.
> He makes me the first of maidens,
>   nor does he grieve my heart.
>
> *Egyptian Love Songs VII, PH500 10:7–8, from AB, in SSHS p.36*

Understood mystically, the "bed" is the inner bridal chamber
where the soul finds the Beloved "brother" in great bliss and "gladness beyond all measure". "Together with him", she "wanders"
through the "beautiful", heavenly pastures of the soul.

In another of these songs – interpreted mystically – the Lover
likens herself to a "plot of land", fragrant and fertile through the
"water" or "wind" of the Spirit which courses through her:

> I am your darling sister.
> I am to you like a piece of land
>   with each shrub of grateful fragrance.

Lovely is the water conduit in it,
   which your hand has dug,
   while the north wind cooled us.
     Egyptian Love Songs VIII; cf. from AB, in SSHS p.36

Whether or not this interpretation is what the original writer had in mind is, of course, unknown. In any case, only a few of these Egyptian songs can be interpreted in this manner. Others are undoubtedly ordinary love songs. Even so, Egypt was renowned for its mystic wisdom, and it is only to be expected that some of their songs would carry a mystic meaning.

Other similarities to the imagery of the *Song of Songs* are to be found among the liturgies and psalms associated with the religious cults of pre-Judaic Palestine, particularly the sacred marriage of Tammuz and Ishtar. Mesopotamian in origin, there is no doubt that the cult of Tammuz and Ishtar was practised in ancient Palestine, for it is denounced by some of the Jewish prophets.[29]

There are also similarities between the *Song* and the religious literature of ancient Mesopotamia. Unearthed at Assur, one of the main cities of ancient Assyria, is a catalogue of Assyrian psalms, liturgies and other songs dating from the mid-first millennium BC. Many of these were ancient when this list was compiled for it speaks of them as Akkadian – a Semitic language of the third millennium BC. Included among this list of rather beautiful titles are found a number that are reminiscent of imagery used in the *Song of Songs*:

She Seeks out the Beautiful Garden of Your Abundance.

O Come Down to the Garden of the King
   that Reeks with Cedar!

The Fragrance of Cedar is Your Love, O Lord.

Hasten Joyfully, O King!

By Night I Thought of You.

O Bird of Life, Harbinger of Light,
    like Honey is Your Voice.

Your Love is indeed a Jewel, my Longing is indeed Gold.

O How I Long for the Couch of the Sons.

After I Lay in the Bosom of the Son.

Mesopotamian Psalm Titles; cf. SSFC pp.74–78

Since these Mesopotamian songs were included among religious texts, it is not unreasonable to suppose that they too were intended to convey a spiritual meaning.

Many other examples of parallel imagery can be found as well. But although it can be readily demonstrated that the writer of the *Song* – like any other writer – was influenced by the literature of his own time, both secular and sacred, few other conclusions can be drawn from this observation. It certainly cannot be used to prove that the *Song of Songs* is a song in praise of worldly love. After all, there is much in the *Song of Songs* that is not to be found in the love lyrics of ancient Egypt or the psalms of Mesopotamia.

Four Levels of Meaning

In the *Song of Songs,* then, allegory, symbolism and *double entendre* are the poet's stock-in-trade. Even the most orthodox commentators have observed this. It is little wonder, therefore, that it has been the subject of so much controversy. In fact, not only is the imagery open to diverse interpretations, but it seems to me that the poet writes simultaneously at three, and sometimes four, interwoven levels of meaning. This helps to explain why there are so many varied opinions concerning the meaning of the *Song:* interpreters have tended to see just a part of the picture, but have mistaken the part for the whole.

The first level of meaning is that of an extraordinarily intense love of a physical kind. The second alludes to the Jewish cultural and religious belief in release from exile and slavery. This includes the finding of the promised land, and the hope of a new dawn when Yahweh will destroy their enemies, creating a new age on earth. But although some commentators have read this meaning into every verse,[30] it is only clearly present on occasion, and then only by allusion.

The third level of meaning is the deep inner love of the soul for the Lord. The fourth, closely allied to the third, is the love of the mystic devotee for the living Saviour, and the yearning to meet him in his spiritual form in the heavenly realms within. Of these, it is the last two interpretations which fit the most consistently throughout, the first two being used only metaphorically in pursuit of the primary theme. The first is thus the literal meaning. The other three are allegorical.

Taking the *Song* literally – as a story of the love between a man and woman – it soon becomes clear that there are considerable difficulties reconciling its various events with a coherent story line. To make this interpretation fit the *Song,* many scholars have despaired, concluding that the text is corrupt, that passages are missing, that some of the poems are out of order or have been added later by other hands, that the poems are a collation of previously separate pieces, and so on. Confusion abounds, for instance, as to how many Lovers and Beloveds there are. For the Beloved is both a king (sometimes King Solomon) and a shepherd, while the Lover appears as a prince's daughter, a shepherdess and a simple country girl living in a humble cottage with lattice windows. The scenes also switch rapidly between the city and the country. All this is possible in the realm of allegory and metaphor, but not if the characters are to be taken in an entirely literal sense.

To account for this confusion, two mutually incompatible literal interpretations have been proposed – each with its own spread of variants. One theory suggests that the *Song* is *either* a single, unified love song; *or* it is a compilation of between six and fifty-four (depending on the scholar) individual love songs woven into a whole, either by original design or by a later editor; *or* it is a cycle of wedding songs; *or* it is the remnants of a liturgy associated with an ancient fertility cult.

The other theory supposes that the *Song* is a drama in which King Solomon, on a visit to the country, becomes enamoured of a peasant girl, enticing or abducting her from her shepherd lover. Back in the royal palace, the girl rejects the king's advances, dreams of her shepherd, and is eventually reunited with him.

There are variants of the drama theory, too, but the major difficulty with this proposal is that none of the events conjectured are actually described in the *Song*. They all need to be presumed. And the dialogues of the *Song* then require an outsize shoehorn to make them serve the purposes of the drama.

It is because the overall, unifying theme of spiritual love between the loving disciple and her Saviour is not generally recognized by scholars that there is such a spectrum of opinion and debate. Lacking an understanding of this underlying theme, the considerable evidence of unity in both authorship and content have often been explained away in the attempt to figure out how the *Song* has been put together.

Historically, the literal interpretation of the *Song* found few advocates before recent times. All the same, especially in Jewish circles in ancient times, there has always been an undercurrent of uneasiness that perhaps the *Song* was, after all, no more than a human love song. It was these misgivings that prompted a review of its canonicity in the early second century AD, resulting in a reconfirmation of its allegorical nature.

The first recorded Christian dissenter to the spiritual interpretation of the *Song* appears to have been the fifth-century Bishop Theodore of Mopsuestia (*d.*428 AD). Bishop Theodore openly rejected the allegorical method in regard to the Bible in general, declaring the *Song* to be no more than a song concerning physical love. For this approach to the scriptures, he was later condemned by the Councils of Ephesus (431 AD) and Constantinople (553 AD).

Literal interpretations again surfaced in the fifteenth century when a German edition divided the *Song* into fifty-four separate love songs, and in the sixteenth century when Chateillon proposed that the *Song of Songs* should be expelled from the canon on grounds of immorality. Other proponents of a literal meaning, Jewish and Christian, have arisen from time to time, but it was not until the late eighteenth century that the idea began to gain any significant support. Until then, allegorical interpretations held the day.

As regards the second level of meaning, that of the relationship of love between Yahweh and his chosen people, there is little doubt that the poet does allude to the aspirations and traditional history of the Jewish religion and culture. This interpretation appears to have been well established in Judaism by the first century AD. This is how the *Targums* (early Aramaic interpretative renderings of the Hebrew Bible) explain the *Song of Songs*. There is also a passage in the *Mishnah* (compiled in the late second century AD) where a passing reference to Solomon's wedding in the *Song of Songs*[31] is understood as the giving of the *Torah* (Law) and the building of the Temple.[32] More indirectly, the biblical *Hosea* (from the eighth century BC) and the apocryphal *4 Ezra* (from the first or early second century AD) both use the metaphors of "lily" and "dove"[33] in reference to Israel, imagery also found in the *Song of Songs*. In later centuries, the *Midrash* (biblical interpretations written 400–1200 AD) and medieval Jewish commentators such as Sa'adia Gaon (*c.*882–942), Rashi (*c.*1040–1105) and Rabbi Abraham ben Isaac ha-Levi (*d.c.*1390) appear to have accepted this interpretation without question, though – once again – there are variations in the details.

This traditional Jewish interpretation of the *Song* is part of a far bigger picture. Large portions of the Bible are understood as an expression of the relationship between God and his chosen people – the children of Israel. This is an essential characteristic and belief of both ancient and modern Judaism. Books·as dissimilar as *Genesis, Isaiah* and the *Psalms* are all interpreted in this manner. In fact, there is little doubt that much of the Bible was written out of this belief.

Nonetheless, there is also much in the Bible that is general, and speaks more universally of the love between God and the soul. And when the metaphors of God and Israel are used to describe this love, it can lead understandably to uncertainty about the meaning intended by the original author.

The minimal use of such imagery in the *Song of Songs* is insufficient to warrant the assumption that it was written wholly as an allegory of the love between God and Israel. Given the ancient tradition, it is understandable how the *Song* came to be interpreted in this manner. But the reality is that to provide an interpretation along these lines, the meaning has to be continually forced. The result is therefore unconvincing and unsatisfactory if it is taken as the only and primary theme and meaning of the *Song*. The majority of the *Song* has nothing to do with traditional Jewish belief and history. And a closer study reveals that where such allusions do occur, they are being used simply as symbols of the higher divine love or as metaphors to explain particular mystic truths. They are the references to local culture and history that all writers consciously or unconsciously employ in the attempt to communicate their particular message.

The poem's third level of meaning, as a description of the divine love between the soul and the Lord, has been recognized by both Jewish and Christian commentators and mystics alike. Josephus, the great first-century Jewish historian, inclines to this point of view when he includes it among four books which he describes as "hymns to God and precepts for the conduct of human life".[34] Likewise, respected Jewish teachers such as Rabbi Akiva (c.50–135 AD) and Moses Maimonides (1155–1204), over a thousand years apart, both held the *Song of Songs* in high regard.

As a young man in his twenties, Rabbi Akiva was among the most influential of the Rabbis responsible for reshaping Judaism and holding it together in the years following the Roman destruction of the Temple at Jerusalem in 70 AD. According to a famous passage in the *Mishnah*, during a dispute regarding the nature of the *Song of Songs*, Rabbi Akiva observed:

> All the ages are not worth the day on which the *Song of Songs* was given to Israel; for all the Writings (*i.e.* the *Hagiographa*, part of the Bible) are holy, but the *Song of Songs* is the holy of holies.
>
> *Mishnah 6, Yadaim 3:5, TM p.782*

Following in this tradition is an anecdote related in the Jewish Kabbalist 'bible', the medieval *Zohar*. According to the story, Rabbi Akiva is visiting his Master, Rabbi Eliezer, as the latter is about to depart from this world. Full of love for his Master, Rabbi Akiva is naturally distressed to realize that they will soon be parted:

> And he (Rabbi Eliezar) then taught him (Rabbi Akiva) … two hundred and sixteen meanings of verses from the *Song of Songs*, and Rabbi Akiva's eyes streamed with tears, and the fire (of love) returned as at the beginning.
>
> When he came to the verse, "Support me with dainties, refresh me with apples, for I am love sick",[35] Rabbi Akiva could no longer bear it, and he raised his voice, weeping and moaning…. (And) he (Rabbi Eliezar) taught him all the profundities and the celestial mysteries contained in the *Song of Songs;* and he made him swear not to use a single verse from it, in case the Holy One, blessed be He, should destroy the world thereby, for it was not his wish that his creatures should make use of it, owing to the great sanctity that it contained.
>
> Rabbi Akiva then departed, lamenting, his eyes gushing with water. "Alas, my Master," he said, "alas, my Master, that the world should be orphaned of you."
>
> *Zohar I:98a–99a, WZ1 pp.224–25*

Rabbi Akiva is normally credited with having taken the *Song* as an allegory of the love between God and Israel. But this is only an assumption, for the extant evidence is less than slender. The *Zohar* clearly considers that Rabbi Akiva and his Master saw a higher spiritual meaning in the *Song's* "profundities and celestial mysteries".

More than a thousand years after Rabbi Akiva, the *Song of Songs* was still considered to be a writing of the greatest spiritual significance. Moses Maimonides was explicit in his interpretation:

> What is the correct form of love? It is in the man who loves God with a love so great, abundant and mighty that his soul is bound to the love of God, and he devotes himself to it continuously, whether he is in repose, or active, eating or drinking. Stronger than this is the love of God in the hearts of those who love him and devote themselves to the love of him continuously, as we have been commanded, "with all your heart and with all your soul".[36]
>
> And this is what Solomon meant metaphorically when he said, "I am lovesick".[37] In fact, the whole book of the *Song of Songs* is an allegory of the subject.

Moses Maimonides, Mishneh Torah, Hilkhot Yesodei ha-Torah 2:2, in WZ3 p.978

Moses Maimonides was one of the earliest known Jewish personalities to have been influenced by Sufism. Sufism spread widely and rapidly among Jewish communities during the twelfth century, and probably earlier, reaching many countries. In fact, it was generally understood that the Jewish patriarchs and prophets of biblical times had been mystics of the same order as the most spiritually evolved among the Sufis.

Among these Jewish Sufis was Rabbi Abraham he-Hasid (*d.*1223), whom Abraham Maimonides, son of Moses Maimonides, refers to as "our Master in the path of the Lord".[38] Fragments of some of Rabbi Abraham he-Hasid's writings were discovered in a Cairo synagogue in 1896, in a stash of Jewish literature. Among these was a commentary on the *Song of Songs,* interpreted as a mystical guide for the soul on her journey to God.

The spiritual importance of the creative Power or Word was also well understood by many of these Jewish mystics. 'Obadyah Maimonides, son of Abraham, was later to write *The Treatise of the Pool* in which he extols the virtues of "Reason" – the *Logos* or Creative Word:

> If a man devote his entire being to Reason, then he will think little of bodily matters and they will no longer bother him as before.... It is possible for man to remain for days on end without requiring food because of his concentration on and his utter absorption with this pursuit (*i.e.* his meditation on the Word).
>
> 'Obadayah Maimonides, Treatise of the Pool XVIII, TP p.111

He then goes on to quote a passage from the *Song of Songs* in which the soul or Lover is compared by the Beloved to a "lily among thorns", explaining:[39]

> Therefore, my son, take care to repulse the affairs of the body as much as possible, for this will ease the restlessness that you will experience at the very beginning of your Path. Upon being delivered from the snare of the body, the soul has been compared to a shred of silk that had fallen among thorns.
>
> 'Obadayah Maimonides, Treatise of the Pool XVIII; cf. TP p.111

In his short treatise, he cites the *Song of Songs* on several other occasions, too, always interpreting it as an allegory of the love between the soul and the Lord.[40] Speaking of the individual's absorption with "Reason" or the Word, he says:

> All the while, your heart should contemplate this pursuit, and your thoughts be pre-occupied therein. As it is said, "I am asleep (to the world), but my heart is awake (to Reason)."
>
> 'Obadayah Maimonides, Treatise of the Pool, Exhortation; cf. TP p.116

Again, he is citing an oft-quoted line from the *Song of Songs*.[41]

Later Jewish mystics were to follow in the same tradition, including the writers of Moorish Spain. Yosef ibn 'Aknin, who lived in Spain during the twelfth and thirteenth centuries, wrote an allegorical and mystical commentary on the *Song of Songs* in Arabic. It is again a treatise on the love of the soul for God, employing a great deal of Sufi terminology. Ibn 'Aknin also quotes freely from early Sufi mystics, for whom he had the greatest regard, even describing Ibrahim ibn Adham (*d.c.*780) as a "perfect Saint".[42] Demonstrating his universal approach to spiritual wisdom, he also quotes extensively from Plato, Galen and other Greek philosophers and mystics.

The Jewish Kabbalists of medieval Spain, especially at the end of the twelfth and during the thirteenth centuries, also regarded the *Song of Songs* as a sacred text. To their way of thinking, it contained detailed esoteric information concerning the Kabbalist hierarchy of creation. Rabbi Abraham ibn Ezra of Gerona (1092–1167), for example, a disciple of Nachmanides, wrote a commentary on the *Song* which was used as a source by the writer of the *Zohar*. In Kabbalist thought, in common with other mystical interpretations, the Beloved is the Lord. The Lover, however, although occasionally interpreted as the soul,[43] is usually understood to be the *Shekinah*. In Jewish mystical thought, the *Shekinah* is the radiance by which God visibly manifests his immanent presence in creation whenever he so wishes, as in some of the biblical stories. This interpretation also appears in the *Midrash*.

Christians, too, have found great mystical inspiration in the *Song of Songs*. Well-known personalities who have interpreted the *Song* as a mystic allegory include Origen (*c.*185–254), St Athanasius (*c.*296–373), St Gregory of Nyssa (*c.*335–394), St Jerome (*c.*347–420), (pseudo)-Dionysius the Areopagite (*c.*500 AD), St Bernard of Clairvaux (*c.*1090–1153), St Francis of Assisi (*c.*1181–1226), St Thomas Aquinas (1225–1274), Meister Eckhart (*c.*1260–1327), Johan Tauler (1290–1361), Henry Suso (*c.*1295–1365), Richard Rolle (*c.*1300–1349), Walter Hilton (*d.*1396), Jean Gerson (1363–1429), Martin Luther (1483–1546), St Teresa of Ávila (1515–1582), Luis de León (*c.*1527–1591), St John of the Cross (1542–1591), St Francis de Sales (1567–1622), Bar Hebraeus (*d.*1286), and many of the ascetic fathers of the Eastern Church as recorded in that inspiring compendium of Christian spiritual teaching, the *Philokalia.* Even the well-known heresy basher, St Hippolytus (*c.*170–236) is recorded as having written an allegorical commentary on the *Song of Songs,* now extant in only a few fragments.

Thomas Aquinas, Bernard of Clairvaux, Gregory of Nyssa and Origen all wrote long commentaries on the *Song of Songs.* For Thomas Aquinas and Bernard of Clairvaux, the *Song of Songs* was the subject of their final works. St Bernard died without completing his extended series of sermon-commentaries, his work being taken up by John, Abbot of Ford, followed by Gilbert, Abbot of Swineshead in England. Thomas Aquinas is said to have died with hands joined, his eyes raised towards heaven, uttering the line from the *Song of Songs,* "Come my Beloved, let us go to the fields (of heaven)".[44] Likewise Jean Gerson, Chancellor of the University of Paris, renowned for his erudition and holiness alike, although appearing to be in excellent health, died three days after expounding fifty aspects of divine love as described in the *Song of Songs.* He, too, is said to have died with a line from the *Song* on his lips: "not death itself is so strong as your love, my God."[45] *The Song of Songs* would seem to be a dangerous book!

St John of the Cross unashamedly took the *Song of Songs* as the inspiration for his *Spiritual Canticle,* in which he borrows and interprets much of the imagery of the *Song.* St Teresa of Ávila, a contemporary of St John of the Cross, also wrote a full commentary on the *Song.* But those were the days of the Inquisition, and Diego de Yangues, a renowned theologian and preacher, as well as St Teresa's confessor for some time, ordered her to burn her manuscript. He considered it an improper subject for a woman.

Christian writers have varied in their identification of the

Lover and the Beloved. For many, the Lover represents the soul, while the Beloved has either been understood as God or as Jesus, the focus of their personal love. Some have interpreted the Beloved as Christ and the Lover as the Church, while others have viewed Mary the mother of Jesus as the Bride of God. But it is inconceivable that Jesus, his mother or the Church could have figured in the poet's mind so many centuries before their time. This can only be a later interpretation. Nor is there any hint that the *Song of Songs* was written as a prophecy of the coming Messiah, who could have been understood by Christianity as Jesus.

But there were other interpretations. Bernard of Clairvaux, John of the Cross and Gregory of Nyssa interpreted the *Song* as depicting the love between the soul and the Creative Word. Calling the *Song* the "sacred text", Gregory writes of its allegorical nature:

> The sacred text uses expressions the obvious meaning of which would suggest carnal passion; and yet it does not slip into any improper meaning, but rather uses such words to instruct us by chaste concepts in the life that is divine.
>
> *Gregory of Nyssa, On Canticles 1, GGGN p.155*

And again:

> In the sacred text, we shall find the soul clothed, in a sense, in the garment of a bride to prepare it for a pure and spiritual marriage with God that has nothing to do with the body.
>
> *Gregory of Nyssa, On Canticles 1, GGGN p.153*

Throughout his commentary, he identifies the Beloved with the Word. Describing the evolution of the soul's love, he writes:

> We see the Word, then, leading the Bride up a rising stair-case, as it were, up to the heights by the ascent of perfection.... Then he bids the Bride draw near to the light.... Then she proceeds even further. Becoming more clear

sighted, she begins to comprehend the beauty of the Word.
She marvels how he descends in shadow to the bed of this
life, under the shade, as it were, of the matter of his human
body.

Gregory of Nyssa, On Canticles 5, 6, GGGN pp.190, 198

Origen, too, understood the Beloved to be the Word, seeing the
Lover as either the Church or the soul. As he says at the outset of
his commentary:

> It seems to me that this little book is an *epithalamium*, that
> is to say a marriage song, which Solomon wrote in the form
> of a drama, and sang under the figure of the Bride about to
> wed, and burning with heavenly love towards her Bride-
> groom, who is the Word of God. And deeply indeed did she
> love him, whether we take her as the soul made in his image,
> or as the Church.

Origen, On The Song of Songs I:1, OSS p.21

In accordance with Christian doctrine, these mystical writers
understood Jesus to have been the only personification or incarnation of the Word. Nevertheless, they are very close to the
Song's fourth level of meaning – the love existing between all
Masters of the Word and their disciples. And it is this interpretation that provides both an overall structure as well as a
precise understanding of many of the details in the imagery of
the *Song*. Included in this interpretation is the love of the soul
for God and for the Word, since God, the Word and a true
Saviour are all one. Essential 'technical' details of the inner
journey are also given, using common mystic metaphors, as we
will see. But although the love of the soul for God and for a
Saviour who has passed is acknowledged, it is often difficult for
people to understand the love for a living Saviour. But this is
something that has been the same between all Masters and their
disciples, in all ages and in all cultures. It is universal, and will
always be so.

The majority of people do not know that such a love even exists in the world today. They do not realize that the love that existed between Jesus and his disciples is present between all Masters and their disciples. But, at least initially, the Master and the disciple must both be living in this world at the same time. Love for a Master who died long ago can only be the product of imagination, encouraged by emotion. It is the living devotee of a living Saviour who can really understand the nature of this divine love affair.

Even so, the Christian mystics achieved what they did by an intensely personal love for the long-departed Jesus and a deep yearning to meet him inside. Imaginary or real, it is this personal love that provides the mind with something conceivable upon which to focus. This is one of the reasons why Christianity insists on the need of Jesus and the Word as intermediaries between the soul and God.

It is very difficult for a human being to love God directly, without a divine intermediary. How can we truly love a little understood divine power through the force of our own imagination, even though he be of our own essence? Love is a matter of experience, not of reason, intuition or imagination. Love is far more real when it is for someone with whom we have had direct personal experience, human to human. As the writer of the *Odes of Solomon* puts it:

> For I have a Helper to the Lord.
> He made himself known to me,
>   without grudging, in his generosity:
> For in his kindness,
>   he set aside his majesty.
> He became like me,
>   in order that I might accept him.
> In appearance, he seemed like me,
>   that I might be clothed in him.

And I did not tremble when I saw him,
>   because he had compassion for me.
He became like my nature,
>   that I might come to know him;
And like my form,
>   that I might not turn away from him.

Odes of Solomon 7:3–6, OSD p.30

The Lord comes in the form of a true Saviour, a personification of Wisdom, the Word, the *Logos*. He is a sage, a "man of understanding", a "Friend of God". And he is so kind, so beautiful and graceful, so full of wisdom, so selfless in his capacity to give, so – as the *Song* says – "altogether lovable",[46] that he melts and captures the hearts of those who are lucky enough to know him. Having attached the soul to himself in his physical form, he then draws the soul inside, first to meet his radiant, spiritual form on the threshold of the inner mansions, and then to take the soul back to the Lord, to the kingdom of God, to the real home of the exiled soul. This is the fourth and most sublime meaning of the *Song of Songs*.

The Content of the Song of Songs

In the arrangement presented here, following that of the *Jerusalem Bible*, the *Song of Songs* consists of a suite of five poems, plus a prologue and finale. Although these five poems are all centred on the theme of divine love, a definite organization, including a description of the evolution of that love, can be discerned among them. In addition to the prevailing theme, the poet also touches on other aspects of the perennial mystic path.

In the title and prologue, the keynote of love is declared, and the song is ascribed to Solomon, the archetypal king of mystic or divine Wisdom. The poet's intention to speak of divine love is expressed at the outset. As the lover says:

> Your love is more delightful than wine....
> How right it is to love you.
> >> *Song of Songs 1:2, 4, JB*

The first poem then concerns the hidden beauty of the soul, held captive in human form. The soul says:

> I am black but lovely.
> >> *Song of Songs 1:5, JB*

And the Beloved responds:

> As a lily among the thistles,
> >> so is my love among the maidens.
> >>>> *Song of Songs 2:2, JB*

The soul is beautiful, yet caught in the travail of human imperfection. But her Beloved, who is a shepherd at the beginning of this poem and a king at the end, is there to guide her and to take care of her spiritual interests. As she says:

> In his longed-for shade I am seated,
> >> and his fruit is sweet to my taste.
> He has taken me to his banquet hall,
> >> and the banner he raises over me is love.
> >>>> *Song of Songs 2:3–4, JB*

The second poem opens with the coming of the Beloved from the heavenly regions, making a dwelling for himself within the disciple. The Lover cries:

> I hear my Beloved.
> See how he comes,
> >> leaping on the mountains,
> >> bounding over the hills.
> >>>> *Song of Songs 2:8, JB*

The Beloved travels fleetly through the inner realms and comes to the 'house' of the soul – the body:

> He looks in at the window,
>   he peers through the lattice.
>
> *Song of Songs 2:9, JB*

The "voice" of the Beloved is given prominence. It symbolizes the Creative Word or Wisdom as the Voice of God or the divine Melody. The Beloved calls to the soul. As a result, she longs to see his spiritual form:

> Show me your face,
>   let me hear your voice;
> For your voice is sweet,
>   and your face is beautiful.[47]
>
> *Song of Songs 2:14, JB*

Responding to his call, the sleeping soul awakens, enjoying the sweetness of spiritual springtime in her yearning to reach her Beloved within. At length, she finds him in the heavenly "pastures", and is united with him in mystic rapture:

> My Beloved is mine and I am his.
> He pastures his flock among the lilies.
>
> *Song of Songs 2:16, JB*

In the third poem, the poet begins by describing the Beloved as the mystic King who comes to the desert of this world to rescue captive souls. Here, the Beloved is identified specifically with Solomon and by inference with Moses – who led the children of Israel from Egypt through the desert to the promised land, guided by a "pillar of cloud"[48] or a "column of smoke". The divine nature of the Beloved is thus indicated once again:

What (who) is this coming up from the desert
   like a column of smoke,
   breathing of myrrh and frankincense,
   and every perfume the merchant knows?
See, it is the litter of Solomon.

Song of Songs 3:6–7, JB

The poem then continues with an expression of the great love
borne by such a Saviour towards his disciples. The Beloved
praises the innate virtues and beauty of the soul, filling her with
encouragement for the arduous spiritual journey ahead. Her true
nature, he says, is like "milk" and "honey", while "Lebanon"
symbolizes the eternity of her inner being:

Your lips, my promised one,
   distil wild honey.
Honey and milk
   are under your tongue;
And the scent of your garments
   is like the scent of Lebanon.

Song of Songs 4:11, JB

The soul responds by inviting the Beloved to enter the "garden"
of her soul – an invitation he accepts, inviting all his friends (his
disciples) to eat and drink their fill of his spiritual treasures:

I come into my garden,
   my sister, my promised bride;
I gather my myrrh and balsam,
   I eat my honey and my honeycomb,
   I drink my wine and my milk.
Eat, friends, and drink:
   drink deep, my dearest friends.

Song of Songs 5:1, JB

The fourth poem, like the second, opens with the awakening call of the Master, beckoning from within:

> I sleep, but my heart is awake.
> I hear my Beloved knocking.
>
> *Song of Songs 5:2, JB*

The soul, now a more seasoned devotee, becomes intensely aware of the Beloved's inner presence, and tries to reach him. She speaks of withdrawing from the world and from the body:

> I have taken off my tunic,
>   am I to put it on again?
> I have washed my feet,
>   am I to dirty them again?
>
> *Song of Songs 5:3, JB*

This time, the Beloved only permits her a glimpse of himself before withdrawing further into the inner pastures. This fleeting sight of him serves to intensify and purify her longing, and she breaks into a paean of loving praise for her Beloved. This, *par excellence,* is the song of longing and separation – the joy of being with the Beloved followed by the intense pang of separation that only serves to deepen and purify her love. The interplay of union and separation is an essential part of the spiritual purification of any disciple. The chorus of devotees then calls out:

> Where did your Beloved go,
>   O loveliest of women?
> Which way did your Beloved turn,
>   so that we can help you look for him?
>
> *Song of Songs 6:1, JB*

And she replies that he has gone to the heavenly regions, leaving her behind:

My Beloved went down to his garden,
to the beds of spices,
to pasture his flock in the gardens
and gather lilies.

Song of Songs 6:2, JB   ·

The fifth poem begins with the Beloved's expression of his eternal love for the soul and – most importantly – with the purpose of his coming into the world (the "nut orchard"). He has come to help the seekers of spirituality (the "vines" and "pomegranate trees"):

I went down to the nut orchard
to see what was sprouting in the valley,
to see if the vines were budding
and the pomegranate trees in flower.

Song of Songs 5:11, JB

This is followed by a portrayal of the soul incarnate in human form as a "dance of two camps" – symbolizing the human struggle between the seemingly opposing forces of spirit and matter:

Why do you gaze on the maid of Shulam[49]
as a dance of two camps?

Song of Songs 7:1, JB

The beauty, nature and spiritual purpose of the human form is then further described, the poem culminating in the soul's plea to be taken into the pastures of heaven, and with an expression of her undying love for her Beloved:

Come, my Beloved,
let us go to the fields.
We will spend the night in the villages,
and in the morning we will go to the vineyards....
Then I shall give you the gift of my love.

Song of Songs 7:12–13, JB

The short, concluding poem begins with a description of the liberation or salvation of the soul from the desert of the world. The Beloved describes how he has awakened the soul. He speaks of the strong, unbreakable bond of love between the soul and the divine Beloved. The *Song* then ends, as it began, with the praise of divine love:

> Love no flood can quench,
>   no torrents drown.
>
> *Song of Songs 8:7, JB*

A number of additions follow the poem, made by various scribes and others, and somehow incorporated into the manuscripts we have today. One of these is poignantly beautiful and clearly expresses the mystic understanding which that particular reader or scribe derived from the *Song*. It is set as an epilogue:

> You who dwell in the gardens,
>   the companions listen for your voice;
> Deign to let me hear it.
>
> *Song of Songs 8:13, JB*

The unknown devotee begs the Beloved who lives in the "gardens" of the higher realms to be given the grace to hear the divine Voice of God. This is the prayer of all disciples.

It can be readily observed from this synopsis that there is a structure to this suite of poems. At the outset, the theme is stated and the role of the divine Beloved is outlined. A picture is painted of the soul's condition in the world, and the Beloved's part in releasing the soul from this captivity is described.

The game of love then begins. The Beloved comes to dwell within the devotee and sounds the mystic call. The soul awakens, and has her first taste of inner communion with him. The role of the Saviour is further elucidated and the interplay of love continues, the soul again meeting her Beloved on the inner planes.

But the course of true love never runs smooth, else it is taken for granted. So, like a good dramatist, adding tone and character to his theme, the poet introduces a setback in the unfolding of the divine love affair. Rising up from the body in the ecstasy of her love, the soul is full with the expectation of meeting her Beloved within. But the Beloved only gives a glimpse of himself before withdrawing. The soul's love is thereby intensified and deepened.

Finally, of course, the Beloved restates his love for the soul – not that it was ever really in doubt – and his purpose in coming to the world. And the soul begs to be taken into the inner realms and back to her original home. The *Song* then ends with the release of the soul from the desert of the world, and a reiteration of the power of divine love.

PART II

The Song

Title and Prologue

Your Love is more Delightful than Wine

The themes of wisdom and divine love are introduced.

TITLE: The Song of Songs, which is Solomon's.

LOVER: Let him kiss me with the kisses of his mouth.
Your love is more delightful than wine;
Delicate is the fragrance of your perfume;
Your name is an oil poured out,
and that is why the maidens love you.

Draw me in your footsteps, let us run.
Take me, O king, into your chambers.[1]
You will be our joy and our gladness.
We shall praise your love above wine;
How right it is to love you.

The Song of Solomon

TITLE: The Song of Songs, which is Solomon's.

This is the greatest of all songs:
the mystic song of the divine King, the Sage.

In the title line, the poet states his intention. This song or poem is the "Song of Songs". No song is greater than the song of divine love. It is a melody in the soul and a sweetness of the spirit, a blissful intoxication and an ecstasy of mystic transcendence. It is the power that returns the soul to God, a healing balm that removes all sorrows. It is the one song that eclipses all other songs. Truly, divine love is the song of songs. The loves of this world pale to insignificance by comparison:

> Only the touch of the Spirit can inspire a song like this, and only personal experience can unfold its meaning. Let those who are versed in the mystery revel in it; let all others burn with desire to attain to this experience than merely to learn about it. For it is not a melody that resounds abroad, but the very music of the heart; not a trilling on the lips, but an inward pulsing of delight.
>
> *Bernard of Clairvaux, On The Song of Songs 1:12, WBC1 pp.6–7*

The *Song* is also the Song of "Solomon", the song of the one epitomized in Jewish mysticism as the source and fountainhead of all divine wisdom. The *Song* is written in this mystic tradition. It is stated at the outset to be a song of pure love between the divine soul and the mystic Beloved. It contains the essence of all the several thousand psalms and songs said to have been written by Solomon.[2]

The Kisses of his Mouth

LOVER: Let him kiss me with the kisses of his mouth.

May he draw me with the intensity of his love,
with the power of his Word.

The soul is a part of God, a drop from his ocean, a spark from his fire. No union is closer than that of a drop merging into an ocean, of a flame into a fire. Here the soul, the Bride or Lover, expresses her inner, divine love in intimate terms.

"Kisses" signify the inward closeness of the Lover and the Beloved who become one in mystic transport. The "kisses of his mouth" also refer to the Creative Word that issues out of the "mouth" of God. The human mouth speaks words, so – metaphorically – what proceeds lovingly out of the mouth of God is his Wisdom, his Creative Word, his creative Power:

A kiss is an operation of the sense of touch: in a kiss two pairs of lips touch. There is, however, a spiritual faculty of touch, which comes in contact with the Word, and this is actuated by a spiritual and immaterial sense of touch.

Gregory of Nyssa, On Canticles 1, GGGN p.156

His living, active Word is ... a kiss, not indeed an adhering of the lips that can sometimes belie a union of hearts, but an unreserved infusion of joys, a revealing of mysteries, a marvellous and indistinguishable mingling of the divine light with the enlightened mind, which, joined in truth to God, is one spirit with him.

Bernard of Clairvaux, On The Song of Songs 2:2, WBC1 p.9

The soul is kissed by God when she is elevated above all temporal things and beholds only God's countenance. God then inclines his countenance and kisses her, and his kissing is simply a dissolving of love with Love. One gazes at the other, and neither can do anything without the other. By love are they bound together.

Book of the Poor in Spirit III:IV.2, BPS pp.182–83

> Deathless Life has embraced me,
>   and kissed me;
> And from that Life is the spirit within me,
>   and it cannot die, because it is Life itself.
>
> *Odes of Solomon 28:6–7, OSD p126*

According to an interpretation of the Bible given in the *Talmud,* the prophets Moses, Aaron and Miriam all died by a kiss from God:

> The sages (in the *Talmud*) have indicated with reference to the deaths of Moses, Aaron and Miriam that the three of them died by a kiss. They said[3] that the dictum (of Scripture), "And Moses the servant of the Lord died there in the land of Moab by the mouth of the Lord,"[4] indicates that he died by a kiss. Similarly, it is said of Aaron, "by the mouth of the Lord, and died there".[5] And they said of Miriam in the same way, "she also died by a kiss". But with regard to her it is not said, "by the mouth of the Lord"; because she was a woman, the use of the figurative expression was not suitable with regard to her.
>
> Their purpose was to indicate that the three of them died in the pleasure of this apprehension due to the intensity of passionate (divine) love. In this dictum, the Sages – may their memory be blessed – followed the generally accepted poetical way of expression that calls the apprehension that is achieved in a state of intense and passionate love for him – may he be exalted – a "kiss", in accordance with its dictum: "Let him kiss me with the kisses of his mouth", and so on....
>
> (The Sages) – may their memory be blessed – mention the occurrence of this kind of death, which in reality is salvation from death, only with regard to Moses, Aaron and Miriam.
>
> *Moses Maimonides, Guide of the Perplexed III:51, GP2 pp.627–28*

The nineteenth-century scholar, Adolphe Franck, similarly quotes the *Zohar* on the real nature of such kisses:

"In one of the most mysterious and most exalted parts of heaven, there is a palace of love. The most profound mysteries are there; there are all souls well beloved by the celestial King, the Holy One, praised be He, together with the holy spirits with whom he unites by kisses of love."[6] Hence, the death of the righteous is referred to as God's kiss.... This kiss is the union of the soul with the Substance (Source) from which it springs.

Adolphe Franck, KRPH p.136

To "die by a kiss from God" is to go through the process of 'dying while living' while retaining full consciousness and control. It is the withdrawal of the soul and mind from the body, leading ultimately to the union of the soul with God.

More Delightful than Wine

LOVER: Your love is more delightful than wine.

The sweetness and ecstasy of your love
excel all intoxications of this world.

"Wine" is intoxicating in a worldly sense, but the wine of divine love is blissful, ecstatic and far more intoxicating, "delightful" and inwardly overpowering than the effect of any outward wine:

Spiritual love is wine and fragrance.
All those who anoint themselves with it take pleasure in it.

Gospel of Philip 77–78, NHS20 p.199

Satisfy yourself with the true wine in which there is no drunkenness nor error. For it marks the end of drinking since there is in it (the power) to give joy to the soul and the mind through the Spirit of God. But before you can drink of it, you must cultivate your meditation *(logismos)*.

Teachings of Silvanus 107–8; cf. NHS30 pp.340–41

[Good is the] wine that is pressed,
   all full of good Wisdom.
He that shall drink of it, his eyes shine in his head,
   his thought is firm in his heart.[7]
He has remembered the great [and true] … Vine.

Psalms of Thomas XIX, Manichaean Psalm Book; cf. MPB p.225

The Fragrance of your Perfume

LOVER: Delicate is the fragrance of your perfume.

*How subtle, hidden and delightful is the Breath
and Fragrance of divinity, of the Creative Word
that is your essence.*

The soul experiences that the Master, outwardly as well as within, is surrounded by an atmosphere, an intense vibration or "perfume", a subtle, "delicate", yet overwhelming "fragrance" – the fragrance of the Word:

> The smell of the divine perfumes does not proceed from the smell of our nostrils but from a spiritual faculty, which draws in the sweet odour … by an inhalation of the spirit.
>
> *Gregory of Nyssa, On Canticles 1, GGGN p.156*

> The sense of smell, by which the Bride and the maidens perceived the fragrance of the Bridegroom's ointments, denotes not a bodily faculty, but that divine sense of scent, which is called the sense of the interior man.
>
> *Origen, On the Song of Songs I:4, OSS pp.80–81*

> It is not the (outer) ears that scent this Fragrance. It is the soul (*lit.* breath) that has the (necessary) faculty, being attracted by the Fragrance and becoming merged in this Fragrance of the Father, to the extent that she takes shelter in it and is taken to its place of origin.
>
> *Gospel of Truth 33–34; cf. NHS21 p.105*

That soul only is perfect who has her sense of smell so pure
and purged that it can catch the fragrance of the spikenard
and myrrh and cyprus that proceed from the Word of God,
and can inhale the grace of the divine odour.

Origen, On the Song of Songs II:11, OSS p.168

The Fragrance of my Kinsmen (the Masters),
  [do you, (O Word), send] to me.
The sweet Breath of the Spirit
  [do you breathe into] this charnel house (the body).

Manichaean Psalm Book; cf. MPB p.152

Your Name is an Oil

LOVER: Your name is an oil poured out,
and that is why the maidens love you.

Your mystic, holy Name brings peace,
comfort and healing to the soul.
That is why your devotees have so much love for you.

No name of the world, whether of God or anyone else, can of
itself bring true and lasting comfort, and peace of mind. Names
are words created by man, with a history in time. They are
symbols by which to remember something or someone. The
"name" must have another meaning. In fact, it has two.

The name of the Beloved, the name of God, indicates the
memory or thought of him. The Lord is within the soul and, for
a disciple, so too is the Master. Whenever a disciple thinks
lovingly of the Master, there is an immediate response, for he is
the one who is pulling the soul towards himself. He is the one
who is prompting the soul to remember him. His memory
induces an indrawing current of bliss and love to flow through
the mind, healing sorrows and dispelling the weariness of being
in the world.

The "name" is also synonymous with the creative Power. It is
one of the oldest terms for his creative Utterance, used by

mystics of many ages and nations. God is One, without any
name. Where there is only oneness, there are no names, for who
is to name who? A thing can only be named when there are two
or more. Therefore, God's First-born Power, his Creative Word,
his Wisdom, the creative Power or Life Force within everything
in his creation, has commonly been called his "Name".[8] It is
God's

> First-born *Logos* ... of many names; for it is called Beginning
> (Source), and Name of God, and *Logos*.
>
> *Philo, On the Confusion of Tongues 28; cf. TGH1 p.234*

It is this Name of God that performs the role of Saviour,
mediator and comforter, both as the outward, human Master
and as the inwardly audible and visible Life Stream, experienced
mystically as sound and light. The first thing we do when we
wish to make contact with someone is to discover their name.
Similarly, the way to contact God is through his mystic or hidden
Name. It is his signature or Sign in all things.

The soul says that this "name" – whether as the remembrance
of the Saviour or as the creative Power – is an "oil poured out".
"Oil" is used as a salve, a comforter for the wounded and the
weary. She says that the "name" represents an oil of this kind to
the one who is tired of life in this world:

> He not only bestows a fragrant comfort, ...
> but actually seems to be comfort and fragrance itself.
>
> *St Francis de Sales, Love of God 8:7, LG p.331*

It gives light; it nourishes; it anoints. It feeds the flame; it
nourishes the body; it relieves pain. It is light, food, medicine.
And is not this true too of the Bridegroom's name? When
preached, it gives light; when meditated it nourishes; when
invoked it relieves and soothes.

> *Bernard of Clairvaux, On The Song of Songs 15:5, WBC1 p.109*

It is the experience of this divine "name" or "oil" that makes the "maidens" or devotees of the Lord love him, for the mystic Sound is inwardly sweet and captivating, while the light is deeply entrancing.

The symbols of "maidens" and "oil" were later used by Jesus in his parable of the Bridegroom, where the oil is the spiritual practice or interior prayer used to keep the lamp of the soul alight and burning:

> We knocked at the door, the door was opened to us,
>   we went in with the Bridegroom.
> We were numbered in the number of the virgins
>   in whose lamps oil was found.
>
> *Manichaean Psalm Book, MPB p.170*

> Since you knew, O soul who loves God,
>   that it is yet a weak house in which you dwell,
> you have lit your lanterns and put oil in your lamps,
> and have not allowed them to go out,
> until they came and summoned you.
>
> *Manichaean Psalm Book CCLVIII; cf. MPB p.70*

In some translations of the *Song,* the "maidens" are rendered as "virgins",[9] which makes the meaning clearer. "Virgins" are symbolic of purity, in all senses of the term, and only those who are pure in mind are capable of loving the divine Beloved. Divine love fills the mind. Therefore, only one whose mind is empty of material thoughts, desires and activities of the world can experience this higher spiritual love:

> Receive me into your bridal chambers, you my Saviour....
> I am a maiden (devotee) unspotted and holy.
>
> *Manichaean Psalm Book CCLXIII; cf. MPB p.79*

In your Footsteps

LOVER: Draw me in your footsteps, let us run.

Draw me after you; let us waste no time.

The "footsteps" of the Beloved lead to the inner realms; they trace the path of the divine Word, the Name of God, leading to eternity:

> You ascended with great glory,
>   and you took up with you
>   all who sought refuge with you,
>   and marked out for them the Path leading up on high;
> And in your footsteps all your redeemed followed.
>
> *Acts of Thomas 8; cf. AAA p.288*

The soul asks to be drawn because she knows that of her own power she cannot follow where the Beloved leads. By the magic of his inner grace and love, he has to pull or "draw" the soul after himself.

"Let us run," the soul then pleads in her eagerness:

> Draw me even against my will, and make me docile; draw me despite my indolence, and make me run.
>
> *Bernard of Clairvaux, On The Song of Songs 21:9, WBC2 p.11*

"You begin," she means, "for I cannot waken by myself. I am unable to move without an impulse from you. Once you have given me that impulse, however, why then, dear Bridegroom of mine, 'we hasten', the pair of us. You run on ahead, drawing me after you, further and further. As for me, I follow in your footsteps, accepting your graces, yielding to your attractions. Let no one think you are drawing me behind you like an unwilling slave or an inanimate cart – O no, I am following you 'by the very fragrance of those perfumes allured!'[10] I am following you, not because you are dragging me, but because you are attracting me. Yet, though your attractions are powerful, they are not violent, since their strength lies in their gentleness." Only the charm of perfume renders it capable of attracting; and such attraction – can it be anything else but charming, pleasant?

St Francis de Sales, Love of God 2:13, LG p.85

When a soul, prompted by grace, feels God's initial attractions and consents to his charms, she begins to sigh as though awakening from a long coma: "My Bridegroom, my friend, draw me, I beg you. Take me by the arm, else I cannot move. Only if you draw me, shall we hasten, both of us: you, in alluring me by the very fragrance of your perfumes." ...

The soul would not be praying were not God prompting her; but as soon as he does, as soon as she feels his attraction, she prays to be drawn. If she is drawn, she runs; but she runs only if the perfumes which attract her ravish the heart by their fragrance. The swifter the soul's progress and the nearer she comes to the Bridegroom, the more delightfully she experiences his charms; until, at last, he enters the soul, soothes the heart like tranquillizing balm. Then the soul exclaims in surprise at such unexpected, undreamed-of delight: "My Bridegroom, your perfumes pour themselves into my heart like the flow of oil; what wonder that man should love you?"

St Francis de Sales, Love of God 2:21; cf. LG pp.106–7

Through the attractive power of his grace and love, a Master takes souls out of this world so rapidly that they can be said to "run" with him. The soul has been lost in the creation for billions of lifetimes, enmeshed in an incredible tangle of associations, attachments and involvements of all kinds. Impressions of all these are stored within the mind, drawing the soul back to the physical realm in birth after birth. Yet mystics say that love for them and for their inner reality – the creative Power – frees the soul from this bondage in practically no time at all. Even rebirth in this world is only for exceptionally recalcitrant individuals. Once a soul has met a Master, the end is in sight. After that the Master "runs" with the soul, straight back to God.

As a consequence, the soul begs:

Into your Chambers

> LOVER: Take me, O king, into your chambers.

> *Take me up, my Beloved,*
> *to meet with you in the heavenly realms.*

In the symbolism of the poem, the "king" is King Solomon, the wise sage, the mystic sovereign, the Master of the mystic Wisdom. The "king" is therefore the Saviour and "his chambers" are the inner mansions – the inner regions of creation. They are the "bridal chambers" of which many mystics have spoken, where the soul and the Beloved meet:[11]

> Take me into your bridal chambers
>   that I may chant with them that sing to you.
>   *Manichaean Psalm Book; cf. MPB p.117*

The soul is begging the Master to take her into the inner realms of creation, where she seeks the divine and radiant form of her spiritual "king":

> My heart is stirred by a noble theme:
>   I address my poem to the King;
>   my tongue as ready as the pen of a busy scribe.
> Of all men, you are the most handsome,
>   your lips are moist with grace,
>   for God has blessed you forever.
>   *Psalms 45:1–2, JB*

This King whom you have is forever invincible,
   against whom no one will be able to fight,
   nor say a word.
This is your King and your Father,
   for there is no one like him.
The divine Teacher is with you always.
He is a Helper, and he meets you
   because of the good that is in you.

Teachings of Silvanus 96–97; cf. NHS30 pp.308–11

How Right it is to Love you

LOVER: You will be our joy and our gladness.
   We shall praise your love above wine;
   How right it is to love you.

You are my source of happiness and bliss. Love for you is greater by far than the intoxication of wine. There is nothing higher than love for you. It is the essence of Truth.

A Master is always surrounded by an atmosphere of great bliss and happiness. Held by the strength of his loving presence, the Lover soon forgets all her worldly cares. Her heart is filled with an inner joy. This intoxication of love is far superior to "wine" – symbolic of the world's commonest source of 'happiness':

Yahweh, you have given more joy to my heart
   than others ever knew, for all their corn and wine.

Psalms 4:7, JB

You have turned my mourning into dancing:
   you have stripped off my sackcloth,
   and wrapped me in gladness;
And now my heart, silent no longer, will play you music:
Yahweh, my God, I will praise you forever.

Psalms 30:11–12, JB

To love God and to find him within with the help and guidance of the divine Beloved is actually the spiritual purpose of life. It is not "right" for the royal soul to give her love to anything or anyone but the King: the Lord and the Master are the only "right" ones to love.

First Poem

I am Black but Lovely

The soul, though imprisoned in human form, speaks of her own essential and inherent beauty, a theme reiterated by the Beloved. The soul goes on to praise the beauty of her Beloved. The two then express their feelings in a dialogue of mutual love and divine intimacy.

LOVER: I am black but lovely, daughters of Jerusalem,
like the tents of Kedar,
like the pavilions of Salmah (Solomon).
Take no notice of my swarthiness,
it is the sun that has burnt me.
My mother's sons turned their anger on me,
they made me look after the vineyards.
Had I only looked after my own!

Tell me then, you whom my heart (soul) loves:
where will you lead your flock to graze,
where will you rest it at noon?
That I may no more wander like a vagabond
beside the flocks of your companions.

CHORUS: If you do not know this, O loveliest of women,
follow the tracks of the flock,
and take your kids to graze
close by the shepherds' tents.

BELOVED: To my mare harnessed to Pharaoh's chariot
I compare you, my love.
Your cheeks show fair between their pendants,
and your neck within its necklaces.
We shall make you golden earrings
and beads of silver.

LOVER: While the king rests in his own room,
my nard yields its perfume.
My Beloved is a sachet of myrrh
lying between my breasts.
My Beloved is a cluster of henna flowers
among the vines of Engedi.

BELOVED: How beautiful you are my love,
how beautiful you are!
Your eyes are doves.

LOVER: How beautiful you are, my Beloved,
and how delightful!
All green is our bed.

BELOVED: The beams of our house are of cedar,
the panelling of cypress.

LOVER: I am the rose of Sharon,
the lily of the valleys.

BELOVED: As a lily among the thistles,
so is my love among the maidens.

LOVER: As an apple tree among the trees of the orchard,
so is my Beloved among the young men.
In his longed-for shade I am seated,
and his fruit is sweet to my taste.
He has taken me to his banquet hall,
and the banner he raises over me is love.
Feed me with raisin cakes,
restore me with apples,
for I am sick with love.

His left arm is under my head,
his right embraces me.

BELOVED: I charge you,
daughters of Jerusalem,
by the gazelles, by the hinds of the field,
not to stir my love nor rouse it,
until it please to awake.

Take no Notice of my Swarthiness

LOVER: I am black but lovely, daughters of Jerusalem,
          like the tents of Kedar,
    like the pavilions of Salmah (Solomon).
      Take no notice of my swarthiness,
        it is the sun that has burnt me.

From my external appearance, I may seem impure,
but my soul within is beautiful and perfect.
I may look like an old and worn out wineskin,
but inside I am full of the finest fragrant wine.
My Beloved, please ignore my unbecoming aspect.
It is only my body and my mind – my outer garments –
that have become imperfect
through exposure to physical existence.

At the very outset, the soul acknowledges her situation – that she is swarthy, that she has been burnt black by the sun. The Hebrew word used here denotes the ruddy hue caused by long exposure to the sun. Being burnt is symbolic of undergoing an ordeal, in this case, of living in the physical world, of travelling through innumerable births under the influence of the mind.

The soul, whose real home is with God, is caught by the mind in countless snares. She thus remains in the whirlpool of birth and death, tossed by the waves of lust, anger, greed and egotism, and caught by attachments and entanglements of every kind to the physical realm of the creation. Life after life, taking one form after another in thrall to the mind, the soul is subject to this ordeal. She is burnt black by the turbulent fire of the mind and senses. But, like a princess lost in a far-off land, the soul's essential royalty is never lost – only forgotten. The soul's intrinsic beauty and comeliness remain hidden under layers of blackness and darkness:

Do not condemn me because I am black, for my blackness is all external. It is due to touching and bearing this image of sin (the body), but it is not a blackness of soul.

Walter Hilton, Ladder of Perfection II:12, LP p.135

She is black only on the outside, "like the tents of Kedar". The nomadic tribesmen of Kedar, who traced their descent from Ishmael, son of Abraham and Hagar (handmaid of Sarah), lived in black goat-hair tents. "Kedar" comes from the Hebrew root *keder,* meaning 'dark' or 'black'. The people of Kedar were also famed for their riches. Their tents were rumoured to conceal a treasury of diamonds and precious stones. Similarly, the soul after her long existence in this world may appear black on the outside due to the imperfections of mind and body, but inside she never loses her divine value and royal estate. An untold spiritual wealth and treasure is hidden within her:

Our bodily dwelling-place … is neither a citizen's residence nor one's native home, but rather a soldier's tent or traveller's hut. This body … is a tent, a tent of Kedar, that now intervenes to deprive the soul for a while of the vision of the infinite light.

Bernard of Clairvaux, On The Song of Songs 26:1, WBC2 p.59

She is also comely, "like the pavilions of Salmah (Solomon)". Pavilions are ornate and decorative shelters, suitable for royalty, more beautiful within than without, to provide peace and delight while resting. She is being compared to the dwelling place of Solomon, eternity, another allusion to her divinely royal origin.

So the soul says that after all her experiences, she may look as weather-beaten as an old, black and well-travelled tent. Nevertheless, she still claims her royal birthright; she reminds the Beloved that underneath it all she is still beautiful, still fit for the love of a king:

Be like a jar of wine,
    firmly set upon its stand;
For the outside indeed is a piece of pottery
    covered with pitch,
    while inside it is a fragrant wine.

Psalms of Thomas XIII, Manichaean Psalm Book, MPB p.220

The "daughters of Jerusalem", addressed occasionally by both
the Lover and the Beloved as an imaginary audience, are the
Lover's fellow devotees – those who worship at the mystic shrine
within. Just as the Jerusalem of this world became a place of
pilgrimage and worship, so symbolically was the kingdom of
God referred to as the heavenly Jerusalem.[1]

My Mother's Sons

LOVER: My mother's sons turned their anger on me,
        they made me look after the vineyards.
        Had I only looked after my own!

*The negative forces in creation, by creating human
imperfection and the illusion of the world, have made me
waste my time in the pursuit of material mirages.
How I wish I had attended
to my own spiritual welfare instead!*

The soul now explains how she has come to be so sunburnt. She
points out that it was not really her fault for, "my mother's sons
turned their anger on me". The "mother" of the soul, another of
the age-old mystic symbols, is Wisdom, the Creative Word, the
Holy Spirit – a feminine noun in both Greek and Hebrew. The
soul is given life and existence by the Holy Spirit. The relationship is one of love, like that of a child and a mother. It is one of
complete dependence and selflessness. The essence of the soul is
the Holy Spirit. Mystically and allegorically, therefore, the Holy
Spirit is the divine Mother,[2] while the soul is the divine child:

Return, my son, to your first Father, God,
and Wisdom your Mother,
from whom you came into being from the very first.

Teachings of Silvanus 91; cf. NHS30 pp.296–97

We shall … be quite correct in saying that the Architect who
made this universe is at the same time the Father of what has
been brought into existence; while its Mother is the Wisdom
of him who has made it.

Philo, On Drunkenness VIII; cf. PCW3 p.333

The "mother's sons" are the forces that keep the soul separate from
God. Everything in creation is created, ordered and sustained by
the one creative Power, the divine Mother. This includes appar-
ently negative forces. Mystics speak of a negative power or a
'devil' – the universal mind and architect of all multiplicity –
which is primarily responsible for the soul's entanglement in the
creation. This negative power and its sub-powers, which include
all the human energies and faculties of a physical and mental
nature, are hence the "sons" of this creative Power. The divine
Mother is the primary emanation of God, and everything else is
an emanation or projection from her. All forces and powers in
creation are her "sons".

Metaphorically, these "sons" turn their anger on the soul in the
sense that faculties used in normal human life become enemies
when they are permitted to draw the soul into the world. From
faculties, they become imperfections:

"The children of my mother have striven against me". The
children are all the lower powers of the soul, they all strive
against her and attack her.

Meister Eckhart, Sermon 21, MEST1 p.174

When a spiritual overview of life is lost, the natural need to
acquire and possess the basics of life becomes greed for more and
more, and attachment to material things. Likewise, the procreative

faculty can degenerate into self-indulgence and lust. The ability to act and to get things done can turn to anger and resentment when the events of life frustrate our goals and intentions. And a balanced sense of human identity, underlain by a spiritual awareness of the soul as a child of God, becomes an illusory sense of personal ego, pride and separateness, the root cause of all other imbalances, weaknesses or imperfections:

> With the help of Wisdom
>> I have been at pains to study
>> all that is done under heaven.
> O, what a weary task God has given mankind to labour at!
> I have seen everything that is done under the sun,
>> and what vanity it all is,
>> what chasing of the wind!
>
> *Ecclesiastes 1:13–14, JB*

Through these imperfections, the soul comes to work as a slave in the "vineyards" of the world, slaving for others under the hot sun of worldliness and human weakness. As a consequence, she forgets to work in her own spiritual vineyard, to undertake the work that, as a human being, is her own natural work. She works for her "mother's sons" in their "vineyards", and neglects her own. This is how she has come to be so badly sunburnt, something that she now regrets.

Where will you Lead your Flock?

> LOVER: Tell me then, you whom my heart (soul) loves:
>> where will you lead your flock to graze,
>> where will you rest it at noon?

> *Show me, my Beloved, where you lead your disciples,*
> *and where you give them spiritual nourishment.*
> *Where do you take them to escape the fires of the world?*

The Beloved, at first depicted as Solomon the mystic King, is now the Shepherd, the protector of his "flock" of disciples, and the guardian of the soul. As with everything else in life, it is destiny which brings souls to a Master. They are his flock from the beginning. So the soul asks the love of her heart, "Where will you take your band of souls?" –

> Show me then the place of pasture,
>   make known to me the Waters of Rest,
>   lead me out to the good grass,
>   call me by name that I, your sheep,
>   may listen to your voice:
> And may your call be the gift of eternal life.
>
> *Gregory of Nyssa, On Canticles 2; cf. GGGN p.158*

But it is a rhetorical question, for she knows full well that her Beloved leads his "flock" to the inner pastures, the heavenly realms, to "graze" upon the spiritual food of the Word.

"Noon" symbolizes the height of happiness attained by the "sheep" of the Beloved, the Good Shepherd of his people. They know no greater joy than being with their Shepherd – inside or out. For at noon, the shepherd finds a place shaded from the extreme heat of the day, resting there, surrounded by his sheep. The intense heat of the noon-day sun is the fire of the human mind and human imperfection. It is the fire of this world that rages fiercely, though many are unaware of it. It burns the souls black and swarthy. But the mystic Shepherd leads his devotees out of the intense heat of the physical universe:

> The Lord is my Shepherd; I shall not want.
> He makes me lie down in green pastures:
>   he leads me beside the still waters.
> He restores my soul:
>   he leads me in the paths of righteousness
>   for his Name's sake.
>
> *Psalms 23:1–3; cf. KJV*

The ancient shepherds of the Middle East used to lead their flocks, unlike the Western practice of following behind with a dog. The shepherd would also whistle or call his sheep, and they would come to recognize the voice of their shepherd and no other. The call of the mystic Shepherd, recognized by the devotees, is the Voice of God, the celestial Sound, which draws souls away from the dangers of this world:

> I am your sheep: you are my Good Shepherd.
> You came after me and saved me
> from the destructive wolves.
> I listened to your words (Word),
> I walked in your laws (Law),
> I became a stranger in the world
> for your Name's sake, my God.
>
> *Manichaean Psalm Book CCLI; cf. MPB p.60*

It is an easily understood pastoral example, appealing at all times, and commonly used by mystics of that period:

> He that enters by the door
> is the shepherd of the sheep.
> To him the porter (doorkeeper) opens,
> and the sheep hear his Voice:
> And he calls his own sheep by name,
> and leads them out.
> And when he leads forth his own sheep,
> he goes before them,
> and the sheep follow him: for they know his Voice....
>
> My sheep hear my Voice, and I know them,
> and they follow me:
> And I give unto them eternal life,
> and they shall never perish;
> Neither shall any man pluck them out of my hand.
>
> *John 10:2–4, 27–28; cf. KJV*

Like a Vagabond

LOVER: That I may no more wander like a vagabond
beside the flocks of your companions.

For I yearn to reach that place,
to wander no more in spiritual homelessness
amid the throng of your devotees.

The soul compares her "wanderings" in creation to those of a
"vagabond" who wanders aimlessly, moving here and there on
the whim of the moment, at the mercy of circumstance. A
"vagabond" is also destitute, just as the soul who has lost her
royal inheritance is devoid of spiritual wealth. She is like the
prodigal son, the son of a rich father who finds himself poverty-
stricken and eating with the pigs. She is a sheep lost in the
wilderness:

> O wandering sheep,
>   your Shepherd seeks you.
> O noble one despised,
>   your King searches for you.
> *Manichaean Psalm Book; cf. MPB p.146*

"The flocks of your companions" are the disciples who automatically flock around a Master, like sheep around a shepherd, all
desiring his attention. The soul expresses her desire to be taken
inside, to remain no longer in this world where so many souls
constantly surround the Beloved:

> The soul that enjoys God's love is bold enough to say to
> him: "Tell me, good Shepherd, where you graze your Sheep,
> and where you rest your lambs at noon, so that by following
> them I may avoid becoming like one encircled by the flocks
> of your companions."
> *Ilias the Presbyter, Philokalia, Gnomic Anthology IV:96, P3 p.59*

> Where are you going, O Chosen Righteous One,
>   whom all your companions seek –
> For whom all your companions long and desire
>   your appearance among them?
>
> *Mandaean Prayer Book 129; cf. CPM p.120*

A Master has many kinds of disciple, for all have charted different paths through millions of lifetimes, carrying many varied impressions and characteristics with them. So the soul prays that she may be taken inside, and no longer have to clamour like a beggar or a vagabond, along with the myriads of his other disciples. This is the desire of many a devotee who has longed to have time alone with their Master. But this longing can only be adequately fulfilled inside.

The Tracks of the Flock

> CHORUS: If you do not know this, O loveliest of women,
>   follow the tracks of the flock,
>   and take your kids to graze
>   close by the shepherds' tents.

> *Dear divine soul, so full of love,*
>   *if this really is unknown to you,*
>   *then follow in your Beloved's footsteps.*
>   *Find any reason to be close to him within.*
>   *Follow the mystic path trodden by the devotees,*
>   *and discover his inner dwelling place.*

The 'chorus' are the "daughters of Jerusalem". It is a literary device, an imaginary audience of devotees used to emphasize a point or to introduce a theme. Here, the soul is described as the "loveliest of women" because there is nothing that makes a soul more beautiful than being saturated with divine love.

The "tracks of the flock" signify the inner pathway travelled by the devotees in their spiritual practice, leading to the inner meeting with the spiritual form of the Beloved:

> Blessed are you, road of the Teachers,
>   path of the Perfect,
>   track that rises up to the place of light.
>   *Mandaean Prayer Book 71; cf. CPM p.58*

The "shepherds" are the Masters. They know where and how the Divine is to be found. Their "tents" are wherever they are, either in this world or in the inner pastures. "Find some pretext for being close to them," suggest the devotees.

Your Cheeks show Fair

> BELOVED: To my mare harnessed to Pharaoh's chariot
>   I compare you, my love.
>   Your cheeks show fair between their pendants,
>   and your neck within its necklaces.
>   We shall make you golden earrings
>   and beads of silver.
>
> *Beautiful you are, dear soul,*
> *though blinkered by your imperfection.*
> *Your divine heart is pure, but encompassed by impurity.*
> *But have no concern. I will restore your spiritual hearing,*
> *and grant you inner light.*

Using a different metaphor, the divine Beloved echoes the opening thoughts of the Lover. She is beautiful within, but her beauty is concealed by external paraphernalia. He knows the soul to be like those enslaved in Egypt, the physical domain, and in thrall to Pharaoh, symbolic of the 'lord' of this world, the negative power. But though in slavery, the soul is still fair and beautiful to the Beloved's eyes, for the soul is a particle of God's light. He promises to replace the cheap shackles of slavery – the "pendants" and the "necklaces" – with gold and silver. He promises to exchange the fetters of the body and the tawdry quality of life here for the true inner riches of the soul.

In ancient times, as in some places today, a fine horse was seen as an object of great beauty, a treasured companion of kings and noblemen. The fine "mare" of the Beloved is the steed upon which he 'rides' – the creative Power. The essence of a soul is also this Creative Word. But she is "harnessed to Pharaoh's chariot" – she is enslaved by the 'lord' of this world. Against her inclinations, she is held in Egypt and forced to perform menial tasks, to carry Pharaoh upon her back, wearing his shackles around her.

But the Master sees the beauty of the soul shining fair beneath her wrappings of mind and body. He sees her "cheeks and neck showing fair" behind Pharaoh's encumbrances of iron pendants and necklaces, wound tightly around the throat, choking her vitality. Despite the coverings that surround her, diminishing her natural light and glory, the Beloved still sees the soul shining within. Despite the shackles of mind and body that keep the soul prisoner, the soul remains beautiful and bright, though concealed.

The coverings over the soul, robbing her of her innate light and knowledge of herself as a pure being, are aspects of the greater mind. Mystics have used a variety of ways to express the increasing density of the coverings over the soul as it descends from God through the heavenly realms, to its lowest dwelling, incarnate in a physical body. Some have described three such coverings, known in modern times, as the causal, the astral and the physical. These relate to the three worlds of the mind, and are the vehicles of the soul or her means of communication in their respective realms. The causal is the highest region of universal mind; the astral is the intermediate zone, and the physical is the universe with which we are presently familiar.

But like a precious stone that has fallen into the mud, or like the fair skin of the Lover beneath her shackles, the soul never loses her value in the eyes of the Beloved. The beauty of the soul is never lost.

"Golden earrings" are probably an allusion to the inner hearing faculty of the soul, which hears the divine Song within. "Silver" is evocative of light, as in the expression, the "silvery moon". The "beads of silver" thus refer to the soul's faculty of inner vision and to the sparkling radiance of the soul herself. The divine Beloved will exchange the heavy blinkers and coverings of this world for garments of spiritual light and sound:

> There is another lesson that we are incidentally taught by the deeper study of this book: it is that we have two sets of senses, one corporeal and the other spiritual.
>
> *Gregory of Nyssa, On Canticles 1, GGGN p.156*

Many mystics have spoken of the soul's ability to both hear and see within.[3] These are the two primary faculties by which the soul travels the inner journey. Even in this world, perception of sound and light are the two faculties without which life becomes very difficult. To a disciple, experience of sound and light come as a gift of grace from the Master. Hence, the Beloved says, "we shall *make* you golden earrings and beads of silver" – they are *made* by the Master; they are his gift to a soul.

A Sachet of Myrrh

LOVER: While the king rests in his own room,
my nard yields its perfume.
My Beloved is a sachet of myrrh
lying between my breasts.
My Beloved is a cluster of henna flowers
among the vines of Engedi.

My divine king dwells within me in the spiritual realms,
and the scent of my love reaches up to him.
He is a healing fragrance in the innermost part of my being.
He is a rare herb among common plants,
a precious treasure among worthless trinkets.

The "king" is the Master, and the "room" or chamber of this king lies beyond the single eye, on the threshold of the heavenly regions. From here he calls the soul, pulling her slowly inward, away from the entanglements of physical life and the physical body. He "rests in his own room" – he does not reveal himself in his radiant form below this level:

> The bedroom of the King is to be sought in the mystery of divine contemplation.
>
> *Bernard of Clairvaux, On The Song of Songs 23:9, WBC2 p.33*

Perhaps there is a double meaning too, for the "King" is also a metaphor for the Lord himself, who – say the mystics – stays aloof from his creation, "in his own room", though he is within every particle and vibration of it.

The soul speaks of the fragrance of her "nard". "Nard" is spikenard, a valuable aromatic root once used in herbal medicine. The precious, healing perfume of the soul is her love and devotion for the divine King.

The Beloved, too, is compared to a fine, intoxicating, fragrant and healing essence, a "sachet of myrrh lying between my breasts", a cosmetic custom of the ancient Orient. The Beloved dwells in the most intimate of places – he is enshrined in the spiritual heart of the disciple:

> Who is so blessed as to have the Word of God as guest in the seat of his heart, between his breasts, in his bosom? Such indeed is the meaning of what is sung here.
>
> *Origen, On the Song of Songs, Homily II:3, OSS p.287*

Just as the fragrance of a perfume continually refreshes the one who wears it, so too does love for the Beloved refresh the mind, filling it with life-giving currents of bliss. The Lover never forgets her Beloved, awake or asleep:

> All fruits wither: all sweet odours pass away;
> But not the Fragrance of the gnosis of Life,
>   which comes not to an end nor yet passes away.
>
> *Mandaean Prayer Book 34; cf. CPM p.34*

In his beauty and purity, the Beloved also resembles – like a rose among thorns – a "cluster of precious flowers" among the "vines of Engedi", among the unenlightened souls of this world.[4]

Your Eyes are Doves

> BELOVED: How beautiful you are my love,
> how beautiful you are!
> Your eyes are doves.

> *Dear one, divine love makes your soul shine*
> *with an incomparable beauty.*
> *Your gaze of love is pure and spiritual.*

The soul and her Saviour now become lost in the interplay of divine love. The Beloved sees only the beauty of the soul; and the soul sees only the beauty of the Beloved:

> Rightly does the Word say to the soul that has been made beautiful: "You have drawn nearer to me by your rejection of any contact with sin. By coming closer to the inaccessible Beauty, you have yourself become beautiful, and like a mirror, as it were, you have taken on my appearance."
>
> *Gregory of Nyssa, On Canticles 4, GGGN p.171*

"Your eyes are like doves," says the Beloved:

> He calls the soul a little 'white' dove by reason of the whiteness and cleanness which it has received of the grace that it has found in God. And he calls it 'dove' … to denote the simplicity and gentleness of its nature and its loving contemplation. For the dove is not only simple and gentle, without gall, but it also has bright and loving eyes.
>
> *St John of the Cross, Spiritual Canticle XXXIV:3, CWJC2 pp.352–53*

The "dove" has long been a symbol of peace, purity, gentleness
and spirituality. It was so in the ancient Hebrew world; we find
it among Jesus' teachings; and it is present in later Christian and
Manichaean belief as a symbol of the Holy Spirit:[5]

> The living kingdom shall be revealed again,
>   the love of God, the white dove.
> For the Holy Spirit was likened to a dove,
>   but the unclean Spirit was likened to a snake.
> The dove and the snake are enemies to each other,
>   the dove does not dwell in a pool unclean.
>
> *Manichaean Psalm Book, MPB p.156*

The soul is compared to a dove because, like a pure and spiritual
person, a dove never does anybody any harm. Moreover, just as a
pure soul can be in the body when she wants to and can fly to
the higher regions whenever she desires, so too can the dove land
on the earth or fly high into the sky, at will. Doves are also
among the fastest flyers of all birds, just as the soul flies with the
speed of the spirit through the heavenly realms:

> In that place they shall forget this world.
> There they have no want,
>   and they shall love one another with an abundant love.
> In their bodies there shall be no heaviness,
>   and lightly shall they fly "as doves to their windows".[6]
>
> *Aphrahat the Persian Sage, Demonstrations XXII:12, HEDA pp.405–6*

Doves, too, have always been kept as domesticated birds, and
many mystics have likened the soul in the body to the plight of a
free-flying bird confined to a small cage. Again, the capacity of
doves to find their way home has been known since ancient
times. Similarly, the spiritual soul seeks her divine home with an
unerring and instinctive sense of direction, once she is connected
to the Word within. A pair of doves are also very attentive,
affectionate and devoted to each other, epitomizing the inherent
love of the soul for God and for all other souls.

So from many different points of view, the metaphor of the dove is apt. "Eyes like doves" symbolize the purity and spirituality of the soul, as expressed in the eyes of the devotee.

The Lover then responds to the outpouring of the Beloved's love:

All Green is our Bed

> LOVER: How beautiful you are, my Beloved,
> and how delightful!
> All green is our bed.

> *Beloved one, your beauty is entrancing;*
> *I am overjoyed to gaze at you.*
> *When I see you, my soul ascends to the spiritual pastures.*

The Lover sees the Beloved with her inner, spiritual eye. The purer her heart, the more she will see his beauty, radiance and vitality:

> (The Beloved) is said to be good and beautiful, and the more closely he can be contemplated with the eyes of the spirit, so much the lovelier and more beautiful is he found.
>
> *Origen, On the Song of Songs III:2, OSS p.174*

The "green"-ness of "our bed" alludes, perhaps, to the legendary fertility of Palestine, the promised land, after the return of the exiles. But esoterically, the really fertile land that flows with milk and honey, full of life and vibrancy, refers to the inner regions where the soul and the Beloved 'eat' and 'drink' their fill of the divine music and divine light that come from above, and lead on to the highest. This is the "green" and fertile land, found after escape from the captivity of the body:

> I (Yahweh) am like a cypress, ever green,
> all your fruitfulness comes from me.
>
> *Hosea 14:9, JB*

The Beloved replies:

Beams of Cedar

BELOVED: The beams of our house are of cedar,
the panelling of cypress.

*We will make our home in the mystic temple of Wisdom,
built from the substance of eternity.*

The evergreen "cedar" and "cypress" were commonly used as
symbols of life, renowned for their natural resistance to rot and
decay, symbolic of divine incorruptibility. They were also precious
materials from the legendary wealth of Lebanon, used in the
holiest Jewish shrine, the Temple at Jerusalem, as well as in the
palace of Solomon.[7] Solomon, as we have seen, was always
portrayed as the great Sage, the Master of Wisdom, and the
palace or "house" of such a mystic is no palace of this world. His
"house", built of precious, incorruptible wood, is to be found
among the inner mansions, in the realm of eternity. It is the
inner kingdom of God, the most precious and holy of all
"houses".

A "house" is also where a person *lives,* and the poet evokes
this meaning, too. The essence of life is the Lord. He is the
inward Source of all being. That is why he is also called the
Living God. His creative Life Essence is the Word. A Master is a
personification of the Word. In the Word, he has his real
dwelling; the Word is his real "house".

Perhaps, too, the house being built of the finest wood that
resists decay is an allusion to the creative Power or Wisdom as
the Tree of Life:

I (Wisdom) have grown tall as a cedar on Lebanon,
as a cypress on Mount Hermon.

Wisdom of Jesus Ben Sirach 24:13, JB

Sometimes, the Masters themselves are described as "Trees of Life":

> [For you] set a plantation
> of cypress, pine, and cedar for your Glory,
> Trees of Life beside a mysterious Fountain
> hidden among the trees by the water;
> And they put out a shoot
> of the Everlasting Plant.
>
> *Thanksgiving Hymns 18:5–10 (XVI); cf. CDSS p.278*

In other places, it is the souls who are likened to "trees":

> The virtuous flourish like palm trees,
> and grow as tall as the cedars of Lebanon.
> Planted in the house of Yahweh,
> they will flourish in the courts of our God,
> still bearing fruit in old age,
> still remaining fresh and green,
> to proclaim that Yahweh is righteous –
> My rock in whom no fault is to be found!
>
> *Psalms 92:12–15, JB*

Characteristically, the imagery of the *Song* evokes multiple, but allied, meanings.

So, the Beloved says to the soul, it is in "our house" of the Word where we will live forever. The holy Word is the reality of our house:

> Surely goodness and mercy shall follow me
> all the days of my life:
> And I will dwell in the house of the Lord forever.
>
> *Psalms 23:6, KJV*

Then the Lover says:

The Rose of Sharon

> LOVER: I am the rose of Sharon,
>   the lily of the valleys.

I am fresh and beautiful, filled with the energy of life,
like the flowers of springtime.

"Sharon" is a plain in western Israel, lying between the Mediterranean and the hills of Samaria, extending from Haifa to Tel Aviv. The "rose of Sharon" is the meadow saffron or crocus, while – in this context – the "lily of the valleys" is the red Palestinian anemone that carpets the countryside in spring.[8] Both are bright heralds of springtime, the 'new age' after the rebirth that comes to every soul who has been reborn into the spiritual family of a Master. The soul is comparing herself to a spring flower: newborn, fresh and full of new life:

> From above, he gave me immortal rest,
>   and I became like the land that blossoms,
>   and rejoices in its fruits.
>   *Odes of Solomon 11:12, OSD p.52*

But the Beloved cautions:

A Lily among Thistles

> BELOVED: As a lily among the thistles,
>   so is my love among the maidens.

Yes, beautiful you may be, but surrounded by imperfection.
Few have your degree of spiritual purity.

The devotee has compared herself to a "lily". But the Beloved responds, "you may be a lily – but among thistles!" It has a double meaning. Firstly, the beautiful soul is entangled with the thorny mind and senses. Every movement results in deeper captivity:

> Upon being delivered from the snare of the body, the soul has been compared to a shred of silk that had fallen among thorns.
>
> *'Obadayah Maimonides, Treatise of the Pool XVIII;*
> *cf. TP p.111*

Secondly, it refers to the spiritual devotee living in this world among materially minded people. She is like a lily – pure and fragrant. But they are prickly, impure and may even be hostile, like thistles. From among these "thistles" the pure and devoted soul has to escape, travelling through the magic, secret door behind the eyes to the inner *rendezvous* with her Beloved.

Continuing the exchange of horticultural compliments, the Lover then expresses the delight she feels at being in her Beloved's presence:

His Longed-for Shade

LOVER: As an apple tree among the trees of the orchard,⁹
so is my Beloved among the young men.
In his longed-for shade I am seated,
and his fruit is sweet to my taste.

My Beloved is the greatest among men.
He is the Tree of Life, giving shade to all creation.
How I have longed for the comfort of his holy presence,
to find a safe haven with him.
Now I am at peace, and enjoy the sweet fruit
of spiritual experience that comes from knowing him.

The soul praises her Beloved. "See how he stands out among the sons of men," she says. She compares him to a young man, for a Master is full of the elixir of life. His face and his eyes sparkle with life and love at all times, and the atmosphere around him is full with life-giving vibrations. Like the Creative Word from which he has sprung, a Master is an embodiment of eternity. He is older than creation, and younger than a flower:

> When the lovely virgins and maidens (devotees),
>   sprung from the *Nous* (divine Intelligence, the Word),
>   saw you, they all with one accord blessed you,
>   O faultless Youth.
> *Manichaean Hymns; cf. GMU p.306ff., RMP at; cf. GSR p.44:1.2, ML p.120*

> On the bank of the river (of Living Water), ...
>   there is a Youth sitting, making music;
> The Youth sits there and makes music
>   in the Fragrance of Life that dwells upon him.
> *Psalms of Thomas V, Manichaean Psalm Book; cf. MPB p.211*

The "apple tree", perhaps because of its rich and abundant harvest, is portrayed as the greatest of all the trees in the orchard. Like the vine, it symbolizes the Tree of Life, the creative Power:

> I (Wisdom) am like a vine putting out graceful shoots,
>   my blossoms bear the fruit of (spiritual) glory and wealth.
> *Wisdom of Jesus Ben Sirach 24:17, JB*

On the Tree of Life hangs the "fruit" of immortality:

> Come, marvel at the Tree,
>   that grows without watering;
> And on which hangs the Fruit of Light.
> *Isaac of Antioch, IADS1 p.256; cf. MEM p.140*

The soul tastes this "fruit" from the Beloved's "tree", and she finds it sweet":

You are the flourishing fruit of the unperishing Tree....
Good the Tree, good the Fruit,
   good the sweet taste too.

Manichaean Psalm Book; cf. MPB p.185

A tree of love, loaded with fruit,
   is planted in my heart and gives me nourishment.
It works such a change in me that it casts forth
   all that there was in it of self-will.

St Francis of Assisi, Canticle of Love, WFA p.122

The rivers of the grace of God pour forth, and the more we taste of them, the more we long to taste. And the more we long to taste, the more deeply we press into contact with him. And the more deeply we press into contact with God, the more the flood of his sweetness flows through us and over us. And the more we are thus drenched and flooded, the better we feel and know that the sweetness of God is incomprehensible and unfathomable. And therefore the prophet says: "O taste, and see that the Lord is sweet."[10] But he does not say how sweet he is, for God's sweetness is without measure. ... And this is also testified by the Bride of God in the *Song of Songs,* where she says: "I sat down under his shadow, with great delight, and his fruit was sweet to my taste."

Jan van Ruysbroeck, Sparkling Stone X, JR pp.211–12

The sweet fruit of the "apple tree", the Tree of Life, is the bliss, the mystic consciousness and the intoxication of the Creative Word of Wisdom, the Power behind all other powers. The soul relaxes in the sense of well-being that comes from conscious contact with the Word. She finds refuge with her Beloved – "in his longed-for shade I am seated":

My joy lies in being close to God.
I have taken shelter in the Lord.

Psalms 73:28, JB

The soul has known great longing to be with her Beloved. Now her heart's desire has borne fruit, and she rests in the shadow of his love:

> The Bride-soul now sits upon the green bough, delighting in her Beloved.... She now drinks the clear water of most high contemplation and the Wisdom of God – water which is cold, signifying the refreshment and delight that she has in God.... (She) likewise settles beneath the shadow of his protection and favour, which she had so greatly desired, wherein she is comforted, pastured and refreshed after a delectable and divine manner, even as she declares joyously in the *Songs*, saying: "I sat down under the shadow of him that I had desired, and his fruit is sweet to my palate."
>
> St John of the Cross, Spiritual Canticle XXXIV:6, CWJC2 p.354

Coming under her divine Beloved's spiritual protection and guidance also means that she is baptized, spiritually, into the Word and, in this way too, she comes under the protection of her Master. Just as the shepherd is responsible for the welfare of his sheep, so too is a Master responsible for seeing his flock of souls safely to their spiritual home. He arranges the liberation of the soul from the mind, ensuring that all debts or sins are accounted for in one way or another.

In his Banquet Hall

> LOVER: He has taken me to his banquet hall,
> and the banner he raises over me is love.
> Feed me with raisin cakes,
> restore me with apples,
> for I am sick with love.

> *He has taken me to the heavenly realms*
> *where I drink the intoxicating wine of divine love.*
> *The banner of his love has been raised on high,*
> *and I have seen who he really is.*

I have been stricken with the disease of love.
Now the only medicine which can cure me
is the sweet and spiritual food from the mystic vine
and the divine apple tree,
fruit from his eternal Tree of Life.

At first, the Beloved was her King. Then he was her Shepherd. Now he is her King again, for only a King has a "banquet hall" (*lit.* the 'house of wine', the 'wine cellar').[11] But the Beloved's "banquet hall" refers to the inner realms where the Word resounds; where the heavenly table is forever laid with divine 'food' and 'drink'; where the cup of the soul forever "overflows".[12] This is the intoxication of divine love experienced by the soul in her mystic rapture and union with the spiritual form of the Beloved:

> She reclined in the bride chamber.
> She ate of the (spiritual) banquet
>   for which she had hungered.
> She partook of the immortal Food (of the Word).
> She found what she had sought after.
> She received rest from her labours,
>   while the Light that shines forth upon her does not set.
>
> *Authoritative Teaching 35, NHS11 pp.287–89*

"He has taken me" there, she says, for she knows full well that she could not have reached there by her own unaided efforts:

> "The king led me into his wine cellar." ... In other words: when I forsook the drunkenness of bodily desire and worldly pleasure, which are (bitter) like wormwood, and sought the King of all bliss, ... (he) led me in. He first led me into myself, so that I might see and know myself. Then he brought me into his cellar, transporting me out of myself into him. And he gave me to taste of his wine, which is his own spiritual sweetness and heavenly joy.
>
> *Walter Hilton, Ladder of Perfection I:80, LP p.98*

The "banner" or the flag raised over the soul is the standard carried by all kings, bearing their coat of arms. It represents who the king is and what he stands for. It is his insignia. The Saviour is the representative of love, and his "banner" is divine love. It is raised in the "wine cellar" to show who the true host is at this festival of divine intoxication:

> You are the Sovereign who gives as a gift
> the diadem, the banner,
> and the (pure) white Sign (of the Word).
>
> *Manichaean Hymns, MM3 p.883, RMP bk; cf. GSR p.58:4.1, ML pp.138–39*

The emblem of the Beloved is always that of love. God is love. The Master is love. The Word is love. The essence of the soul is love. Nothing attracts a soul more than love. The Master, more than anyone else, is aware of this great fact. Everything a Master does is steeped in love, from its beginning to its end.

He feeds the soul tenderly, like a mother her child, with the sweetest and healthiest of foods – "apples" and "raisin cakes"; for the soul "is sick with love":

> The Brother disturbs my heart with his voice:
> he causes a sickness to seize me.
>
> *Egyptian Love Songs, Beatty C1:8, LLSS p.178*

The soul has taken refuge with the Beloved. She has seated herself in his shade. Only the spiritual fruit of the Tree of Life can heal her lovesickness now:

> There is no one more blessed than he who dies because he loves so much. No creature can love God too much. In everything else, what is practised in excess turns to evil, but the virtue of love is such that the more it abounds, the more splendid it becomes. A lover will languish if he does not have the object of his love near him. Which is why the scripture says, "Tell my Beloved that I languish for love," as

if it were saying, "It is because I cannot see him whom I love; my very body is wasting away with the intensity of my devotion!"

Richard Rolle, Fire of Love, FL p.99

Her inner being burns in the sweet fire of divine devotion:

If there is anyone anywhere who has at some time burned with this faithful love of the Word of God; if there is anyone who has received the sweet wound of him who is the "chosen dart"; … if there is anyone who has been pierced with the loveworthy spear of his knowledge, so that he yearns and longs for him by day and night, can speak of nought but him, would hear of nought but him, can think of nothing else, and is disposed to no desire nor longing nor yet hope, except for him alone – if such there be, that soul then says in truth: "I have been wounded by charity (love)." And she has received her wound from him of whom Isaiah says: "And he has made me as a chosen dart, and in his quiver has he hidden me."[13]

Origen, On the Song of Songs III:8; cf. OSS p.198

His Right Arm Embraces me

> LOVER: His left arm is under my head,
> his right embraces me.

He supports me from without and draws me from within.

With one "arm", his 'outer' or "left arm", he supports and guides the outer life of the disciple. With the other, his "right" or 'inner' "arm", he pulls and beckons the soul from within. What more could a lover ask of her Beloved? The Right Hand of God, another Middle Eastern metaphor for the creative Power,[14] is implied here, as the Power that inwardly "embraces" and encircles the soul:

The Right Hand of the Lord is with you,
   and will be your Helper.
                    Odes of Solomon 8:6, OSD p.38

In a moment, my God, your mercy became one with me.
Because of your strong protection,
   lo, my diseases passed far from me.
Lo, joy has overtaken me
   through your Right Hand that came to me.
                    Manichaean Psalm Book; cf. MPB p.153

I am the first, I am also the last.
My Hand laid the foundations of the earth
   and my Right Hand spread out the heavens.
                    Isaiah 48:12–13, JB

The Beloved then concludes:

Until it Please to Awake

BELOVED: I charge you,
   daughters of Jerusalem,
by the gazelles, by the hinds of the field,
   not to stir my love nor rouse it,
      until it please to awake.

I tell you, do not try to engender divine love by force.
Let it awaken naturally from within the soul.
Let it be free and graceful,
like the wild mountain gazelles and the deer of the field.

The Beloved says that the soul's love for him is not to be aroused
by force. He leaves the soul as free as the "gazelles" and the
"hinds of the field". Only by her own natural awakening and by
her coming to him of her own accord can the desired result be

achieved. A true mystic never uses argumentative, proselytizing or any other forceful means to bring souls to himself. He knows that he cannot use the ways of the mind to attract souls away from their entanglement with the mind. Therefore, he never advertises or coerces. He works silently from within, with love, slowly awakening the soul to the splendours of her innate inner treasure.

As his authority, the Beloved cites the "gazelles" and the "hinds of the field", and scholars have puzzled over the meaning. Some say that the line cannot be adequately translated because the original Hebrew embodies a play on the sound of the words. *Ayyaloth* (gazelles) and *sebaoth* (hinds) suggest the Name of the Lord of Hosts *(Elohei Sebaoth)*, implying that the Beloved wears the mantle of the Name of the Lord. By divine decree, he is an embodiment of the mystic Name. This expression appears several times in the *Song*.

But gazelles are common in southern Lebanon where they are admired for their grace, and are regarded as symbolic of beauty. So, understood more simply, they could simply point to the graceful purity of the free and loving soul. Perhaps the poet had both ideas in mind.

SECOND POEM

I Hear my Beloved

In the prologue and first poem, the poet speaks of the essential beauty of the soul, and the natural attraction and love of the soul for the divine Beloved. The second poem describes how the Beloved comes from the highest heaven to call the exiled soul homewards.

LOVER: I hear my Beloved.
See how he comes,
leaping on the mountains,
bounding over the hills.
My Beloved is like a gazelle,
like a young stag.
See where he stands
behind our wall.
He looks in at the window,
he peers through the lattice.
My Beloved lifts up his voice,
he says to me:

BELOVED: "Come then, my love,
my lovely one, come.
For see, winter is past,
the rains are over and gone.

"The flowers appear on the earth.
The season of glad songs has come,
the cooing of the turtledove is heard in our land.
The fig tree is forming its first figs,
and the blossoming vines give out their fragrance.

"Come then, my love,
my lovely one, come –
My dove, hiding in the clefts of the rock,
in the coverts of the cliff."

LOVER:[1] Show me your face,
let me hear your voice;
For your voice is sweet,
and your face is beautiful.

Catch the foxes for us,
the little foxes
that make havoc of the vineyards,
for our vineyards are in flower.

My Beloved is mine and I am his.
He pastures his flock among the lilies.

Before the dawn wind rises,
before the shadows flee:
Return! Be, my Beloved,
like a gazelle,
a young stag,
on the spicy mountains.[2]

On my bed at night, I sought him
whom my heart (soul) loves.
I sought but did not find him.
So I will rise and go through the city;
In the streets and the squares,
I will seek him whom my heart (soul) loves.
I sought but did not find him.

The watchmen came upon me
on their rounds in the city:
"Have you seen him whom my heart (soul) loves?"
Scarcely had I passed them
than I found him whom my heart (soul) loves.
I held him fast, nor would I let him go
till I had brought him
into my mother's house,
into the room of her who conceived me.

BELOVED: I charge you,
daughters of Jerusalem,
by the gazelles, by the hinds of the field,
not to stir my love, nor rouse it,
until it please to awake.

See how he Comes

LOVER: I hear my Beloved.
See how he comes,
leaping on the mountains,
bounding over the hills.
My Beloved is like a gazelle,
like a young stag.
See where he stands
behind our wall.
He looks in at the window,
he peers through the lattice.

I hear the divine Voice of my Beloved,
the harmonies of the celestial Symphony.
He travels freely among the heavenly realms,
yet he has stooped down from the heights to visit me.
He comes to my soul, captive in the body.
He dwells within me,
aware of everything I do from behind the veil
that hides the inner door.

The soul, caught up in a mood of spiritual yearning, is enraptured by the inner presence of her Beloved. She *hears* her Beloved; she hears the divine Melody. Literally, the Hebrew reads, "Hark! My Beloved!" –

This … is the sound of a voice that calls the soul through its spiritual sense of hearing to a contemplation of the mysteries.

Gregory of Nyssa, On Canticles 5, GGGN p.199

He comes from the "mountains" and the "hills" – the spiritual heights of the inner creation:

To the mountains I say:
"How fragrant are your scents,
   how delightful your perfume!
Within you, all is full of brightness!"
   Mandaean Prayer Book 157; cf. CPM p.135

Send out your Light and your Truth;
Let these be my guide,
   to lead me to your holy mountain
   and to the place where you live.
   Psalms 43:3, JB

The Beloved travels as easily and swiftly as a "gazelle" or a "young stag" among rocky places, for these high regions are well known to him. He also comes in the Name of the Lord, as the Hebrew wordplay perhaps implies. He descends to the house of the soul, the body. He comes and stands "behind the wall", behind the inner veil of darkness. He looks in through the "lattice window", the inner door, the single eye. He gazes on his dear and loving disciple from within:

> This is no mere imagination but a most certain truth, for though we cannot see him, he certainly looks down upon us.... So we can truly say: "He is standing on the other side of this very wall ... looking in through each window in turn, peering through every chink."
> *St Francis de Sales, Introduction to the Devout Life II:2, IDL p.55*

The Hebrew word for "peer" also implies 'to sparkle'. His sparkling, radiant form lies on the other side of the "window". Feeling his presence, the soul cries out silently and tearlessly in her longing to see him and to be with him.

Come then, my Love

LOVER: My Beloved lifts up his voice,
        he says to me,

BELOVED: "Come then, my love,
        my lovely one, come.
      For see, winter is past,
      the rains are over and gone.
      The flowers appear on the earth.
      The season of glad songs has come,
the cooing of the turtledove is heard in our land.
      The fig tree is forming its first figs,
and the blossoming vines give out their fragrance.

      "Come then, my love,
        my lovely one, come –
My dove, hiding in the clefts of the rock,
      in the coverts of the cliff."

  The divine call of my Beloved comes to me.
        "Awake," he says,
  "from the dark winter's sleep of materiality.
    Your spiritual springtime has come.
  Let your heart blossom; let love appear.
    Hidden in the flowering of your heart
    is the promise of an abundant harvest.
  So come, dear soul, do not hide your face
      in the narrow byways of this world.
    Fly like a dove to the inner skies."

The Beloved "lifts up his voice": he makes the Word, the divine
Melody, the real Song of Songs, ring within the soul. He also
"lifts up" the soul to the single eye, so that she may hear his
voice, for the real Sound is not heard below this centre. He
beckons the soul, calling endearingly and affectionately, as only

he knows how. For he is the Lord of love himself and his mission is one of love and mercy. "See," says the Beloved, "the dark days of winter are over. The hard rain has passed. Now is the season of spring and summer." The soul's long sentence of captivity in the creation is coming to an end. The dark days of illusion and spiritual ignorance, of being knocked helplessly in all directions by the wild, unconscious impulses of the mind – of living in hatred, jealousy, anger, greed, selfishness, desire and attachment to materiality – those days are nearly over:

The Word has spoken to the Bride, calling her "my love" because she is close to him and "my dove" because she is beautiful. He now goes on to say that the sadness of winter no longer dominates our souls. For the cold cannot resist the rays of the sun. "Behold," he says, "winter is now past, the rain is over and gone." Sin is given many different names in accordance with its different effects. It is called winter, rain, drops – each name suggesting a different sort of temptation. In wintertime everything that is lovely withers away. All the leaves, which are the natural crown of the beauty of the trees, fall from the branches and are mingled with earth. The song of the birds is silent; the nightingale flies away, the swallow sleeps, and the dove leaves its nest. Everything imitates the oppression of death. The blossom perishes; the grass dies; the branches are stripped of their leaves like bones of their flesh; and what was once lovely flower and leaf is now an ugly spectacle.

Gregory of Nyssa, On Canticles 5, GGGN p.187

The soul is not made one with the Word of God, and joined to him, until such time as all the winter of her personal disorders and the storm of her vices has passed.... When, therefore, all these things have gone out of the soul, and the tempest of desires has fled from her, then the flowers of the virtues can begin to burgeon in her.

Origen, On the Song of Songs III:14, OSS p.240

Man's nature in the beginning flourished while it was in paradise, growing fat and thriving on the Water of the Fountain there; and he flourished so long as he had the blossom of immortality and not the leaves. But when the winter of disobedience came and withered its roots, the blossom was shaken off and fell to the ground. Man was thus stripped of his immortality; the grass of virtue was dried up; the love of God was chilled by repeated sin; and the passions were stirred up into a great swell by stormy winds, causing many souls to be shipwrecked.

Gregory of Nyssa, On Canticles 5, GGGN p.188

But then the warmth of the soul's spiritual springtime comes. "The flowers appear": the soul expands, blossoms and fills with the love of God:

But then came the one who brought spring to our souls. And whenever an evil wind churned up the sea, he scolded the winds and spoke to the sea: "Peace, be still."[3] And thus all was brought to peace and calm. Our nature began once again to blossom and reveal its beauty with its own flowers. For the flowers of life are the virtues, which blossom now, and bring forth their fruit in season.

Gregory of Nyssa, On Canticles 5, GGGN pp.188–89

And all this comes about through the grace of the Word, the "Water of Emancipation", the "Great Law":

Pray give me the fragrant Water of Emancipation....
   cleanse my wonderful soul from dust and dirt....

Send down the springtide of the Great Law
   to prosper the ground of my soul:
And cause the flowers and fruits
   of the tree of my soul to thrive....
Compel the sun of the Great Law to shine universally,
   and make my heart and soul always bright and pure.

Manichaean Hymns; cf. LSMH p.178:30–32

"The season of glad songs" has arrived. Now is the time to listen
to the harmonies of the celestial Music. This is the gladdest of all
songs for, in the heavenly realms,

> [all is filled] with happiness
> and sweet delightful Song.
> *Manichaean Hymns, Huwidagman I:60, MHCP p.75*

> The chariots of light are the gate to the (eternal) kingdom:
> joyful is the song that sounds from them.
> *Manichaean Hymns, MM3 p.887ff., RMP bj;*
> *cf. GSR p.57:3.2, ML p.140*

Yet, even before this inner Sound has been heard, the devotees of
the mystic path can enjoy a state of inexpressible happiness,
especially when they are with the Beloved. Then their "song" is
one of great gladness and joy of heart:

> You (Lord) are a hiding place for me:
> You guard me when in trouble,
>   you surround me with Songs of Deliverance.
> *Psalms 32:7, JB*

"Turtledoves" are symbols of spiritual peace, and their "cooing"
is probably another allusion to the heavenly Sound:

> Surely … he speaks of the "(voice of the) turtledove" as of
> the unutterable and unknown Wisdom.
> *Origen, On the Song of Songs III:14, OSS p.241*

"Cooing" is also a part of the courtship ritual of doves, here
symbolizing the soul's approach to the Divine. The "turtledove"
is also a bird of passage, a migratory species whose calling is a
herald of springtime. The "turtledove" is hence another symbol
for the soul, since she too is a migrant who has wandered far, but
is now homeward bound.

"Our land" – of the Beloved and the soul – implies the inner, heavenly realms, where the mystic Symphony – the "cooing" – can be heard, and where the courtship of divine love is consummated.

The harvest is beginning to grow, the first green figs are forming, and the spring vines, welcome for their sweet fragrance, "are blossoming". Both portray the gradual awakening of the soul to the springtime of new life and spiritual consciousness:

> And what else is there that fits the opportuneness of this time and its delightfulness? "The fig tree," he says, "has put forth her buds." The spirit of man, of which the fig tree is a figure, does not yet bear the fruits of the spirit – love, joy, peace, and the rest; but it is beginning now to put forth buds thereof.
>
> *Origen, On the Song of Songs III:14; cf. OSS p.241*

> Tranquillity, then, comes to the soul when the Word of God appears to her, and sin ceases to be. And so at last, when the vineyard is in flower, the virtues and the orchards of good fruits will begin to bud.
>
> *Origen, On the Song of Songs III:14, OSS p.242*

The Beloved calls the soul his "dove". Doves nest in inaccessible places, sitting tight when in danger of discovery, reluctant to leave. The soul is a spark of pure spirituality, hiding concealed, even from herself, in the rocky crevices of matter. "So come," says the Beloved, lovingly and coaxingly, "do not hide fearfully in the dark rock clefts of this world! Come up to me!" –

> Arise and come to me, O my beautiful dove,
>   my holy Bride, my pure field;
> And I will take you into my garden with me,
>   and array you with my myrrh and my spice,
>   and spread beneath you the garments of fine linen.
>
> *Falling Asleep of Mary I:VII; cf. CAG p.53*

Beckoned from within by such a love, the soul can only respond, though to begin with she hardly understands the real nature of the pull and the seeking urge she feels. But as time passes, she becomes a helpless captive of his love, longing to be with the Beloved at all times. Then she cries within, in the ecstasy of divine yearning:

Show me your Face

> LOVER: Show me your face,
>   let me hear your voice;
> For your voice is sweet,
>   and your face is beautiful.[+]

> *Show me the radiance of your spiritual form.*
> *Let me hear the divine Symphony that encircles you.*
> *Nothing is sweeter than that Music,*
> *nothing more beautiful than your form of light.*

"Show me your face," she says, "show me your real form. Let me hear the inner Melody of God. That 'voice' is so intoxicating, your radiant face so full of light and beauty":

> Your beautiful Image, my Father,
>   reveal it to me and your unsullied brightness....
> Reveal your face to me,
>   O holy and unsullied brightness;
> For you are my good Shepherd.
> *Manichaean Psalm Book CCLII; cf. MPB p.61*

> For me the reward of virtue is to see your Face,
>   and, on waking, to gaze my fill on your Likeness.
> *Psalms 17:15, JB*

> Every voice, I have heard,
>   no other Voice pleased me but yours.
> *Manichaean Psalm Book; cf. MPB p.154*

This voice of the Spouse (Beloved), who speaks to the Bride in the inmost part of the soul, she perceives to be the end of her ills and the beginning of her blessings. And, in the refreshment and protection and delectable feeling which this causes her, she likewise lifts up her voice, as does the sweet philomel (nightingale), in a new song of jubilation to God.

St John of the Cross, Spiritual Canticle XXXIX:9, CWJC2 pp.377–78

But, despite her longing, the soul has a problem:

Catch the Little Foxes

> LOVER: Catch the foxes for us,
> the little foxes
> that make havoc of the vineyards,
> for our vineyards are in flower.
>
> *It is my wayward desires and thoughts*
> *that keep me from seeing you within.*
> *Control my mind for me.*
> *My heart may be full of love,*
> *but my mind still disturbs me.*

She pleads, "Catch the little foxes of the mind and senses":

These foxes represent temptations.

Bernard of Clairvaux, On The Song of Songs 64:1, WBC3 p.169

All this chorus of desires and motions of the senses, the soul here calls foxes, because of the great similarity which at this time they have to them.

St John of the Cross, Spiritual Canticle XVI:5, CWJC2 p.264

"They are making havoc of the spring and summer," she says, "when 'our vineyards are in flower'." Love and devotion are coming into full bloom, but still the mind wanders and upsets the flowering of the vines. And if the flowering is disturbed, there can be no fruit – and there will be no meeting with the Beloved.

As before, the "vineyards" are this world and the "vines" are the unemancipated souls caught in the creation:

> To a wise man, the vineyard means his life, his soul, his conscience.
>
> *Bernard of Clairvaux, On The Song of Songs 63:2, WBC3 p.162*

But the "vineyards are in flower". The soul is beginning to flower after the long hard winter, yet still the little foxes of the mind and its desires distract the soul as she comes into bloom. In the folklore of many lands, the fox is portrayed as mischievous and cunning. Similarly, the mind – at this stage, the enemy of the soul – cleverly beguiles the soul, weaving its spells of illusion and desire:

> How much longer will you hide your face from me?
> How much longer must I endure grief in my soul,
>   and sorrow in my heart by day and by night?
> How much longer must my enemy
>   have the upper hand of me?
> Look and answer me, Yahweh my God!
>
> *Psalms 13:3, JB*

He Pastures his Flock

> LOVER: My Beloved is mine and I am his.
> he pastures his flock among the lilies.

> *My Beloved, I am yours, you who lead your flock of souls
> into the gardens of heaven.*

"My Beloved is mine and I am his," she says. Divine love is an ocean in which the Lover and the Beloved bathe together:

O for the day when I can cast my soul into his heart, when
he will pour his heart into my soul! Such blissful unity – a
life that knows no parting!

St Francis de Sales, Love of God 1:9, LG p.23

"He cares for his flock," she continues, "among the lilies and the
flowers":

He leads me out to pasture among the lilies of his perfec-
tions, which afford me delight.

St Francis de Sales, Love of God 8:2, LG p.319

He showers his spiritual children with love and comfort, leading
them to the best of inner pastures, where the souls graze on the
pure music of the divine Word itself, and drink the indrawing
nectar of his Wisdom:

Good Shepherd,
    you who have given yourself for your own sheep,
    and have vanquished the Wolf
    and redeemed your own lambs,
    and led them into a good pasture:
We glorify and praise you and your invisible Father,
    and your Holy Spirit, the mother of all creation.

Acts of Thomas 39; cf. ANT p.384, AAA p.181

The soul then speaks of her longing to be with her Beloved:

On the Spicy Mountains

LOVER: Before the dawn wind rises,
        before the shadows flee:
        Return! Be, my Beloved,
            like a gazelle,
            a young stag,
        on the spicy mountains.⁵

Before morning comes, in my night prayer,
come to me, my Beloved, in your spiritual form.
Draw me up into the higher realms;
take me to your promised land.

The real lovers of the Lord live for the night when they can be
with him. This is the best time for spiritual practice. The busy
activity of the world is hushed in slumber, and the atmosphere is
calm, peaceful and without disturbance. The mystic lovers learn to
keep awake for at least some part of the night. In time, even while
the body sleeps, they discover how to remain conscious within,
awaiting the coming of their Beloved in his form of light.[6]

In the opening lines of this poem, the soul was full with the
expectation of his imminent arrival. Here, she is still longingly
awaiting him. "Return to me," she says, "like a gazelle or a
young stag" – imbued with grace and love, 'accompanied' by the
Name of God, come 'bounding' through the heavenly regions –
the "spicy mountains" of the soul.[7]

Night also refers symbolically to the brevity of human life.
The end of life is the "dawn". The soul is hence praying to the
Beloved, "let my life be spiritually fruitful. While I live, permit
me to meet with you in the heavenly realms."

On my Bed at Night

LOVER: On my bed at night, I sought him
whom my heart (soul) loves.
I sought but did not find him.

Concentrated in contemplation at the single eye,
I sought to meet the love of my spiritual heart.
I sought him, but he did not come.

Alone within herself, in the dark solitude of the night, the soul
seeks her Beloved in mystic prayer:

I speak to my heart, within me, this prayer:
"My Great One is afar from me tonight,
   and I am like one in my grave (my body)."
         Egyptian Love Songs, PH500 10:4; cf. LLSS p.173

The soul yearns for her Beloved, but he does not reveal himself. This game of hide and seek fills the soul with greater longing, cleansing her of the last traces of human imperfection, insincerity, self-consciousness and mental distraction:

He may visit her from time to time, indeed, and yet from time to time she may be forsaken by him, too, that she may long for him the more.
         Origen, On the Song of Songs III:13; cf. OSS p.232

The "bed" of the soul is its place of rest, inside. Specifically, the "bed" where the Beloved is met lies just beyond the single eye or eye centre, on the threshold of the heavenly realms:

On my bed I think of you,
   I meditate on you all night long,
   for you have always helped me.
         Psalms 63:6–7, JB

The seat of the mind and soul in the human form is in the forehead – between the eyebrows – at the eye centre, though this centre is entirely non-physical in nature. Just as the physical heart lies at the centre of bodily activities, so too does the eye centre lie at the centre of human spiritual activity. Consequently, many mystics have also referred to this centre as the spiritual heart.

It is from this spiritual centre behind the eyes that the currents of the mind and soul flow out into the body, and – through the senses – into the world. The mind and soul, woven tightly together, make up the attention or human consciousness. Flowing outward, this attention or consciousness becomes scattered and diffused into the world. So distracted does the mind become, and so absorbed in matter, that it completely identifies with the body, coming to feel that there is no reality other than its physical covering and the material world.

The single eye is like the bed or bedroom of the body. When we wish to sleep, we withdraw from the world, remove our daytime clothes and get into bed. The same is true spiritually. The attention is withdrawn from the world, and then from the garment or clothing of the body. The attention focuses at the single eye. The mind becomes motionless, but increasingly attentive, inside. As concentration deepens further, the mind and soul leave the body altogether and go within. They pass through the portals of death and enter the heavenly, astral world. And there, on the threshold of this realm of light, the radiant and loving form of the Beloved Master is encountered.

In a similar analogy, this is the bride chamber where the soul meets the Beloved:

> In the Holy of Holies, which cannot be described,
>   the Son of the King has built for his Bride
>   a glorified bride chamber.
>   *Chaldaean Breviary, BCB 3:425; cf. MEM p.116*

This is where the soul gathers herself together in quiet contemplation, longing to meet with her Beloved:

> Help me, O Saviour, my God:
>   let me see your Image …
> Make me, even me, worthy of your holy bridal chambers.
>   *Manichaean Psalm Book CCLII; cf. MPB p.62*

This is what the Lover means by "on my bed at night, I sought him whom my heart (soul) loves". Here, the Hebrew word translated as "heart" *(nefesh)* is more commonly rendered as "soul". The soul withdraws to the "bed" or "bride chamber" of the body – the single eye. And there she seeks her Beloved: she struggles to hold her attention fully focused, intent upon the inner meeting. But whether or not he comes to her is not under her control; that is up to him. In this instance, she fails to find him, for it takes time to still the mind, to purify it of all outward tendencies, and to hold the attention fully concentrated at the inner centre. "I sought him, but did not find him," says the soul.

I Will Seek Him

> LOVER: So I will rise and go through the city;
>   In the streets and the squares,
>   I will seek him whom my heart (soul) loves.
>   I sought but did not find him.

> *I have risen up from my body.*
> *All consciousness has been withdrawn*
> *in preparation for the inner ascent.*
> *I have sought him in my soul, but he has not come.*

The "city" is Jerusalem, where the holy Temple was situated, the highest place of worship. Here, the "city" is a symbol for the soul, wherein – within the inner sanctum – the Beloved is to be found and worshipped.

"I will rise," says the soul. "I will rise up within the city of my soul. I will search for him within my own heart, within the hidden recesses of my being." But she does not find him, for he can only be found when he wishes to be found:

> I am here, calling for your help,
>   praying to you every morning:
> Why do you reject me?
> Why do you hide your face from me?
>   *Psalms 88:13–14, JB*

The soul continues her narrative:

I Found him whom my Heart Loves

LOVER: The watchmen came upon me
on their rounds in the city:
"Have you seen him whom my heart (soul) loves?"
Scarcely had I passed them
than I found him whom my heart (soul) loves.
I held him fast, nor would I let him go
till I had brought him
into my mother's house,
into the room of her who conceived me.

The distractions of the mind, encompassing the soul,
keep guard on the inner citadel, and hold me back.
They are the ones who know where my Beloved is
and why I cannot find him.
Only when I rose up past them did I find him.
Then my soul merged into his,
travelling higher until we came to the source of Wisdom,
the essence of my existence.

The "watchmen" are the lower impulses and imperfections of the human mind which keep a close "guard" on the entry to the heavenly realms. "Scarcely having passed them" – having hardly overcome all these lower impulses, reaching only just above the physical body, only just beyond the single eye – the soul at last finds the Beloved; or rather, the Beloved reveals himself. Then she "held him fast": she becomes united to him in mystic transcendence and bliss. The soul clings to him until she reaches "her mother's house", entering "into the room of her who conceived me":

My Bridegroom has taken me to his bride chamber,
I have rested with him in the land of the immortal.
Manichaean Psalm Book CCLIII, MPB p.63

As before, the "mother" of the soul is *Hokhmah* or Wisdom, the *Torah*, the Law, the *Logos*, the Word, the mystic Name, the creative Power of God in the creation:

> Surely we would be right in understanding the mother here
> as the First Cause of our being.
>
> *Gregory of Nyssa, On Canticles 5, GGGN p.203*

A Saviour is a manifestation of this great Power, and so too is the soul. Indeed, there is nothing but this Power in the entire creation. It is the Power behind all powers. It underlies all vibration and movement in mind and matter. It is the Power by which the existence of all creation is sustained. And just as vibrations in the air can be heard by the ear, so too can this great cosmic motor, this primal Power, be heard by the inner hearing faculty of the soul and mind.

So the soul listens to the voice of the Beloved, just as the poem said at the outset. And rising on that current, in intimate company with the Beloved, she returns to the One who gave her birth, who created her. First she enters her "mother's house" – the inner creation – and then the very "room" or place of her "conception", the true origin or home of the soul.

There is an alternative interpretation. The various commentators differ over the identity of the "watchmen", particularly since – in a later poem – the same watchmen beat and wound the soul.[8] Bar Hebraeus considers them to be the imperfections of the mind,[9] as interpreted above. But others, like Gregory of Nyssa and Meister Eckhart, take them as friendly 'guardians' of the "city" – as the angels who inhabit the heavenly Jerusalem of the inner realms.

In this interpretation, the soul seeks for her Beloved throughout the heavenly realms, in all the "streets and the squares" of creation. But she does not find him, nor – when she asks them – do the inhabitants know where he can be found:

Their only answer to the question is silence; and by their silence they show that what she seeks is incomprehensible to them.

Gregory of Nyssa, On Canticles 5, GGGN p.202

The spiritual home of the Beloved is above all the lower creation, whether it be the heavens or this world. He dwells in the bosom of the "mother's house"; he has his being in the Word:

She found angels and many things, but she did not find him her soul loved.... The soul that is to find God must leap over and pass beyond all creatures.

Meister Eckhart, Sermon 42, MEST1 p.294

The Beloved can only be found when the soul withdraws her attention from all the distractions of creation – higher or lower:

I abandoned all creatures, and passed by all that is intelligible in creation; and when I gave up every finite mode of comprehension, then it was that I found my Beloved.

Gregory of Nyssa, On Canticles 5, GGGN p.202

Until it Please to Awake

BELOVED: I charge you,
daughters of Jerusalem,
by the gazelles, by the hinds of the field,
not to stir my love, nor rouse it,
until it please to awake.

Divine love is mine and will awaken at my pleasure.
Such love cannot be forced.

In the poem, as in reality, the Beloved has the last word. He tells the devotees of the holy Temple within, the "daughters of Jerusalem" – his loving disciples – that his love cannot be stirred or awakened until he so wishes it:

> To the cultivation of this field every soul – who is now called a daughter of Jerusalem because she knows her mother is the heavenly Jerusalem – must of necessity bring some contribution; and she must desire this in order to be made worthy of being a heavenly possession.
>
> *Origen, On the Song of Songs III:10; cf. OSS p.204*

No one by their own will can storm the inner citadel and take divine love for themselves. It is a gift of God which he gives when he sees fit.

THIRD POEM

Who is this Coming Up from the Desert?

The third poem begins by describing the greatness of the Beloved who comes to the desert of the world as a mystic King to take his army of souls, his "champions", back to his own throne room. The greater part of the remainder of the poem is then taken up with an expression of the Beloved's love for the souls under his protection.

The Beloved praises the beauty and virtues of the soul, likening her to the beautiful things of this world. He then compares her to a garden, full of the rarest fruits and sweet-smelling herbs, all fed from a fountain of living water. But the garden is enclosed; its fruit and flowers are out of sight; and the fountain is sealed so that no water flows.

This depicts the soul in human form, unaware of her hidden, spiritual potential and inner treasure. The Beloved is describing the hidden beauty of the soul in order to awaken love and yearning in the heart of his devotee.

The soul responds by praying that the Beloved will bring life and vitality to the garden of her soul. And the ever loving Beloved enters her garden, telling his "friends" – his disciples – to eat and drink to their heart's content of the inner banquet.

NARRATIVE: What (who) is this coming up from the desert,
like a column of smoke,
breathing of myrrh and frankincense,
and every perfume the merchant knows?

See, it is the litter of Solomon.
Around it are sixty champions,
and flowers of the warriors of Israel;
All of them are skilled swordsmen,
veterans of battle.
Each man has his sword at his side,
against alarms by night.

King Solomon
has made himself a throne
of wood from Lebanon.
The posts he has made of silver,
the canopy of gold,
the seat of purple;
The back is inlaid with ebony.

CHORUS: Daughters of Zion,
come and see King Solomon,
wearing a diadem with which his mother crowned him
on his wedding day, on the day of his heart's joy.

BELOVED: How beautiful you are, my love,
how beautiful you are!
Your eyes, behind your veil, are doves;
Your hair is like a flock of goats,
frisking down the slopes of Gilead.
Your teeth are like a flock of shorn ewes
as they come up from the washing.

Each one has its twin,
not one unpaired with another.
Your lips are a scarlet thread
and your words enchanting.
Your cheeks, behind your veil,
are halves of pomegranate.
Your neck is the tower of David,
built as a fortress,
hung round with a thousand bucklers,
and each the shield of a hero.
Your two breasts are two fawns,
twins of a gazelle,
that feed among the lilies.
You are wholly beautiful, my love,
and without a blemish.

LOVER: Before the dawn wind rises,
before the shadows flee,
I will go to the mountain of myrrh,
to the hill of frankincense.

BELOVED: Come away with me to Lebanon,
my promised bride;
Come away with me to Lebanon,
come on your way.[1]
Lower your gaze from the heights of Amana,
from the crests of Senir and Hermon,
the haunt of lions,
the lairs of leopards.[2]

You ravish my heart,
my sister, my promised bride.
You ravish my heart
with a single one of your glances,
with one single pearl of your necklace.
What spells lie in your love,
my sister, my promised bride!

How delicious is your love, more delicious than wine!
How fragrant your perfumes,
more fragrant than all other spices!
Your lips, my promised one,
distil wild honey.
Honey and milk
are under your tongue;
And the scent of your garments
is like the scent of Lebanon.

She is a garden enclosed,
my sister, my promised bride;
A garden enclosed,
a sealed fountain.

Your shoots form an orchard of pomegranate trees,
bearing precious fruit;[3]
Nard and saffron,
calamus and cinnamon,
with all the incense-bearing trees;
Myrrh and aloes,
with the subtlest odours.

Fountain that makes the gardens fertile,
well of living water,
streams flowing down from Lebanon.

LOVER: Awake, north wind,
come, wind of the south!
Breathe over my garden,
to spread its sweet smell around.
Let my Beloved come into his garden,
let him taste its rarest fruits.

BELOVED: I come into my garden,
my sister, my promised bride;
I gather my myrrh and balsam,
I eat my honey and my honeycomb,
I drink my wine and my milk.
Eat, friends, and drink:
drink deep, my dearest friends.

Like a Column of Smoke

NARRATIVE: What (who) is this coming up from the desert,
            like a column of smoke,
      breathing of myrrh and frankincense,
      and every perfume the merchant knows?
      See, it is the litter of Solomon.

Who is this ascending from the material realm
            in a column of glory,
full of the healing fragrance of God's creative Power,
the Breath of God that all the great sages have known?
      It is the mystic King, the Master.

The "desert" is the physical universe where life is difficult and
arid, parched of conscious contact with the Living Water of the
creative Power. The "column of smoke" is the cloud of dust
thrown up by the advancing cavalcade. Symbolically, it is probably an allusion to the "pillar of cloud" – one of the two 'signs'
from Yahweh that served as beacons to lead the captive Israelites
out of Egypt, through the Sinai desert, to the promised land, in
the company of Moses:[4]

> Yahweh went before them, by day in the form of a pillar of
> cloud to show them the way, and by night in the form of a
> pillar of fire to give them light; thus they could continue
> their march by day and by night. The pillar of cloud never
> failed to go before the people during the day, nor the pillar
> of fire during the night.
>
> *Exodus 13:21–22, JB*

The creative Power is like a "pillar" or column of glory and
radiance, leading back to God. The Lord has his "throne" at the
head or source of this "pillar":

> I (Wisdom) came forth from the mouth of the Most High,
>   and I covered the earth like mist.
> I had my tent in the Heights,
>   and my throne in the pillar of cloud.
>
> *Wisdom of Jesus Ben Sirach 24:3–4, JB*

The "pillar of fire" represents the light of this creative Power. The "pillar of cloud", by alluding to thunder, signifies its sound.

The Beloved is also being likened to Moses, the Saviour who releases souls from captivity, and has the authority of Yahweh, of the Lord himself. The opening words "what is this …" also mean "who is this …". The ambiguity is by design since the Master is both the personal form and the essential power of the Word; the two are merged into one.

As before, the fragrance and perfume of the Master refer to the sublime atmosphere of love and peace that surround and emanate from him. In fact, "Fragrance" or "Perfume" was another term used for the Word of God as his Essence, his Emanation or his Breath. Significantly, the fragrant herbs and spices, "myrrh and frankincense", were known for their healing qualities, for there is no greater healer than the creative Power, the eternal healer of the eternal soul:

> I (Wisdom) have exhaled a perfume
>   like cinnamon and acacia;
> I have breathed out a scent like choice myrrh,
>   like galbanum, onycha and stacte,
>   like the smoke of incense in the tabernacle.
>
> *Wisdom of Jesus Ben Sirach 24:15, JB*

The "merchants" who know these "perfumes" and this Fragrance are the Masters who are intimately acquainted with the divine attributes, and are dealers in the divine treasures. They 'sell' this Fragrance to their disciples, though the only fee they charge is that of love – a commodity that is also their gift. They carry the soul to God:

He (the Living Spirit) spread out this great sea (of creation):
He built the ships and launched them on it,
    the ships of the Great Traders, the faithful Men of Truth;
The barks of the Merchants,
    that will convey up the distilled part (the soul) to Life.

Psalms of Thomas VII, Manichaean Psalm Book, MPB p.213

"See, it is the litter of Solomon." Solomon, the godly ruler and messianic king of Jewish tradition, also symbolizes the divine sage or Master, as we have seen. The poet is describing the ascent of the Master, who – as an emissary of the Lord – comes up from the desert of the world like a guiding and protecting beacon, escorting souls on their homeward journey.

Veterans of Battle

NARRATIVE: Around it are sixty champions,
    and flowers of the warriors of Israel;
    All of them are skilled swordsmen,
        veterans of battle.
    Each man has his sword at his side,
        against alarms by night.

The companions of the mystic King, his advanced and
*   dedicated disciples, are with him.*
Every one of them has fought long in the holy war.
Each one has the sword of God's mystic Word with him,
*   to cut through the darkness and debris of the mind*
*   in his night prayer.*

The "sixty champions" and the "flowers of the warriors of Israel" are the souls being guided home from exile in the desert of the world. They are all "skilled swordsmen" and "veterans of the battle" with the mind and senses. They have gained enough experience to be able to come up from the desert with the spiritual King – to travel with him into the heavenly gardens of the soul:

> O my Father, my God, my Saviour, my King:
>   I will be a champion for you,
>   I myself will go out and fight.
>>   *Manichaean Psalm Book; cf. MPB p.148*

> Fight, O sons of light:
>   yet a little while and you will be victorious.
> He that shirks his burden will forfeit his bride chamber.
>>   *Manichaean Psalm Book CCXLIX, MPB p.58*

Each one of them is constantly watchful and vigilant against the diversions and distractions of the mind and senses, against all the 'enemies' who can pull the soul and mind out into the world again. They have been armed by their Master with a technique of spiritual practice and by contact with the "sword" of the Word:

> All those who are familiar with the hidden meanings and the concepts of the scriptures must surely understand this reference, and are aware that the sword is the Word.
>>   *Gregory of Nyssa, On Canticles 6; cf. GGGN p.207*

They have their "sword at their side":

> Take onto yourself the whole armour of God, that you may be able to withstand the evil day.... Stand therefore, having your loins girt about with truth, and having on the breastplate of righteousness.... Above all, take the shield of faith, with which you will be able to quench all the fiery darts of the wicked. And take the helmet of salvation, and the sword of the Spirit, which is the Word of God: praying always with all prayer and supplication in the Spirit, and watching thereunto with all perseverance.
>>   *Ephesians 6:13–14, 16–18; cf. KJV*

Great "skill" or technique is required for the soul to leave the body. It is not a matter of sentiment or a haphazard romantic adventure, but a specific spiritual practice or science that must be performed correctly and with application if results are to be achieved. The devotee must become a "warrior" in order to overcome all human passions and imperfections, to concentrate the mind, and thereby withdraw all attention from the body and its senses. All the outward tendencies of the mind have to be skilfully and completely severed, as with a "sword". The devotee has to become a "skilled swordsman".

The souls of this world are "veterans of battle" – they have been knocked about for millions of lifetimes in the hurly-burly of physical existence. The devotee who can leave his body has also become a "veteran" of the battle with the mind. This is the true holy war. No one subdues the mind without first undergoing a long and arduous fight. Many things are learnt during this battle, leaving the devotee rich in wisdom and experience.

The "alarms by night" are the disturbances to meditation, and the temptations that arise during the warrior disciple's inner journey. They come "by night" because night is the time when the devotees sit in spiritual prayer, trying to reach the Beloved within. And they come by "night" because the soul, when assailed by the dark forces of the mind, is still in the dark night of the physical realm. "Night", here, has a double meaning.

A Throne of Wood from Lebanon

NARRATIVE: King Solomon
has made himself a throne
of wood from Lebanon.
The posts he has made of silver,
the canopy of gold,
the seat of purple;
The back is inlaid with ebony.

The mystic King has his dwelling in eternity,
the seat and source of all spiritual treasures.

The Hebrew word here translated as "throne" or "palanquin" is used nowhere else in the Bible. But the poet is echoing the biblical description of the throne in Solomon's palace:

> The king made a great throne of ivory, and overlaid it with the best gold. The throne had six steps, and the top of the throne was round behind: and there were stays on either side on the place of the seat.
>
> *1 Kings 10:18–19, KJV*

Esoterically, the "throne" of the Beloved is his inner dwelling place, ultimately that of God himself:

> God of our ancestors, Lord of mercy,
>   who by your Word have made all things, …
> Grant me Wisdom, consort of your throne....
> Dispatch her (Wisdom) from the holy heavens,
>   send her forth from your throne of glory
>   to help me and to toil with me,
>   and teach me what is pleasing to you,
>   since she knows and understands everything.
>
> *Wisdom of Solomon 9:1, 4, 10–11, JB*

The poet indicates the divine character of the "throne" by describing it as being constructed of the most precious, beautiful and regal of earthly materials. It is made of "gold" and "silver", "purple" and "ebony", and "wood from Lebanon", Lebanon being symbolic of eternity. Such precious materials were commonly used in descriptions of the divine Reality:

> Her (Wisdom's) yoke will be a golden ornament,
>   her reins, purple ribbons;
> You will wear her like a robe of honour.
>
> *Wisdom of Jesus Ben Sirach 6:30–31, JB*

The Hebrew text actually says that the throne is "inlaid with love", rather than "inlaid with ebony". It also adds "by the daughters of Jerusalem". But modern scholars have usually considered the text corrupt, and have changed it accordingly. Perhaps a word-play is intended, for the mystic throne is certainly adorned with love, as its essential characteristic:

> By purple, in the divine Scripture, is denoted love. Kings are clad in it and use it…. Thus all these virtues in the soul are, as it were, hung with the love of God…. They are … bathed in love, because all and each of them are ever enkindling the soul with love for God…. This is to be hung with purple.
>
> This is well expressed in the divine *Songs;* for there it is said that the seat or bed that Solomon made for himself, he made of the woods of Libanus, and the pillars of silver, the couch of gold and the hangings of purple. And it says that he arrayed it all by means of love. For the virtues and gifts which God places in the bed of the soul, which are denoted by the woods of Libanus, and the pillars of silver, have their couch and resting-place of love, which is the gold. For … the virtues are grounded and preserved in love.
>
> St John of the Cross, Spiritual Canticle XXIV:7; cf. CWJC2 p.303

Crowned with a Diadem

CHORUS: Daughters of Zion,
come and see King Solomon,
wearing a diadem with which his mother crowned him
on his wedding day, on the day of his heart's joy.

Come, see the mystic King.
He has been appointed by Wisdom
with which he has become one.

By allusion, it is made clear who is meant by "King Solomon": he is "wearing the diadem with which his mother crowned him on his wedding day". The mystic King is the Master. The "mother" of a Master, as of all souls, is Wisdom or the Holy Spirit:

> Hold her (Wisdom) close, and she will make you great;
> Embrace her, and she will be your pride;
> She will set a crown of grace on your head,
>   present you with a glorious diadem.
>
> *Proverbs 4:8–9, JB*

A Master is "crowned" or appointed to be a Master. No Master appoints himself. Inwardly, he is appointed to this 'office' by the Word, his "mother", with whom he is one. Outwardly, he is appointed by his own Master, while his Master is still living in the body.

The "wedding", symbolizing love and union, represents mystic union with God. The Master's "wedding day" would perhaps be the day on which he himself attained union with the Lord. But maybe the Master had always been one with God, with no vestige of separation. In that case, every day would have been his "wedding day", for in the eternity beyond time there are no days. Either way, there can be no greater "heart's joy" for a soul than the triumphant consummation of the divine marriage.

The "wedding day" could also be the day on which he was appointed Master, though it is doubtful whether a Master would really call such a day his "wedding day". To take on the role of a Master in the spiritual desert of the physical creation is not a duty to rejoice about, as one would at a wedding. The forces of destiny and the need to satisfy the ego which keep worldly rulers going, despite the constant difficulties and problems that beset them, are absent in a Master. Masters derive no egocentric pleasure from their position, nor are they – like the rest of us – the victims of their destiny. In their compassion, they see only the lost, captive and exiled souls, craving for release. They perform their duties only out of love and obedience to the divine will.

But in whatever way the passage is taken, "King Solomon" is the mystic Beloved; "his mother" is the creative Power; and his "marriage" signifies his union with God. And to one of the gnostics of early Christian times, writing nearly two thousand years ago, the "diadem" or "crown" was the Creative Word, the "Name of the All":

> It is (the soul) that the Protogenitor (the Son) saved by means of his own power. Because of this work (of salvation), the Father of the All, the indescribable One, sent a Crown in which is the Name of the All, whether endless, or unutterable, or incomprehensible, or imperishable, or unknowable, or still, or all-powered, or indivisible. This is the Crown of which it is written: "It was given to Solomon on the day of the joy of his heart."
>
> *Untitled Text 12, BC p.250*

The Beloved now takes the stage and describes the beauties of the soul:

How Beautiful you are

> BELOVED: How beautiful you are, my love,
> how beautiful you are!
> Your eyes, behind your veil,
> are doves.

> *Your soul, dear one,*
> *veiled as it may be by mind and body,*
> *is nonetheless pure spirit, and always retains its beauty.*

It was an ancient Middle Eastern custom to sing praises of the bride at her wedding,[5] and the poet now makes use of this tradition. The Beloved reminds the soul of her innate and inner beauty. "How beautiful you are, my love," he says. Were he not to have this deep love for his chosen souls, he would never stay in this world to extricate them from the mess they are in. By reminding them of their real beauty, they are inspired to seek their inner, spiritual treasure. By expressing his love for them, he generates love for himself in their hearts. It is this love that then draws the soul out of the body, towards himself, on the inner planes.

The Hebrew word for "veil" implies confinement. Confined behind the "veil" of mind and body, the soul is pure spirit, here symbolized by the "dove". "The eyes are the windows of the soul," as the popular saying goes.[6] During spiritual practice, the soul and mind must be concentrated behind the eyes, at the single eye. When devotees with such concentration gaze at the Beloved in his physical form, their eyes sparkle with joy, consciousness and depth of being. Their eyes express the love and spirituality within. They have "eyes" like "doves", though the being of the devotee is hidden "behind" the "veil" of the body, for neither the soul, nor even the mind, can be seen with the physical senses.

Wholly Beautiful

> BELOVED: Your hair is like a flock of goats,
>   frisking down the slopes of Gilead.
> Your teeth are like a flock of shorn ewes
>   as they come up from the washing.
>   Each one has its twin,
>   not one unpaired with another.
>   Your lips are a scarlet thread
>   and your words enchanting.
>   Your cheeks, behind your veil,
>   are halves of pomegranate.
> Your neck is the tower of David,
>   built as a fortress,
> hung round with a thousand bucklers,
>   and each the shield of a hero.

Your two breasts are two fawns,
twins of a gazelle,
that feed among the lilies.
You are wholly beautiful, my love,
and without a blemish.

Your loveliness compares with that which is most beautiful.
You are purity and perfection personified.

To modern minds, such comparisons may seem bizarre. Nevertheless, it was traditional in the ancient Middle East to extol the beauty and good qualities of an individual by comparison with the beautiful or striking sights of this world.[7] Here, the writer works a double meaning into the Beloved's paean of praise, though some of the details of the symbolism are obscure after the lapse of so many centuries. All the same, the general drift can be appreciated.

The living soul is hidden beneath the coverings of physical life. Yet the soul still shines like the sun glistening upon the backs of a "flock of goats" on the hillside, whose natural colouring was a glossy black, like the "hair" of most Middle-Easterners. Gilead, a mountainous region east of the Jordan, visible from Jerusalem, was renowned for its rich pastures and many flocks.

Like the clean whiteness of newly shorn sheep, the soul is bright, pure and perfect – but covered – like the "cheeks behind her veil". The soul is the essence of life, here symbolized as her "cheeks" – rosy and fresh, full of life and vitality, like the deep pink of a halved "pomegranate" – a common Eastern comparison.

In the mind's eye of the poet, her stately and beautiful "neck" hung with jewels is seen as a command "tower" hung about with a "thousand bucklers". The Lover wears a fine and shining necklace, each jewel of which is the "shield of a hero", a buckler being a small shield worn on the arm.

"The neck signifies fortitude," says St John of the Cross,[8] and the "thousand bucklers" are the soul's spiritual strengths and virtues. They are the true ornaments of a loving soul, as well as her defence against her lower nature:

> The ... shields are here the virtues and gifts of the soul, which ... serve it ... as a crown and prize, for its work in having gained them. And not only so, but they likewise serve it as a defence, and as strong shields against ... vices.... She says that there are a thousand of them, in order to denote the multitude of the virtues, graces and gifts wherewith God endows the soul in this estate (of love).
>
> *St John of the Cross, Spiritual Canticle XXIV:9, CWJC2 p.304*

The "tower of David" refers to the Lord within, who gives strength to the soul, as in the *Psalms* attributed to David:[9]

> The Lord is my rock,
>   and my fortress, and my deliverer,
>   my God, my strength, in whom I will trust,
>   my buckler, and the horn of my salvation,
>   and my high tower.
>
> *Psalms 18:2, KJV*

Her "breasts" symbolize her spiritual heart – her inner being – likened to the gentle and graceful offspring of a "gazelle". Possibly the word also invokes the untranslatable wordplay that links the gazelle to the Name of God. In the innermost centre of the soul lies the Name of God. The soul is the child of God who can traverse the inner mountains, like the Beloved, and feed upon "lilies" in the heavenly pastures, sustained by the Word of Life. The soul is, in herself, wholly perfect – "without blemish".

The devotee is greatly encouraged to hear this, and to know that despite her imperfections, the Beloved sees only the highest good in her. Always kind, his love for her is unconditional.

To the Mountain of Myrrh

> LOVER: Before the dawn wind rises,
>   before the shadows flee,
> I will go to the mountain of myrrh,
>   to the hill of frankincense.

> *In the stillness of the night,*
> *I will ascend in silent prayer to the blissful, healing,*
> *heavenly regions of the soul to meet with my Beloved.*

Given inspiration by the Beloved's outpouring of love, the soul immediately sits in meditation, wishing to traverse the inner realms. In the peace of the night, "before the dawn wind rises, before the shadows flee", she will spend her time in contemplation, lost in bliss, traversing the inner heavens of light in the company of her divine Beloved.

In Jewish religious symbolism, the "mountain of myrrh" and the "hill of frankincense" are said to represent the site of the Temple, the holiest of places for the ancient children of Israel. Esoterically, they signify the inner realms, the mountains of light, "myrrh" being a healing herb, and "frankincense" well known for its sweet and intoxicating fragrance:

> Bestow great mercy: pray take and adopt me,
>   lead me to the soft and gentle flocks of the Light.
> Admit me to the hills and woods of the Law (Word)
>   on the fair mountains,
>   wandering and walking peacefully,
>   and always without fear.
>   *Manichaean Hymns; cf. LSMH pp. 181–82:66*

Then the Beloved urges:

The Haunt of Lions

BELOVED: Come away with me to Lebanon,
my promised bride;
Come away with me to Lebanon,
come on your way.[10]
Lower your gaze from the heights of Amana,
from the crests of Senir and Hermon,
the haunt of lions,
the lairs of leopards.[11]

Come with me to eternity. Withdraw your attention
from all the lower realms of creation,
from the distractions that hold you back.

The poet is using the topography and geography of Palestine and the surrounding area as symbols of the inner journey. There are a number of instances where mystics of the ancient Middle East have described the inner regions in this way, as with Palestine as the mystic "promised land", and Egypt or Babylon as the physical universe. Other mystics have likewise used the staging posts of a trade route or a long journey to signify the inner levels of creation.[12] These details would have been a part of the secret, esoteric teachings, given only to initiates, and it is possible that, here, the writer is bearing in mind his circle of fellow disciples, and their own particular nomenclature, making allusions that only they would fully understand. It is, after all, unlikely that the poet would have expected his work to be still extant after 2500 years!

In the mystical expression of the ancient Middle East, the inner creation was generally depicted as a hierarchy of seven heavens, a description dating back at least to early Zoroastrian times, around 1500 years before Jesus. There are a number of texts from pre-Christian[13] and later Jewish mysticism,[14] as well as from the gnosticism of the early Christian period,[15] that speak of this hierarchy of heavens or *aeons,* each ruled over by angels or *archons.* These constitute the inner mountains to which the ascending soul may be attracted – and thus detained for some time – on the inner journey. In modern terminology, they are the regions which lie within the dominion of the universal mind, the negative power.

Throughout the *Song of Songs,* Lebanon is used as a symbol for eternity.[16] Here, the Beloved is urging the soul to "come away with me to Lebanon",[17] to eternity – to leave the lower realms of creation – the "heights of Amana" and the mountain peak of "Senir" or "Hermon". According to *Deuteronomy,* Mount Hermon, north of Palestine in Lebanon, was called Senir by the Amorites.[18]

"Come away from those places; turn away your gaze," is the advice of all true Masters. All the heavens within the administration of the universal mind, however enticing, blissful and beautiful they may be, are places from which the soul can easily lose her life to "lions" and "leopards". Even from these heavenly realms, she can descend once again into the realms of rebirth and death in the physical creation. The many powers of the mind, human or higher, are the "lions" and "leopards" that waylay a soul struggling to climb the steep and narrow pathway. They are generally called 'wild beasts', 'enemies', 'persecutors' or 'thieves'[19] in the ancient literature:

> She calls the world 'wild beasts' because, to the imagination of the soul that sets out upon the road to God, the world seems to be represented after the manner of wild beasts, which threaten her fiercely.
>
> St John of the Cross, *Spiritual Canticle II:7, CWJC2 p.205*

> Thoughts which are not good are evil wild beasts…. Do not pierce yourself with the sword of sin. Do not burn yourself, O wretched one, with the fire of lust. Do not surrender yourself to barbarians like a prisoner, nor to savage beasts that want to trample upon you.
>
> *Teachings of Silvanus 85, 108; cf. NHS30 pp.280–81, 340–41*

Compassionate Father of all the souls of light,
  merciful Mother of all the robbed!
Now save me from the jackals and wolves
  as was promised by the Jesus of light.
Manichaean Hymns; cf. LSMH pp.176–77:13

Likewise, the negative power was sometimes described as the 'Lion':[20]

Be sober, be vigilant; because your Adversary the Devil,
  as a roaring lion, goes about,
  seeking whom he may devour.
1 Peter 5:8; cf. KJV

You (Lord) will save me
  as I am ensnared by this lion-faced power;
For you are my Saviour.
Pistis Sophia 47; cf. PS p.86, PSGG p.70

So the "promised Bride" – the soul – is urged on to make her way through the mountain pass leading into Lebanon. Though the precise interpretation of the symbolism is no longer clear, the passage perhaps refers to one of the narrow 'gateways' encountered on the spiritual journey. These are 'places' where the inner ascent is said to be difficult, requiring great love and concentration of all the inner faculties to pass through.

Spiritually, the soul has largely escaped from the worst of the 'wild beasts' – the imperfections of the lower, human mind – when she passes through the narrow passage of the single eye. And she has escaped the realms of the mind when she goes beyond the universal mind. Hence, the Beloved urges the soul to make her way through these narrow gateways, out of the body, away from the physical creation, to find him within and to escape altogether from the mind worlds.

Then, never tiring of his work, never failing in his affection, the Beloved repeats his message of love and compassion. It is hard work climbing the steep mountain path of spiritual ascent, and he knows that the soul needs all the encouragement she can get:

What Spells Lie in your Love

> BELOVED: You ravish my heart,
> my sister, my promised bride.
> You ravish my heart
> with a single one of your glances,
> with one single pearl of your necklace.
> What spells lie in your love,
> my sister, my promised bride!

> *When you gaze at me, dear soul,*
> *love flows between us, enrapturing my heart.*
> *I am made captive by your love.*

Borrowing from Egyptian love lyrics, the Beloved calls the devotee "my sister". She is also "promised" to him, because every soul who comes to a Master is "promised" or destined to do so. She is his "bride" because, inwardly, the soul and the Beloved are one. All sense of self and ego is ultimately dispelled.

There is nothing more "ravishing" than the pangs of divine love. The heart is swept away and the sense of individual self dissolves. Every look or "glance" exchanged by the Beloved and the devotee travels upon waves of love and bliss:

> One glance ... implies a single concentrated gaze, without looking again and again.
>
> St Francis de Sales, Love of God 6:5, LG p.231

Literally, the expression is, "with one of your eyes". The image is of the Oriental woman unveiling one eye when addressing some-one. In so doing, she also reveals some of the ornaments hanging around her neck. The "necklace" or ornamentation of the soul is her love and devotion for the Beloved. One "pearl", one small part of this, has great powers of attraction. This kind of love is "spell"-binding. The Master fosters love in the hearts of his devotees, responding to these "pearls" with an even greater out-pouring of love:

> The eye is the love of man penetrating into God, and with this love the soul compels God, so that he must do what she desires. And this is called "wounding" ("you ravish my heart") because she has potency over God and has mastered him. She stretches her bow and shoots God in the heart, and the bow that she stretches is her very heart. She … shoots with a burning desire at God and hits the true mark. In this way, she attains to the highest degree of perfection.
>
> *Book of the Poor in Spirit II:I.5, BPS p.129*

How Delicious is your Love

BELOVED:[21] How delicious is your love,
more delicious than wine!
How fragrant your perfumes,
more fragrant than all other spices!
Your lips, my promised one,
distil wild honey.
Honey and milk
are under your tongue;
And the scent of your garments
is like the scent of Lebanon.

Sweet and intoxicating is your love,
bearing the incomparable fragrance of the divine Word.
Within your heart, seen on your face
and expressed in your words is the treasure of pure love.
The essence of eternity permeates your being.

There is nothing more desirable – more "delicious" – than divine love. The experience of it is far superior to the effect of wine. The soul is intoxicated with bliss and inner sweetness – an intoxication that increases consciousness rather than diminishes it.

Love is a "perfume" – a "fragrance" rarer than any "spice". Those of developed spirituality possess a subtle perception of the atmosphere of love that surrounds all lovers of the divine. Fragrance, too, is a term that alludes to the blissful music of the Word, as we have seen.

The "lips" automatically express the nature and content of a person's inner being. The character of a person's words indicates what lies within them. "Your lips distil wild honey," says the Beloved. "Honey and milk are under your tongue." Only purity and sweetness lie within the lover of the Lord. All their actions and words testify to this:

> I spoke with the lips of my heart,
>   and when my voice reached him, he heard me.
> And his Word came to me,
>   and gave me the fruits of my labours;
> And gave me rest by the grace of the Lord.
>
> *Odes of Solomon 37:2–4, OSD p.156*

"Milk and honey" are an allusion to the biblical promised land. But the real "land of milk and honey" lies within us. "Milk and honey" symbolize the divine grace and sustenance of the Word. The expression refers to the inner, spiritual bliss, 'tasted' in the mystic transport of meditation. "Taste, and see that the Lord is good,"[22] as one of the psalms says.

Milk is highly nutritious; it is both food and drink; it is that which enables the infant to grow; it is the food given of herself by a mother to her child. Honey is likewise full of goodness, a sweet purveyor of energy and life. It is also a natural preservative against decay. In combination, warm milk and honey make an ambrosial, comforting drink, symbolic of abundance and satisfaction. Similarly, there is nothing more inwardly sweet, spiritually nourishing, unlimited in abundance and full of all good and eternal things than conscious contact with the Word of Life:

> Sprinkle Thy dews upon us, (Lord),
>   and open Thy abundant springs,
>   which pour forth milk and honey to us.
> > *Odes of Solomon 4:10, OSD p.20*

> More than shelter was he to me,
>   and more than a foundation.
> I was carried like a child by his mother,
>   and he gave me milk, the Dew of the Lord.
> > *Odes of Solomon 35:4–5, OSD p.150*

"The scent of your garments is like the scent of Lebanon," says the Beloved, referring to the Oriental custom of perfuming clothes. St Francis de Sales calls this "scent" the "caress of heaven upon our hearts".[23] As before, Lebanon is being used as a symbol of eternity. The "garments" of the soul in the inner regions are its light, its radiance, its devotion to the Word, its love. The "garments" may also be the finer, or more subtle, inner 'bodies', which surround the soul while in the heavenly realms of the greater mind. In this world, too, the physical body is only a "garment". But in a devotee, all these 'wrappings' are imbued with the same fragrance or "scent", the perfume of divine love, the fragrance of the divine Melody:

> Her garments are like the flowers of spring,
>   and from them a waft of Fragrance is borne;
> And in the crown of her head the King is established,
>   who with his immortal Food (ambrosia)
>   nourishes them that are founded upon him.
> > *Acts of Thomas 6; cf. ANT p.367*

The clothing of your virtue, my bride, imitates the divine
perfection, and has become like the transcendent Godhead
because of your purity and integrity. And such is the fragrance
of your divine garments that they may be compared with
frankincense that is consecrated to the worship of God.[24]

Gregory of Nyssa, On Canticles 8, GGGN p.227

What lies within is reflected outwardly. What is seen without
has its origins within. The five physical senses are reflections of
more subtle, mental essences, energies or counterparts within –
though these senses are increasingly merged into one continuous
perception as the soul ascends. And the "scent" of a divine lover
or of the Beloved is infinitely more intoxicating and indrawing
than any fragrance or flower of this world. Ascending souls can
discern this scent, inherent in the being of the Beloved and all
souls who are saturated with the love of the divine Essence.

She is a Garden Enclosed

BELOVED: She is a garden enclosed,
my sister, my promised bride;
A garden enclosed,[25]
a sealed fountain.

The soul is a store of secret treasures.
Within herself, she is a fragrant garden
of colourful blossom and peaceful delight.
And although she may not know it,
the Living Water of the Word flows abundantly within her.

The Beloved compares the soul to a walled "garden" and a
"sealed fountain". An "enclosed garden" may be a haven of peace,
full of the most luxuriant blossom; its trees may be laden with
the sweetest and most nourishing fruit. But, being enclosed, no
one can experience its treasures without a key or the permission

to enter. They may not even know that it is there. Similarly, a "sealed fountain" does not permit the water to flow. There may appear to be no water at all; the surrounding garden may be suffering from drought. Yet there is abundant water within if the means of tapping it are known.

In like manner, the soul, inwardly a garden of the highest heaven or a fountain of Living Water, is "enclosed" or "sealed" in by the many coverings of mind and body. Everything lies within the soul, but her treasures are hidden from external view.

There is another interpretation. Just as a garden is walled in to prevent the intrusion of strangers, so too is the soul veiled and chaste in all her thoughts. No strange, unwelcome or worldly thoughts are permitted entry to her mind:

> "My sister is a garden enclosed and a fountain sealed up" – that is to say, enclosed and sealed up against all things that may enter.
>
> St John of the Cross, Ascent of Mount Carmel 3:3.5, CWJC1 p.221

Her devotion to the Beloved within is so focused that no ray of her attention can escape outside. She has walled herself in with the treasures of love. Her thoughts and attention revolve only around her Beloved, to the exclusion of all else. It is only with such one-pointed love that the soul can leave the body and meet the Beloved inside. The soul goes where the desires of the mind take her. Only when the mind has been purified of all worldliness and thoughts of self can the inner meeting with the Beloved take place. Similarly with a "sealed fountain":

> A pure soul can truly be called "a chosen vessel",[26] "an enclosed garden", "a sealed fountain", and "a throne of perceptiveness".[27] But a soul polluted with filthy impurities stinks like a sewer.
>
> St Theodoros, Philokalia, A Century of Spiritual Texts 36, P2 p.20

Water being scarce in the East, the owners of springs or fountains would seal them with clay, which – hardening rapidly in the sun – prevented loss, rendering it their own personal water supply. In this way, too, the soul becomes rapt in divine love. She drinks from the ocean without wetting her lips. Love is so well digested within herself that – though she cannot hide her loving and affectionate nature – not one drop of that love is wasted in outer show or vanity:

> Drink the water from your own cistern,
>   fresh water from your own well.
> Do not let your fountains flow to waste elsewhere,
>   nor your streams in the public streets.
>
> *Proverbs 5:15–16, JB*

The water of love flows abundantly within her, but she keeps it hidden from curious eyes.

Fountain that Makes the Gardens Fertile

BELOVED: Your shoots form
an orchard of pomegranate trees,
bearing precious fruit;[28]
Nard and saffron,
calamus and cinnamon,
with all the incense-bearing trees;
Myrrh and aloes,
with the subtlest odours.
Fountain that makes the gardens fertile,[29]
well of living water,
streams flowing down from Lebanon.

The garden of your soul is luxuriant and fragrant;
all that is precious grows and thrives there.
The Living Water of the divine creative Power
flows down from eternity, entering your soul.

The poet now expands on the nature of the "garden enclosed" and the "sealed fountain" that lie concealed within the soul. "Orchard" *(pardes)* is generally thought to be a term of Persian origin, having the same root as the word 'paradise'.[30] The fresh, springtime "shoots" and the promise of a rich harvest of "precious fruit" from this "orchard" indicate the eternal springtime and heavenly fruitfulness of the soul. Her divine love is also likened to the fragrance of precious herbs, spices and oils,[31] and to the healing qualities of "myrrh and aloes". Divine love, too, is rare and transcendent: it is a rare soul who experiences such an intensity of love.

The glories that await the soul when she begins to realize her own true heritage are beyond description. The most beautiful and enchanting sights and experiences of this world are only a dim reflection of what lies within. There, the life-giving, healing and creative vibration of the Word is perceived to underlie everything. The Word is the divine Breath and Fragrance that breathes life into all things. It is the "fountain" that brings life and 'fertility' to all realms of the creation. Everything blossoms and comes into being due to the inward vibration and vitality of the Word. Ultimately, the soul realizes that there is nothing but this primal Word, reverberating through all things. It flows out from "Lebanon", the eternity of God. It is the "well of Living Water" spoken of by many mystics of old,[32] including Jeremiah and Jesus:

> My people have committed a double crime:
>> they have abandoned me,
>> the fountain of Living Water,
>> only to dig cisterns for themselves,
>> leaky cisterns that hold no water.
>
>> *Jeremiah 2:13, JB*

> Whoever drinks of the Water
>> that I shall give him will never thirst;
> But the Water that I shall give him shall become in him
>> a well of water springing up into everlasting Life.
>
>> *John 4:14; cf. KJV*

In dry areas, like much of the Middle East, the availability of water is essential to existence. Without water, there is no physical life. Without the Living Water, there is no creation. Without conscious contact with the Living Water, there is no salvation for a soul sweltering in the heat of physical existence.

Let my Beloved Come into his Garden

LOVER: Awake, north wind,
come, wind of the south!
Breathe over my garden,
to spread its sweet smell around.
Let my Beloved come into his garden,
let him taste its rarest fruits.

*Come, living Spirit, fill my heart
with the fragrance of divine life.
May my Beloved reveal himself within me.
May our love be one.*

Now, the soul responds, calling upon the "wind" to bring life to her garden, to spread its fragrance. The "wind" is the Word, the Holy Spirit. In the Middle East, the north wind brings the infrequent rain, necessary for the crops to grow. But the south wind brings warmth in winter to colder areas such as Palestine. And all winds are of help to seafarers in Mediterranean countries. Hence, both – in their own season – are the harbingers of life, energy and activity:

> This divine Breath of the Holy Spirit is greatly to be desired, and ... every soul (should) pray that he (the Spirit) may breathe through her garden so that the divine fragrances of God may flow. And because this is so necessary, and of such great glory and good for the soul, the Bride desired it and prayed for it in the *Songs*, ... saying: "Rise up hence, north wind, and come, southwest wind, and breathe through my garden; that its fragrances and precious spices may flow."
>
> *St John of the Cross, Spiritual Canticle XVII:9; cf. CWJC2 p.272*

In both Greek and Hebrew, as well as other ancient languages of the Middle East, the words for 'wind', 'breath' and even 'fragrance' are the same as that for 'Spirit'. Consequently, these terms are commonly used as metaphors for the Spirit. Just as breath is indicative of physical life, so too is the Word the essence of inner life and consciousness. This wordplay is found in many places in the ancient mystic literature:

> When that spirit (*or* wind, of the world) blows,
>   it brings the winter.
> When the Holy Spirit (*or* Holy Wind) breathes,
>   the summer comes.
>
> *Gospel of Philip 77, NHS20 p.197*

> He (God) brought clouds of brightness into being,
>   dropping down dew and life;
> He summoned a holy Fire,
>   giving a sweet burning.
> He called forth a Wind and an Air (of the Spirit),
>   breathing the Breath of the Living.
> He called forth holy mountains,
>   sending up fragrant roots.
>
> *Psalms of Thomas I, Manichaean Psalm Book;*
>   *cf. MPB p.203*

So the soul prays that the wind – the Spirit – may breathe into her – her "garden". She is begging to hear the Sound of the Spirit, the Creation Song, the Song of Life. "Let my Beloved come into his garden," she says, calling the sacred place of her own heart "*his* garden", not even claiming that as her own. "Let him come and play the game of love within me, tasting its finest fruits." Only a soul steeped in love can honestly express such selflessness, such desire to meet with and merge into the Beloved.

And the Beloved responds to the purity of her love:

Eat, Friends, and Drink

BELOVED: I come into my garden,
my sister, my promised bride;
I gather my myrrh and balsam,
I eat my honey and my honeycomb,
I drink my wine and my milk.
Eat, friends, and drink:
drink deep, my dearest friends.

I will reveal myself within your soul.
We will enjoy the sweet healing of divine love.
Spiritual food and drink are plentiful at my table,
so come and take your fill.

The Beloved enters the garden of his devotees to gather the abundant harvest of love. He appears within the devotee, drawing the soul upwards. The poet is using rich imagery to describe the divine meeting. "Myrrh", "balsam", "honey", "honeycomb", "wine" and "milk" are all symbolic of the soul's delight within when taking her fill of the divine, life-giving Spirit:

Into his garden, the divine Bridegroom comes, when he visits a devoted soul. Since his "delight" is to mix "with the sons of Adam",[33] what more fitting abode can await him than the garden of a soul wearing his own image and likeness? In that garden, his own hands have planted the gratifying love we have for his goodness, the love on which we feed. His goodness, too, delights and feeds on our gratification. This, in turn, grows as we become aware that God is pleased to see that we find our contentment in him. The result of all these mutual delights is a supremely gratifying love, of which the fruit is his, who is happy to find us content with him.

St Francis de Sales, Love of God 5:2, LG p.184

The creative Power is the Beloved's spiritual food and drink – he calls them "my wine" and "my milk", and he urges his devotees to fill themselves from his table. "Eat, friends, and drink," he invites. "Drink deep," he continues, calling his disciples his "dearest friends". What greater friend to the soul could there be than this? –

> You who are my friends ... shall be fed with the spiritual food of the Bread of Life. But you who are my beloved ... shall drink deep of the richest and best wine in my cellar, which is the supreme joy of love in the bliss of heaven.
>
> *Walter Hilton, Ladder of Perfection I:44, LP pp.54–55*

> Come unto me (Wisdom), all you that desire me,
>   fill yourselves with my fruits;
> For my memory is sweeter than honey,
>   my inheritance than honeycomb.
>
> *Wisdom of Jesus Ben Sirach 24:19–20; cf. in OPJG p.61*

The garden of divine love is always open and welcoming.

Fourth Poem

I Sleep, but my Heart is Awake

*Drawn by the love of the Beloved, the soul speaks of her
longing and her efforts to find him within.*

LOVER: I sleep, but my heart is awake.
I hear my Beloved knocking.

BELOVED: Open to me, my sister, my love,
my dove, my perfect one;
For my head is covered with dew,
my locks with the drops of night.

LOVER: I have taken off my tunic,
am I to put it on again?
I have washed my feet,
am I to dirty them again?

My Beloved thrust his hand
through the hole in the door;
I trembled to the core of my being.
Then I rose
to open to my Beloved.
Myrrh ran off my fingers,
onto the handle of the bolt.
I opened to my Beloved,
but he had turned his back and gone!

My soul failed at his flight.
I sought him, but I did not find him,
I called to him, but he did not answer.

The watchmen came upon me
as they made their rounds in the city.
They beat me, they wounded me,
they took away my cloak:
they who guard the ramparts.

I charge you,
daughters of Jerusalem,
If you should find my Beloved,
what must you tell him...?
That I am sick with love.

CHORUS: What makes your Beloved better than other lovers,
O loveliest of women?
What makes your Beloved better than other lovers,
to give us a charge like this?

LOVER: My Beloved is fresh and ruddy,
to be known among ten thousand.
His head is golden, purest gold,
his locks are palm fronds
and black as the raven.
His eyes are doves
at a pool of water,
bathed in milk,
at rest on a pool.[1]

His cheeks are beds of spices,
banks sweetly scented.
His lips are lilies,
distilling pure myrrh.
His hands are golden, rounded,
set with jewels of Tarshish.
His belly a block of ivory
covered with sapphires.
His legs are alabaster columns
set in sockets of pure gold.
His appearance is that of Lebanon,
unrivalled as the cedars.
His conversation is sweetness itself,
he is altogether lovable.
Such is my Beloved, such is my friend,
O daughters of Jerusalem.

CHORUS: Where did your Beloved go,
O loveliest of women?
Which way did your Beloved turn,
so that we can help you look for him?

LOVER: My Beloved went down to his garden,
to the beds of spices,
to pasture his flock in the gardens
and gather lilies.
I am my Beloved's, and my Beloved is mine.
He pastures his flock among the lilies.

My Heart is Awake

LOVER: I sleep, but my heart is awake.

I may be living in the world of the senses
that make men unaware,
but my soul remains conscious within.

The line has a double meaning. The soul says that she "sleeps". She is sleeping in the intoxication of the senses and materiality, unconscious of the Divine within herself. Held captive in the body, exiled from her true home with God, she is unconscious of her royal status. Like the sleeping princess, bound by the spell of the wicked witch (the mind), she awaits the awakening call of the prince (the Master).

So the soul says that she is in the body. Yet, though she appears to be sleeping, inside herself she is spiritually awake and conscious:

> Although I sleep with respect to my natural self, ceasing to labour, my heart is awake, being supernaturally lifted up in supernatural knowledge.
>
> *St John of the Cross, Ascent of Mount Carmel 2:14.11; cf. CWJC1 p.118*

To external appearances, she may seem to be "asleep", like every-body else. But actually, her inner love and consciousness are awakened within:

> She is awake to her Beloved, watching and praying, heart to heart with him.
>
> *St Francis de Sales, Love of God 6:11; cf. LG p.247*

The soul, enjoying alone the contemplation of being, will not awake for anything that arouses sensual pleasure. After lulling to sleep every bodily motion (activity), she receives the vision of God in a divine wakefulness with pure and naked intuition.

> *Gregory of Nyssa, On Canticles 10; cf. GGGN p.242* [2]

There may be a human individual who, through his appre-
hension of the true realities and his joy in what he has
apprehended, achieves a state in which he talks with people
and is occupied with his bodily necessities while his spirit is
wholly turned towards him, may he be exalted, so that in his
heart he is always in his presence, may he be exalted, while
outwardly he is with people, in the sort of way described in
the poetical parables that have been invented for these
notions: "I sleep, but my heart wakes", "It is the voice of my
Beloved that knocks", and so on.

Moses Maimonides, Guide of the Perplexed III:51; cf. GP2 p.623

The line has another meaning. During the day, the devotees of
the Divine attend dutifully to whatever it is they have to do,
according to their own particular way of life. They appear to be
just like everyone else. But at night, when the world sleeps and
the atmosphere is quiet and peaceful, these lovers seek the Lord
within in contemplative prayer. In fact, the time comes when
the soul remains conscious inside at all times. The body and
physical brain may take their needed rest, but the consciousness
does not descend below the single eye into the sleep state.
Rather, it soars within in mystic transcendence, meeting with
the spiritual form of the Beloved, and traversing the spiritual
realms:

> At night my soul longs for you
>   and my spirit in me seeks for you.
> *Isaiah 26:9, JB*

> Lo, I sleep and awake,
>   and I shall no more go to sleep.
> *Acts of Thomas 142, ANT p.427*

The soul then describes how, while she is in this state of divine
wakefulness, her Beloved comes to her:

I Hear my Beloved Knocking

LOVER: I hear my Beloved knocking.

I hear my Beloved calling from within,
trying to awaken me.

When we sleep, we can be awakened by someone knocking on the bedroom door. Mystically, the body is like a house where the soul sleeps. The bedroom of this house is the single eye, the secret door opening inwards, permitting the soul a means of escape from the body. The Master comes and calls the sleeping soul. He 'knocks', and the soul 'hears' the knocking:

> Behold, I stand at the door, and knock:
> If any man hear my Voice, and open the door,
>   I will come in to him,
>   and will sup with him, and he with me.
>
> *Book of Revelation 3:20, KJV*

The soul 'hears' in many ways. She responds to the inner pull of the Master, and her attention concentrates within; she is interested in his teachings and what he has to say; she becomes aware of his presence within; she recognizes the flow of his love, and his guiding hand in all that happens to her. The soul may think that she is interested in the Master – but actually it is his interest in her that starts and sustains the entire process. Yet all this is only the preliminary 'hearing'.

Mystically, hearing the Beloved's voice or "knocking" means that the soul hears the divine Melody, the life-giving, Creative Word or Voice of God, which is the real Master. This is the 'knocking' that awakens the soul and keeps her awake – by day and by night – while the world sleeps on.

The Beloved then calls coaxingly:

My Head is Covered with Dew

> BELOVED: Open to me, my sister, my love,
>   my dove, my perfect one;
> For my head is covered with dew,
> my locks with the drops of night.

> *Dear soul, rise up to the inner door;*
>   *pass through and come to me.*
>   *For my essence is imbued*
> *with blissful showers of spiritual grace.*
>   *It is here that I await you.*
> *My inner form radiates this divine Power.*

With great affection, love and kindness, the Beloved calls to the longing soul to "open" her inner heart – to relinquish the bonds of mind and ego that keep her wrapped up in her small self, unable to find the Beloved within. Out of his purity, he calls her "sister". In recognition of her innate spirituality, he calls her "my dove" and "my perfect one". The "dove", as we have seen, is symbolic of the soul that – when free from mind and matter – becomes the "perfect one". True perfection of the soul is synonymous with salvation – the cleansing of the soul from all its associations with the creation and its return to God.

So the soul hears the radiant Beloved calling her to himself, to receive his inner blessings:

> Says the devoted Bride: "… See, it is he who awakens me; he calls me lovingly; I can tell him by his voice." God awakens us with a start, unexpectedly, by the call of his inspiration. We do nothing in these early stages of grace but feel the impulse "which is God operating in us", as St Bernard says, "but without our co-operation".
>
> St Francis de Sales, *Love of God 2:9, LG p.73*

The "dew" that covers the Beloved's head, forming so copiously

in certain months in the East that it saturates clothing,[3] is the
intoxicating, life-giving atmosphere of bliss, joy and peace which
emanates from him. This is the true 'nectar of the gods', the true
spiritual food and drink that gives life to a soul, long dead from
her continuous wanderings in the physical creation. Essentially,
it is the Creative Word, the power behind all other powers, and
the real nature of the Master:

> Do you not see the food of the soul, what it is? It is the *Logos*
> of God, (raining) continuously like dew, embracing all the
> soul, suffering no portion to be without part of itself.
>
> *Philo, Allegorical Interpretation III:59; cf. PCW5 pp.414–15, TGH1 p.247*

> For the Lord is like the sun,
>   shining upon the face of the land:
> My eyes were enlightened,
>   and my face received the Dew,
>   and my breath (spirit) took pleasure
>   in the pleasant Fragrance of the Lord.
> And he brought me to his paradise,
>   wherein is the abundance of the Lord's pleasure.
>
> *Odes of Solomon 11:13–16, OSD p.52*

> Wash us now therefore in the dewdrops of your joy …
> Open to us passage to the vaults of the heavens,
>   and walk before us to the joy of your kingdom,
>   O Glorious One!
>
> *Manichaean Psalm Book CCXL; cf. MPB p.41*

> He will appear to you … with a face full of joy,
>   he will wash you also
>   and purify you with his pleasant dews.
> He will set your foot on the path of Truth
>   and furnish you with your wings of light.
>
> *Manichaean Psalm Book CCLXXIX; cf. MPB p.100*

Even the dead shall arise,
  nurtured by the dew of light.
                                    Isaiah 26:19 [4]

The "drops of night" refer both to this rain of heavenly grace, as well as to the peace of the night in which the soul communes with him.

I have Taken off my Tunic

> LOVER: I have taken off my tunic,
>   am I to put it on again?
> I have washed my feet,
>   am I to dirty them again?

> *I have withdrawn my attention from the body;*
>   *am I to let it fall again without seeing you?*
> *I have hushed and purified my lower nature;*
>   *am I to return once more to physical existence?*

When the Beloved calls, the soul responds. The two go hand in hand, and by degrees the pull of the Beloved's love draws the soul out of the body. The soul says that she has divested herself of her garment, her "tunic" – the physical body. She has "taken it off" – she has withdrawn all her mind and consciousness from the body and come to the single eye, the 'lattice window' of the second poem:[5]

> I was covered with the covering of Thy Spirit,
>   and I removed from myself my garment of skin.
> For Thy Right Hand raised me up,
>   and caused sickness to pass away from me.
> And I became strong in Thy Truth,
>   and holy in Thy holiness.
>   *Odes of Solomon 25:8–10, OSD p.116*

The gates of the skies (heavens)
   have opened before me through the rays of my Saviour,
   and his glorious Likeness of light.
[I have left] the garment upon the earth,
   the senility of diseases that was with me:
The immortal robe I have put upon me.

Manichaean Psalm Book CCLXIV, MPB p.81

Even during human life, the soul can find her "immortal robe":

But first, you must tear off the tunic (body) that you are
wearing, the robe of ignorance, the foundation of imperfection, the chain of corruption, the carapace of darkness,
the living death, the corpse made of the senses, the tomb you
carry with you, the thief within your house, who through
the things he loves, hates you; and through the things he
hates, bears you malice.

   Such is the tunic, the enemy, that you wear, which strangles
you and pulls you down towards itself; lest you should look
up and, beholding the Beauty of Truth and the Good that
dwells within it, you should come to hate its imperfection –
having discovered the plot that it has hatched against you by
rendering insensible your wits and seeming senses, by stopping
them up with a mass of matter and filling them with loath-
some desire, to keep you from hearing what you ought to
hear, and to keep you from seeing what you ought to see.

Corpus Hermeticum VII:2–3; cf. GS pp.462, TGH2 pp.120–21

The soul also says that she has "washed her feet" – she is no
longer sullied and constrained by the confines of this world and
its body. By Jewish custom, anyone entering the Temple had first
to 'purify' themselves by various rituals. These included washing
the feet. In fact, to wash their dusty feet before entering a house
was expected of all travellers. Likewise, before entering the real
temple or house of the body, the soul must first be purified of
the dirt of this world:

It is surely a divine grace that (the soul) … happens to receive Reason's (the Word's) favour; for all obstacles shall be cast aside before her, especially if her desire for this state be constant, and she remains unperturbed by worldly affairs. As it is said, "I have put off my coat (tunic), I have washed my feet. How then shall I defile them?"

'Obadayah Maimonides, Treatise of the Pool II; cf. TP p.77 [6]

The soul says that she has prepared herself for entry into the true temple – is she to be rejected? She has purified herself by turning her mind away from the world, by focusing all her attention inside, by withdrawing her consciousness from the body – has it been to no avail? –

> When it has rejected evil, let the soul still engaged in ascetic struggle repeat the words of the *Song* to the malicious demons and thoughts that forcibly try to turn her attention once more to vanities and delusion: "I have taken off my coat; how can I put it on again? I have washed my feet; how can I make them dirty?"
>
> *Ilias the Presbyter, Philokalia, Gnomic Anthology IV:95; cf. P3 p.59*

The "feet" also indicate that the body lies at the bottom – at the 'foot' – of the creation. The human form is unique. Many mystics have said that it is a microcosm of the entire creation. Though it lies at the nethermost limit, it contains the entire creation within it. Through this form alone can the entire creation and the Creator himself be fully known. But it must first be purified of the dirt of human imperfection and entanglement with the lower creation. It must first be cleansed: the "feet" of creation must be "washed".

The soul says that this preparation has been made. By purification of the mind, attraction to the world of the senses has diminished and she has been able to respond to the pull of the Beloved. She has "washed her feet". So she asks plaintively and hopefully, "Am I to dirty them again? Am I to return to the body empty-handed, without having seen you within?"

The soul knows that the inner vision of the Beloved is not in her hands; and the Beloved knows that his aim is to purify the soul of all attachment to the physical world. The soul, too, must relinquish all idea of individual self. She must become pliant in her Beloved's hands. All prickles, barriers and walls must be dismantled and discarded. To accomplish this, the Master is well aware that there is nothing so effective as the fire of divine longing combined with the buffets of the world. Gold must pass through fire before it is purified.

Therefore, a soul can never presume that the radiant Master, the "Likeness of light", will appear inside. Everything has to be surrendered to him. It is the Master who pulls and purifies a soul. And having brought the soul thus far, he will not abandon her without response.

The soul then relates what happens next:

The Hole in the Door

> LOVER: My Beloved thrust his hand
> through the hole in the door;
> I trembled to the core of my being.
> Then I rose to open to my Beloved.
> Myrrh ran off my fingers,
> onto the handle of the bolt.
> I opened to my Beloved,
> but he had turned his back and gone!
> My soul failed at his flight.
> I sought him, but I did not find him,
> I called to him, but he did not answer.

My attention being focused in contemplation at the inner door, my Beloved gave me a glimpse of his radiant form. Waves of love coursed through me as I stood before the door. I passed through and thought to see him in all his glory, but he had withdrawn himself. In my longing, I tried to reach him, but he did not come.

The hole in an old-fashioned wooden door was the means of lifting the latch from the other side. It could also be used for checking who was wanting to enter. The "door" is the single eye, the inner door, upon which Jesus said, "Knock and it shall be opened."[7] The knocking is a reference to the effort and longing of the soul to go within.

But it is the Master who sets the process in motion. First he knocks upon the bedroom door from *his* side. It is *his* call that awakens the soul. He is also the only one who can open the bedroom door, and let the sleepy soul come out.

So the soul says that the Beloved, "thrust his hand through the hole in the door" – he gives encouragement to the soul, to help the door be opened. He gives a hint of his presence, a glimpse of himself. The soul "trembles to the core of her being" – she is thrilled by the chords of love:

> And all my heart went out to meet his coming,
>   ere he came.
>
> *Tennyson, The Death of Oenone*

She "rose" from her bed – she rises up from her body, the land of sleep. "This is the soul while she is in the body,"[8] observes the *Zohar*, commenting on this passage. All her love, mind, attention and concentration gather together at the single eye. Every ray of attention becomes fixed and intent upon the inner door, awaiting his coming, at his pleasure. She comes forward to "open" to her Beloved – to let all barriers between them be dissolved.

She is in bliss and ecstasy. "Myrrh" – precious, aromatic and healing – runs off her hands and fingers in generous abundance: she is overwhelmed by the intoxication of his nearness. She feels the powerful vibration of his presence. Her inner being is healed: she is at peace; her mind is quiet. Her inner spiritual heart opens to her Beloved. But he has gone higher! He is playing hide and seek. He is refining the one-pointedness, intensity and sincerity of her love. He is a skilled goldsmith, purifying precious gold.

Myrrh has the property of preservation from decay and was used in olden times to anoint the dead. By association, it thus became a symbol of death. The implication here is that to go within and meet the Beloved, the soul must pass through the door of death:

> In our text the soul has arisen up through death, and, "filled with myrrh", she puts her hands "to the bolt" and desires her Beloved to enter in. But he passes by. And she goes out, not remaining where she was, but rather trying to touch the Word who leads on constantly ahead.
>
> *Gregory of Nyssa, On Canticles 12, GGGN p.263*

"My soul failed at his flight," she says. She is struck by an even deeper love and longing. She cannot find him, for the divine Beloved can only be found as and when he wants to be found. Other renderings have, "my soul passed out with longing for his word"; thus, "my soul longed to hear his voice".[9] This makes the meaning even clearer. She longs to hear the mystic Voice of the Beloved, the divine Music of the inner realms.

So the Beloved gives a fleeting vision of himself through the inner door, and then withdraws. The soul's response is to "call" for him – she longs to see him; her heart goes out to him, but she does not immediately find him. She is given a glimpse, but he then goes higher up, silently 'beckoning' her to follow, through the drawing power of his love. He appears to make no reply, yet the feeling of his presence and pull remains. This only increases her love and longing:

> I have long been calling you, my Saviour,
>   until you should answer me....
> Where is the boiling of your mercies,
>   that you have suffered me to be so long in my prayer?
> If my voice has reached you,
>   then how has your mercy tarried?
> If I have turned to you a little,
>   you ought to turn to me much....

I have wearied of calling you:
   O Doorkeeper, open the door to me.
I will not stem my tears, O Powerful One,
   unless you wipe away my sin.
     Psalms of Heracleides, Manichaean Psalm Book; cf. MPB p.188

The soul then provides the reason why she was given only a glimpse of her Beloved:

The Watchmen Came upon me

> LOVER: The watchmen came upon me
> as they made their rounds in the city.
> They beat me, they wounded me,
>   they took away my cloak,
> they who guard the ramparts.
>
> *My mind again becoming active,*
> *I came back from the inner door.*
> *My human imperfections guarding the entrance*
> *to the spiritual realms robbed me*
> *of my garment of radiance,*
> *leaving me spiritually bereft and destitute.*

The "watchmen" are the physical senses and human imperfections. It is they who guard the "city" of the soul, permitting only the pure to pass by and to go within. The mind is ever diligent and watchful to keep a soul fast asleep in this world; the watchmen of the mind – the senses and the passions – never cease their "rounds". They "guard the ramparts", they prevent the soul from scaling the spiritual heights, from rising up out of the body and entering the "city" of the soul.

    The attention of the mind is scattered by the attraction of the senses and the temptation of human imperfections. These are the forces which "beat" souls in this world:

(They are) the demons that observe the heel of the soul and
bereave it of its glory by the "little foxes that spoil the vines"
– the excitations of the body.

Bar Hebraeus, Ethikon I:V.8; cf. BHBD p.131

None of us is spared; everyone struggles, more or less, to stay
positive and avoid the negative. Compared to the real bliss of the
soul, everyone is constantly miserable and in suffering, however
happy and positive they may appear on the surface. The mind is
the real thief in the city of the soul, taking away her royal
"cloak", her true garment of light, handing out the sad and
tawdry garment of the body in exchange:

> My son, throw every robber out of your gates. Guard all
> your gates with torches which are the words, and by all these
> means, you will acquire inner peace. But he who will not
> guard against these things will become like a city that is
> desolate through being captured. All kinds of wild beasts
> have trampled on it, for thoughts that are not good are evil
> wild beasts. And your city will be filled with robbers, and
> you will not be able to acquire peace for yourself.
>
> *Teachings of Silvanus 85; cf. NHS30 pp.280–81*

Not even a loving devotee is immune from the negative
tendencies of the mind. Not until the pure spiritual realms are
reached, beyond the dominion of the universal mind, is the soul
safe. This is why the soul fails to meet the Beloved within –
because of the impurities that still remain and have yet to be
eliminated. Hence the Beloved plays the game of hide and seek.

There is another interpretation. As in their earlier appearance,[10] the "watchmen" could be friendly – the angels or beings
inhabiting the heavenly realms. They also dwell within the "city"
of the soul. Their beating and wounding is the fire of love, the
pangs of separation from the Beloved that make the Lover – as
she is about to reveal – "sick with love". By this means, they
remove the "cloak" or veil of ego and selfhood from the soul.

Whichever the intended meaning, the Lover continues:

Sick with Love

> LOVER: I charge you,
> daughters of Jerusalem,
> if you should find my Beloved,
> what must you tell him...?
> That I am sick with love.

My dear friends and companions on this path,
if you are fortunate enough to see our Beloved,
tell him that I am consumed with love for him.

When the lover cannot be with the Beloved, the next best thing is to send messages of love through someone else. This helps assuage the heart and keep the fires of love burning. So the soul longingly tells her fellow devotees that if they are lucky enough to meet the Beloved inside, they should let him know of her condition; that despite – or because of – her struggles with the "watchmen", she is "sick" or "wounded" (as the *Septuagint* has it) with love for him:

> Love of loves, why have you so wounded me?
> My heart, torn from its dwelling,
>   is consumed with love.
>   St Francis of Assisi, Canticle of Love; cf. WFA p.122

> I am dying of sweetness,
>   do not marvel at it.
>   St Francis of Assisi, Canticle of the Furnace, WFA p.120

What is more wondrous than divine beauty, or more lovely than the sense of God's magnificence? What longing is so keen and unbearable as that engendered by God in a soul purified of every vice, and truly able to say: "I am wounded with love"?

> Ilias the Presbyter, Philokalia, Gnomic Anthology IV:93, P3 p.59

The Bride … in the *Song of Songs,* pined away with love, when her search for her true love was prolonged. Love bred desire, desire bred urgent search; it was that urgency that caused her to pine away, that would have wasted and broken her heart, if she had known no hope of meeting in the end with the one she was seeking.

St Francis de Sales, Love of God 2:16; cf. LG p.91

Perhaps this is also the strange game of love played by God with his entire creation. He hides himself within every soul and in each particle of his creation. Then the game is simply one of hide and seek.

What makes your Beloved better?

CHORUS: What makes your Beloved better than other lovers,
O loveliest of women?
What makes your Beloved better than other lovers,
to give us a charge like this?

*What makes you think that your Beloved
is more beautiful than all others, O soul?*

The soul is the "loveliest of women" because nothing is lovelier in this world than a divine lover, a spiritualized human being:

We are not human beings seeking spiritual experience:
we are spiritual beings going through a human experience.

Anon.

The soul carries within herself the essence of all beauty and love, and when this begins to shine on a person's face, it beautifies them far more than any cosmetic or social mannerism. Here, the loving soul, deprived of the inner vision of her Beloved, now consoles herself by describing the beauty of his physical form. As in the third poem, the poet describes the Beloved's comeliness by comparison with the beautiful things of the world. But, as before, each of these similes contains a higher, mystical meaning. They refer not only to the spiritual beauty of the Beloved in his physical form, but also to the spiritual form itself, as a manifestation of the Word:

His Appearance as Lebanon

> LOVER: My Beloved is fresh and ruddy,
> to be known among ten thousand.
> His head is golden, purest gold,
> his locks are palm fronds
> and black as the raven.
> His eyes are doves
> at a pool of water,
> bathed in milk,
> at rest on a pool.[11]
> His cheeks are beds of spices,
> banks sweetly scented.
> His lips are lilies,
> distilling pure myrrh.
> His hands are golden, rounded,
> set with jewels of Tarshish.
> His belly a block of ivory
> covered with sapphires.
> His legs are alabaster columns
> set in sockets of pure gold.
> His appearance is that of Lebanon,
> unrivalled as the cedars.

My Beloved is full of spiritual life and energy;
he is unique among men.
His essence is of God, ever young,
untouched by the vagaries of existence.

He sees everything:
nothing escapes his perceptive and penetrating eye.
His presence brings joy and wholeness to all around him.
His words are those of love and wisdom,
imparting hope and courage.
His hands and gestures possess both power and grace.
His radiance is pure and precious.
He stands tall; his soul reaches to eternity,
like the Tree of Life itself.

The loving soul, temporarily denied the vision of the inner Master, seeks solace in considering the beauties of her Beloved. He is "fresh and ruddy", she says, signifying the tremendous vitality and energy with which a Master is imbued. He is radiant with light and life. He stands out in a crowd, even "among ten thousand". The Word, too – the essence of the divine Beloved – is the source of all vitality and life.

His highest part – the head – is made of the purest materials, probably alluding to the Temple that was plated with "purest gold".[12] Pure gold was also used to plate the holies of holies,[13] the innermost shrine within the temple. "Palm fronds", too, were used in the temple decoration.[14] The Beloved is being likened to the holiest shrine of ancient Judaism. He is the true temple in which God dwells. Within him lies eternity. The human form has often been described as the "temple of God":

> Do you not know that you are the temple of God,
> and that the Spirit of God dwells in you?
>
> *1 Corinthians 3:16; cf. KJV*

The difference with a Master is that he has attained full realization of his divinity.

His "black locks" are a sign of his perpetual youth and vigour. Metaphorically, he has no grey hairs, for a Master is never made inwardly old and weary by the jading processes of life. The Word is eternally 'youthful' and life-bestowing.

"His eyes are doves" alludes to the dove as a symbol of love and spirituality; it betokens the purity of soul shining in a Master's eyes. They rest by a "pool of water", signifying the deep peace and serenity surrounding the Beloved. They are bathed in "milk" and honey – in the sweetness of his life-bestowing atmosphere, in the spiritual food and drink of his Creative Word:

> Nobody can perceive and know how great is the splendour of the Word, until he receives dove's eyes – that is, a spiritual understanding.
>
> *Origen, On the Song of Songs III:2, OSS p.172*

His eyes "bathed in milk" also describe the deep black irises and pupils of the Easterner, surrounded by pure white, like milk. A Master has deep and piercing eyes, soft like velvet, far-sighted and all-seeing like an eagle.

The atmosphere around him is full to overflowing with sweet vibrations, like the fragrance of the most precious healing herbs and spices. His face is like a calming "bank" where the soul rests, surrounded by intoxicating scents. His beard flows from his cheeks like banks of sweet herbs. His face is a kingdom in which the soul would dwell.

From his "lips" come only the kindest and the wisest of words, words to cheer and encourage – empowering words – instilling confidence, faith, and love for him and for the Lord's creation. They are full with the fragrance of the Word of God:

> This is why God, your God, has anointed you
>   with the oil of gladness, above all your rivals;
> Myrrh and aloes waft from your robes.
>
> *Psalms 45:7–8, JB*

His hands are beautiful; they are perfectly shaped. His gestures fascinate and beguile the mind. His fingers are "set with jewels of Tarshish". His soft and beautiful hands are so perfectly formed that in the eyes of the lover, even the nails appear to be made of precious stone. Tarshish was an ancient port also mentioned in *1 Kings*,[15] either in southern Spain or in one of the Phoenician colonies of Sardinia. The gem was probably beryl, chrysolite or topaz, any of which come in colours that could be considered appropriate for refined and beautiful fingernails.

"His belly a block of ivory covered with sapphires." "Sapphire", here, is probably the brilliant azure blue of lapis lazuli. "His belly" means his body, the centre of physical existence. The centre or 'body' of the Beloved's existence is the Word or Wisdom of God. A Master's spiritual form, even his physical form for those who have the spiritual eyes to see, is an expression of this great Power. And both the spiritual and physical forms shine with whiteness and purity, radiant and sparkling as if set with precious gemstones – like polished ivory studded with sapphire:

> By the sapphires are denoted the ... mysteries and judgments of the divine Wisdom, which is here denoted by the belly. For sapphire is a precious stone of the colour of the heavens, when they are clear and serene.
>
> St John of the Cross, Spiritual Canticle XXXVII:7, CWJC2 pp.367–68

"His appearance is that of Lebanon, unrivalled as the cedars." He is stately and regal, upright and secure, like the kingdom of Lebanon, fabled for its beauty and fertility, whose tall cedars were famous throughout the world, and whose wood was used extensively in the temple of Solomon. Just as the cedar towers above other trees, so too is a Master's inner stature such that he appears taller than anyone else, even if he is of moderate height. Whenever he enters a room, he fills it with his loving atmosphere, and all souls are attracted to him. Lebanon, too, is used in the *Song of Songs* as a symbol of divinity and the eternity of God. "My Beloved," says the soul, "is divine." His inner reality is that of the Tree of Life.

The soul is describing her Beloved as possessing the qualities of the most beautiful things she can think of in this world. She then concludes:

Altogether Lovable

> LOVER: His conversation is sweetness itself,
> he is altogether lovable.
> Such is my Beloved, such is my friend,
> O daughters of Jerusalem.

> *His words bring gladness to the heart;*
> *his Word is joy itself.*
> *Dear companions, he is my only true friend.*

When he speaks, nothing but love is expressed. The soul wonders how such a thing could be, for no one else has such a constant capacity for love, charm, wisdom and understanding. But a person can only express what they have within themselves, and the Master, being love incarnate, has nothing but the highest love and wisdom to offer. Mystically, his "conversation" is also the divine Speech or Word:

> Wondrous is his Voice,
> and his Converse otherworldly.
> *Mandaean Prayer Book 169; cf. CPM p.147*

(As) it is written, "Your speaking is comely." ... This Voice is sent forth from a profound place in the realms above.
> *Zohar I:246b, WZ1 pp.325*

Therefore, "he is altogether lovable" concludes the soul simply, enraptured with his beauty and his majesty. "Such is my Beloved, such is my friend," she says, for only a Master has the capacity to be a true friend:

Rich Friend of the beings of light!
In mercy grant me [strength
   and] succour me with every gift!
Array [my soul], O Lord respond to me!
[Succour me] in the midst of the foe!
Make pass from me all the ravages of their deceitful body,
   which tortures me with pain.
You are the Friend, praised and beneficent!

Manichaean Hymns, Angad Roshnan I:1–4; cf. MHCP p.113

Trapped by the mind and driven by destiny through the travails of time, no soul can ever be a true friend to another, for we do not possess the freedom to be so. We are constrained by the impressions and entanglements of past lives to give and take, according to our destiny. We come and go according to a preset path. Therefore, we can never be true friends to others, however much we may wish to be so.

But a Master comes from the Lord himself, and is totally free from the constraints of the mind and destiny:

The world shall pass and come to nothing,
   and its works also shall perish with it.
Do you, therefore, O great elect,
   lift up your eyes to the land of light:
You shall see the Friend of the righteous
   standing beyond the world.

Psalms of Thomas XIII, Manichaean Psalm Book; cf. MPB p.219

He alone is the true giver and true friend of the soul, for he comes with the power to take the exiled child back to her true holy land, the kingdom of God within. Such a friend even meets his disciples at death, remaining with them and arranging their further progress towards the final, divine reunion. All other friendships, however sincere and imbued with affection they may be, are temporary. Their course lies beyond our control, and they terminate at death. But friendship with the divine Beloved reaches to eternity:

All the gods and inhabitants (of the inner realms),
    the mountains, the trees, and the springs,
    the spacious and strong palaces and halls
    become joyful at your coming, O Friend.
                Manichaean Hymns; cf. GMU p.306ff., RMP at;
                        cf. GSR p.44:1.2, ML p.120

Then the 'chorus' takes up the theme:

Where did your Beloved go?

>   CHORUS: Where did your Beloved go,
>   O loveliest of women?
>   Which way did your Beloved turn,
>   so that we can help you look for him?

>   *Where, then, can we find this Beloved of yours, O soul?*
>   *For we would help you seek him.*

"Where is this Beloved of yours?" asks the 'chorus', the fellow
devotees, creating the setting for the final scene in this poem.
The soul replies:

Among the Lilies

>   LOVER: My Beloved went down to his garden,
>   to the beds of spices,
>   to pasture his flock in the gardens
>   and gather lilies.
>   I am my Beloved's, and my Beloved is mine.
>   He pastures his flock among the lilies.

>   *Gathering to himself his flock of souls,*
>   *my Beloved has withdrawn into the realms of spirit,*
>   *the fragrant gardens of the soul.*

I have merged into my Beloved;
his essence has become mine.
Now he rests with his disciples in the pastures of eternity.

He has gone away to his "garden", says the soul. He has gone
inside, among the sweet fragrances of the heavenly realms of the
Stream of Life. He is caring for "his flocks" – the sheep that have
been allocated to his care, the ones he has already taken within.
He has given them all a place in the inner pastures and meadows
while, with his love and guidance, they slowly work their way
back to God.

There he "gathers lilies" – he engages in the most sublime and
carefree of 'activities'; he is merged into the Life Stream itself. He
gathers an incredible treasure of the Living Waters to distribute
to his flock:

> Fear not, little flock:
> For it is your Father's good pleasure
>   to give you the kingdom.
>
> *Luke 12:32, KJV*

The souls in a Master's care need have no fears, for the Lord has
sent a Saviour with the express intention of taking them back to
the kingdom of God, whether or not they think they want to go!

"I am my Beloved's," she says. She has totally merged herself
into her Beloved. With the utmost faith she has placed herself in
his hands, for she knows that this is her destiny, and that there is
nowhere else for her to go. He has claimed her as his own, to
return with her to the Father's house.

"And my Beloved is mine." By the same token, when two
become one, what belongs to one belongs to the other. The
unliberated soul has nothing worth retaining or giving. All she
has is her ego, her individuality. In the sphere of being and
spirituality, this is all an individual has to give. But, in exchange,
the soul receives everything that a Master has to offer – the Lord
himself. It is not a bad bargain!

The soul now feels God to be so solicitous in granting her favours ... that she believes that there is no other soul in the world whom he thus favours, nor aught else wherewith he occupies himself, but that he is wholly for herself alone. And, when she feels this, she confesses her feeling in the words of the *Songs:* "My Beloved to me and I to him."

St John of the Cross, Living Flame of Love II:32; cf. CWJC3 p.52 [16]

Her sole attachment will be her Beloved, to the skirt of his raiment will she only cling. As the Sage has said, "I am my Beloved's, and my Beloved is mine." Such a state is most difficult to attain, for how may impure and coarse beings such as we, cling to a luminous and most simple Substance (Spirit)?

'Obadayah Maimonides, Treatise of the Pool II; cf. TP p.77 [17]

"He pastures his flock among the lilies," concludes the soul. He is the good Shepherd who cares for his flock with the utmost concern:

There is a Shepherd giving pasture:
he came seeking his sheep.
Manichaean Psalm Book, MPB p.172

He shares with them his own bounty, the "lilies" – the spiritual peace and bliss of the inner pastures and meadows:

(For) it is he who has made us,
not we ourselves.
We are his people,
and the sheep of his pasture.
Psalms 100:3; cf. KJV

FIFTH POEM

I Went Down to the Nut Orchard

Through the description of the soul's longing, and through the dialogue between the soul and her Beloved, the first poem lays out the fundamentals of the path of divine love. The second relates the travails of the soul in her intense desire to meet the Beloved inside. The third tells of the Master and his love for the soul, while in the fourth the soul again takes centre stage, describing her efforts to reach the spiritual form of the Beloved within.

In this last poem, the soul and the Beloved come together, expressing their mutual love — the poet repeating many of the images and allusions that have gone before. The Beloved or Saviour opens with an expression of his unending love for the soul and his purpose in coming to this world. This is followed by his praise of the soul in human form. His description of the human form as a "prince's daughter", as the "feet" of creation and as a "dance of two camps", also make it clear that he is speaking in general terms of the spiritual purpose of human life. This eulogy is then followed by the soul's response of love.

BELOVED: You are beautiful as Tirzah, my love,
fair as Jerusalem.
Turn your eyes away,
for they hold me captive.
Your hair is like a flock of goats,
frisking down the slopes of Gilead.
Your teeth are like a flock of sheep,
as they come up from the washing.
Each one has its twin,
not one unpaired with another.
Your cheeks, behind your veil,
are halves of pomegranate.

There are sixty queens,
and eighty concubines,
and countless maidens.
But my dove is unique,
mine, unique and perfect.
She is the darling of her mother,
the favourite of the one who bore her.
The maidens saw her and proclaimed her blessed,
queens and concubines sang her praises:
"Who is this arising like the dawn,
fair as the moon,
resplendent as the sun,
terrible as an army with banners?"

I went down to the nut orchard
to see what was sprouting in the valley,
to see if the vines were budding
and the pomegranate trees in flower.
But before I knew ... my desire had hurled me
on the chariots of my people, as their prince.

CHORUS: Return, return, O maid of Shulam;
Return, return, that we may gaze on you!

BELOVED: Why do you gaze on the maid of Shulam
as a dance of two camps?

How beautiful are your feet in their sandals,
O prince's daughter!
The curve of your thighs is like the curve of a necklace,
work of a master hand.
Your navel is a bowl well rounded,
with no lack of wine.
Your belly a heap of wheat,
surrounded with lilies.
Your breasts are two fawns,
twins of a gazelle.
Your neck is an ivory tower.
Your eyes, the pools of Heshbon,
by the gate of Bath-rabbim.
Your nose, the Tower of Lebanon,
sentinel facing Damascus.

Your head is held high like Carmel,
and its plaits are as dark as purple;
A king is held captive in your tresses.
How beautiful you are, how charming,
my love, my delight!
In stature like the palm tree,
its fruit-clusters your breasts.
"I will climb the palm tree", I resolved,
I will seize its clusters of dates."
May your breasts be clusters of grapes,
your breath sweet-scented as apples,
your speaking, superlative wine.

LOVER: Wine flowing straight to my Beloved,
as it runs on the lips of those who sleep.
I am my Beloved's,
and his desire is for me.
Come, my Beloved,
let us go to the fields.
We will spend the night in the villages,
and in the morning we will go to the vineyards.
We will see if the vines are budding,
if their blossoms are opening,
if the pomegranate trees are in flower.
Then I shall give you the gift of my love.
The mandrakes yield their fragrance,
the rarest fruits are at our doors;
The new as well as the old,
I have stored them for you my Beloved.

Ah, why are you not my brother,
nursed at my mother's breast!
Then if I met you out of doors, I could kiss you
without people thinking ill of me.
I should lead you, I should take you
into my mother's house, and you would teach me!
I should give you spiced wine to drink,
juice of my pomegranates.

His left arm is under my head
and his right embraces me.

BELOVED: I charge you,
daughters of Jerusalem,
not to stir my love, nor rouse it,
until it please to awake.

Fair as Jerusalem

BELOVED: You are beautiful as Tirzah, my love,
fair as Jerusalem.

Your soul is a beautiful city,
a fitting residence for the mystic King.

Tirzah – meaning 'she is pleasing' or 'favoured' – was an ancient Canaanite city. It was the first capital of the northern kingdom of Palestine, famed for its grace and used as a royal residence. Jerusalem was capital of the south, described in *Lamentations* as the "perfection of beauty, the joy of the whole world".[1]

Mystically, it means that the soul carries within herself the essence of all loveliness. She is a place fit for the divine King, the royal Shepherd, the Beloved, to dwell. The fairness and beauty of the soul are being likened to the beauty of God. Jerusalem is also symbolic of the true holy city, the heavenly Jerusalem,[2] the eternity within:

> And he (an angel) carried me away in the spirit
>   to a great and high mountain;
> And showed me that great City, the holy Jerusalem,
>   descending out of heaven from God,
>   having the glory of God:
> And her light was like unto a stone most precious,
>   even like a jasper stone, clear as crystal.
>
> *Book of Revelation 21:10–11, KJV*

The angels approached my soul and detached her from the sensible (bodily) faculties. I found myself before the heavenly Jerusalem, which was encircled by an exceedingly vast river, of great beauty and brightness.

Marina de Escobar, VME1 III:1, GIP p.274

The Beloved then continues:

Your Eyes Hold me Captive

> BELOVED: Turn your eyes away,
> for they hold me captive.

I am a prisoner of your love.

The Beloved inspires love in the heart of the lover, who cannot help but respond. The soul, even as an unenlightened human being trapped in a physical form, cannot take her eyes away from the eyes of her Beloved. But the love is one. Love is only responding to love. So the Beloved says that he, too, is a captive of the soul's love, for the Beloved is the personification of divine love. But the love that comes from the soul is returned a hundredfold by the Beloved.

Literally, the expression is, "for they take me by storm" – indicating the power of divine love to sweep aside all other loves.

> BELOVED: Your hair is like a flock of goats,
> frisking down the slopes of Gilead.
> Your teeth are like a flock of sheep,
> as they come up from the washing.
> Each one has its twin,
> not one unpaired with another.
> Your cheeks, behind your veil,
> are halves of pomegranate.

You are the fountain of divine beauty.
Veiled you may be, but shining bright within.

The Beloved repeats the expression of his love first given in the third poem.[3]

Countless Maidens

> BELOVED: There are sixty queens,
> and eighty concubines,
> and countless maidens.

Lovers of all degrees throng around the Beloved.

The "queens" were the full wives in Solomon's harem, while the "concubines" were his slaves. Here, they represent the many devotees of the Master, also including the "maidens who love him" of the first poem. As before, the Master is symbolized as Solomon, and his entourage, his "harem", the throng who love him, are his disciples.

The difference in status between "queens", "concubines" and "maidens" probably represents the many kinds of disciple that are drawn to a Master. Some are spiritually evolved. They are the "queens" who have union with the King. Some – the "concubines" – possess great devotion and steadfastness, but as yet they have not been granted entry to the inner sanctum, the King's chamber. They have not yet met him within, in his radiant form. And there are many others – the "countless maidens" – who strive and struggle upon the spiritual path and will achieve their goal one day. All the "maidens" will one day become "queens". They will all, in due time, be invited into the King's chamber.

The Hebrew word used here for "maidens" denotes young women of a marriageable age. That is, all disciples are in a position to consummate the divine marriage by their personal meeting with the Beloved within. But he is the one who has to call them, which he does only when he considers them to be ready – to be of sufficient inner purity.

My Dove is Unique

> BELOVED: But my dove is unique,
> mine, unique and perfect.
> She is the darling of her mother,
> the favourite of the one who bore her.
> The maidens saw her and proclaimed her blessed,
> queens and concubines sang her praises:
> "Who is this arising like the dawn,
> fair as the moon,
> resplendent as the sun,
> terrible as an army with banners?"

But the true mystic devotee is rare.
She is beloved of the Spirit from whom she sprang.
Others recognize her attainment, her purity,
her spiritual light and power.

"But my dove is unique," says the king. A Master loves all his disciples equally. Every disciple receives his personal care and attention, making them realize that they are each special to him. Even so, in the spectrum of human life, true spiritual devotees are a rarity.

As before, the Spirit is the "mother" of the soul, the spiritual "dove". The soul and the Holy Spirit – the Word or Wisdom – are one. The relationship is of pure love, of utter selflessness, of merging. The soul is the "darling of her mother", Wisdom. She is the "favourite" of the "one who bore her", for the creative Power is the inner essence of the soul:

Surely we know who the mother of the dove is, since we know the tree by its fruits. When we consider man, we cannot doubt that he is born of man. Similarly, if we look for the mother of the chosen dove, we will recognize her in none other than that Dove (of the Spirit). For the nature of the parent is always visible in the offspring. But the offspring of the Spirit is spirit. Hence, if the offspring is a dove, then surely its mother must be that Dove that came down from heaven.... This is the Dove that the maidens call blessed, and the queens and concubines praise. For the path to that blessed happiness is one that is open to all souls from every rank.

Gregory of Nyssa, On Canticles 15, GGGN pp.287–88

The other devotees, the "maidens, ... queens and concubines", cannot help but see the "blessedness" of a soul that is steeped in the love of the Beloved, and they are drawn by that love to express their appreciation. She is as fresh and pristine as the "dawn", as intoxicating as "moonlight", as powerful and majestic as the "sun", the source of light. She is a spiritual champion. She has, within herself, the power of a great and advancing "army with banners", for she is merged into the Power of Powers.

I went Down to the Nut Orchard

> BELOVED: I went down to the nut orchard
> to see what was sprouting in the valley.

> *I descended to the material world*
> *to see which souls were stirring and awakening.*

The "nut orchard" is the physical universe, the image conveying the potential for a rich harvest. The material world is like a "valley", the lowest point in creation, yet potentially rich and fertile if the right seed is sown and nurtured, and harvested in the right season:

> Though I walk through
> the valley of the shadow of death,
> I will fear no evil.

Psalms 23:4, KJV

The day on which the Wind (Spirit)
    bears down upon the valley,
    its people are illumined by its radiance.
        Mandaean Prayer Book 164; cf. CPM p.142

The human form is like a field in which the seed of the Word
can be sown by a Master. From this sowing, a rich spiritual
harvest can be reaped, for it is in the human form that God can
be realized. This is the greatest of all harvests.

A nut, too, has characteristics that lend themselves to mystic
symbolism. Its nutritious fruit is hidden within a hard shell.
Even if it falls into the mud, the kernel remains pure and intact.
Likewise, the soul is encased within the hard shell of the physical
form, obscuring an awareness of the essence within. However
hard and dirty this dense shell may become, the innate purity of
the soul is never lost – only temporarily hidden from view. The
nut, with its shell and kernel, is a symbol of God, the soul and
the creation:

> The entire creation, upper and lower, is organized on this
> principle, from the primal mystic Centre (*Hokhmah,*
> Wisdom) to the very outermost of all layers (this world). All
> are coverings, the one to the other, kernel within kernel, spirit
> inside of spirit (essence within essence), shell within shell.
>
> The primal Centre *(Hokhmah)* is the innermost Light of a
> translucence, subtlety and purity beyond comprehension.
> That inner Point emanates from Itself, manifesting a 'palace'
> (*i.e.* spiritual realms or regions around the King and his
> Throne), which acts as an enclosure for the Centre, and is
> also of a radiance, brilliant beyond the power to know it.
>
> This 'palace' (garment) around the incognizable Inner
> Point, while it is also an unknowable radiance in itself, is
> nevertheless of a lesser subtlety and brilliance than the primal
> Point. The 'palace' then emanates into a garment for itself....
> From thence outward, there is emanation upon emanation,
> each constituting a garment to the one before, just as a shell

surrounds the kernel. But though emanated first as a shell, each then becomes the kernel for the next emanation.

Zohar I:19b–20a; cf. WZ2 p.495, ZBS p.28

In the same way, the soul and mind are encased in the human form:

Everything here below is constructed according to this pattern, so that mortal man is fashioned in the same way as creation: kernel and shell, spirit and body, and all is for the well-ordering of the creation.

Zohar I:20a; cf. WZ2 pp.495–96, ZBS p.29

A soul encased in the human form is like a many-layered nut. The kernel is surrounded by a shell, just as the soul in human form is surrounded by mind and body.

A Saviour, then, comes to the world of human beings to see who is ready to return to God:

If the Vines were Budding

BELOVED: To see if the vines were budding
and the pomegranate trees in flower.

*To see which souls were coming into bloom,
were ready for spirituality.*

The Beloved goes down to the "valley" of the physical world to collect those souls who are ready for the journey home, who are ready to be harvested. The "vines" and "pomegranate trees" are the souls lost in the dark "valley" of the material universe, awaiting the springtime of a Master's coming. The Masters are always here, but the souls have to be "budding", "sprouting" or in "flower" – they have to be ready to understand the Master, ready for spiritual growth. And as the soul breaks into blossom, she begins to long for her salvation. And when she has begun to grow, she seeks more and more of God's love and attention:

There was a vine: you uprooted it from Egypt;
To plant it, you drove out other nations,
  you cleared a space where it could grow:
It took root and filled the whole country....

Please, Yahweh Sabaoth, relent!
Look down from heaven, look at this vine, visit it,
  protect what your own Right Hand has planted.
                              Psalms 80:8–9, 14–15, JB

But the divine Source never neglects his creation and the souls
who dwell in it:

Sing of the delightful vineyard!
I, Yahweh, am its keeper;
Every moment I water it
  for fear its leaves should fall;
Night and day I watch over it.
                              Isaiah 27:2–3, JB

As their Prince

BELOVED: But before I knew ... my desire had hurled me
  on the chariots of my people, as their prince.

*But my compassion made me stay,
to serve them as their Saviour.*

Although most of us are deeply involved in the affairs of physical
living, Masters are correspondingly compassionate. They see the
potential in every soul, and are skilled at encouraging it to sprout
and in bringing it to fruition. This "desire", this compassion,
'hurls' them on the "chariots of my people, as their prince".[4] The
Beloved visitor to the "valley" becomes the Saviour for his chosen
people in order to lead them out of captivity:

Here is my servant whom I uphold,
   my Chosen One in whom my soul delights.
I have endowed him with my Spirit
   that he may bring true justice (spirituality)
   to the nations (to all peoples).

Isaiah 42:1, JB

The 'chorus' then gives encouragement to the soul:

CHORUS: Return, return, O maid of Shulam;
   Return, return, that we may gaze on you!

Come back to your spiritual home,
O soul, O daughter of peace,
so that those who dwell in eternity may greet you.

"Shulam" means 'she who has peace'. There is no greater peace
than that found in the return to God and in being with him.
This is the inward peace that "passes all understanding".[5] So the
exiles, the "budding ... vines", the lost souls, are exhorted to
return and share in the joy of those pure souls who have always
dwelt with God.

In Hebrew, the "maid of Shulam" is the *Shulamith* (Shulamite),
which is also the feminine form of *Shelomo* (Solomon). Both are
derived from *shalom,* meaning peace. *Shulamith* thus identifies
the soul as the Bride or Lover of Solomon, the Master of peace
and wisdom.[6]

A Dance of Two Camps

BELOVED: Why do you gaze on the maid of Shulam
   as a dance of two camps?

How is it that the soul has come to struggle
between her desire for this world
and her attraction to the world of the Spirit?

The soul, the "maid" or maiden struggling to return to God, dances between the "two camps" of this world and the spiritual realms. Sometimes she is drawn helplessly towards the inner Beloved. Sometimes, the events and attachments of material life pull her attention out into the world. So she dances.

These two lines are a prelude to the description of the human form that follows, for it is human destiny to be pulled simultaneously in two directions. We are given the discrimination, the wisdom and the apparent free will to seek and to realize God. Yet that same free will or independent sense of self also gives us the potential for independent wilfulness and worldliness.

We are creatures of light and dark. At every moment, we have the opportunity to move inward towards God or outward into the world. This constant struggle is our human lot, the price of our apparent free will. But, like gold in fire, it is through this "dance" or struggle that we can ultimately be purified, be made whole, and can return to God.

Following on naturally from the description of the Saviour's descent "into the nut orchard" to help humanity, struggling upwards to the Light, the poet is depicting the beauty, the travail and the purpose of being human.

O Prince's Daughter

> BELOVED: How beautiful are your feet in their sandals,
> O prince's daughter!

> *How beautiful you are, O daughter of God,*
> *held captive in the human form at the foot of his creation.*

Using parts of the body as metaphors, the Beloved now inspires the soul by reminding her of the spiritual potential locked up in her humanity.

"Your feet in their sandals" describes the soul in her physical covering – the human form being at the 'foot' of the creation.

The sandals represent the physical body, strapping and enclosing the inner man – the human mind and the innermost soul. Yet, says the Beloved, "how beautiful are your feet". How beautiful is the soul, despite her coverings. She may be held captive, yet her beauty is not completely hidden. Likewise, the Beloved has previously compared the soul to "my mare harnessed to Pharaoh's chariot", to a "dove, hiding in the clefts of the rock", to a "garden enclosed", to a "sealed fountain", and to a "lily among the thistles".[7]

"You are also a 'prince's daughter'," says the Beloved, the epithet also meaning the child of a noble family. "You are a drop of the being of God, a child of royal blood." The initiated soul, too, is a "prince's daughter" – she becomes a child of the mystic Son of the divine King, the Master.

The circle of love is then completed as the Beloved repays the soul's compliments of the previous poem, using similar bodily imagery. Some of the allusions are reasonably clear, others more obscure:

The Work of a Master Hand

> BELOVED: The curve of your thighs
> is like the curve of a necklace,
> work of a master hand.
> Your navel is a bowl well rounded,
> with no lack of wine.

Your human form has been divinely crafted. You are a vessel filled with the sweet intoxication of love.

"You have the potential for perfection," continues the Beloved encouragingly. "You have been designed and made by the supreme Source." The "navel", more or less at the centre of the body probably represents the holy centre or God within. It is filled with "wine". "Your essence," he tells the soul, "is filled with the nectar and ecstasy of divine love."

A Heap of Wheat

> BELOVED: Your belly a heap of wheat,
> surrounded with lilies.

You have within yourself
the divine source of spiritual nourishment.

In ancient times, wheat was threshed and winnowed in the open air. When the chaff had been separated, the wheat was gathered into a heap and surrounded with thorns to keep away cattle and other farm animals. Here, the Beloved says that the devoted soul is like a "heap of wheat" – the essence and sustainer of life. But the soul is no longer surrounded by the thorns of human imperfection; it is protected by the sweet "lilies" of spirituality.

The "heap of wheat" also signifies bread, the staff of physical life, which fills the "belly". The spiritual "bread" and food of the soul is the Word of Wisdom, the Bread of Life, the "manna" fed to the children of Israel when crossing the spiritual desert:[8]

This is the teaching of the hierophant and prophet, Moses, who will say: "This is the bread, the food that God has given to the soul,"[9] for it to feed on, his own Word, his own *Logos;* for this bread that he has given us to eat is this Word.

Philo, Allegorical Interpretation III:60; cf. PCW1 pp.417–19, TGH1 p.247

This is the Bread which comes down from heaven,
that a man may eat thereof, and not die.

John 6:50; cf. KJV

An Ivory Tower

> BELOVED: Your breasts are two fawns,
> twins of a gazelle.

You are a model of purity and innocence.

Breasts are the source of milk for babes, symbolizing the spiritual nourishment and comfort of the Word,[10] while the "gazelle" could again be an allusion to the mystic Name of God. But "fawns" are the essence of innocence and gentleness, while the "gazelle" is the epitome of grace and beauty, so maybe the intended meaning is simply the purity of the soul.

> BELOVED: Your neck is an ivory tower.

Your spiritual ascent within
requires great effort and persistence.

A stately, regal neck has always been considered elegant and beautiful. Symbolically, the "neck" may represent one of the narrow 'gateways' encountered on the inner journey, lying between the major regions of creation, as between the physical and the astral realms, or the astral and causal regions. They are 'narrow places' where all the energies are focused, passing from above to below and from below to above. In the mystic ascent of the soul, such 'gateways' are difficult to ascend through, but easy to fall below; they are as slippery as an "ivory tower".

In the physical body, the neck itself is one of these 'gateways'. From the brain, messages flow out to the entire body, and from the body they travel up to the brain. To fully withdraw the attention from the body below the neck and to bring it up into the head is a very difficult task because the attention is more in the habit of flowing down than rising up. This is why it takes a great deal of effort for the mind and soul to return to their 'bedroom' at the eye centre.

The "neck" also represents the effort, fortitude and determination of the soul in her spiritual endeavour.

The Pools of Heshbon

BELOVED: Your eyes, the pools of Heshbon,
by the gate of Bath-rabbim.

You are an island of peace in a sea of turbulence.

Heshbon was an ancient garden city, situated twenty miles to
the east of the Jordan's point of entry into the Dead Sea. In its
day, it was famous for its lush greenery and lakes. Here, the
Beloved likens the peaceful eyes of the lover to the quiet beauty
of the Heshbon pools. But, he adds, they are "by the gate of
Bath-rabbin". "Bath-rabbin" literally means 'populous city', and
the allusion is rather beautiful.

The mind of a lover becomes peaceful and calm, like the
atmosphere around still waters – the pools of "Heshbon". The
depth of being that is generated by love holds the mind in
concentration at its inner centre. Conversely, the world outside
is full of busy-ness and activity. When involved with the world,
our minds are always buzzing with something or another, and
never rest even for a moment. The world is like the gateway to a
heavily populated city, through which people continually come
and go, but where nobody stays for long.

Therefore, the Beloved compares the soul to pools of peaceful
water beside a busy city gateway. The soul and mind of the lover
are concentrated at the single eye. "You are at peace," he says,
"an inwardly silent observer of a world in a state of continual
agitation."

The Tower of Lebanon

BELOVED: Your nose, the Tower of Lebanon,
sentinel facing Damascus.

Behind your eyes lies the look-out point
of the secret watchtower
whence you can begin your journey to eternity.

"Her nose is praised for its perfect straightness," comments Rabbi Abraham ben Isaac ha-Levi.[11] But the medieval Rashi is less certain. "Since when," he observes, "is a prominent nose a sign of beauty?"[12] But perhaps some "Tower of Lebanon" – now unknown to history or folklore – was fabled for its beauty, perpendicularity and fine proportions. Either way, the symbolism is obscure.

Bearing in mind the previous references to Lebanon as symbolic of eternity, it is perhaps another allusion to the divinity of the soul. Maybe it means that the soul and mind must ascend to the head of this divine tower, to the highest point of the nose, between the two eyes. In this case, it would be a reference to the single eye to which the soul must ascend upon its journey to "Lebanon", to God.

A King is Held Captive

> BELOVED: Your head is held high like Carmel,
>   and its plaits are as dark as purple;
>   A king is held captive in your tresses.

> *Within your head is the holy mountain of God*
> *where the divine Sovereign reigns.*

Mount Carmel is a mountain ridge in northwest Israel whose western promontory is poised in solitary magnificence overlooking the Mediterranean. Metaphorically, mountains are the inner realms, as before, while Mount Carmel signifies eternity:

> Who has the right to climb the mountain of Yahweh,
>   who the right to stand in his holy place?
> He whose hands are clean, whose heart is pure,
>   whose soul does not pay homage to worthless things,
>   and who never swears to a lie.

> *Psalms 24:3–4, JB*

I (the Saviour) ascended the mountain Carmel,
   you I ascended, mountain, Mount Carmel! ...
The man who saw me and discerned me,
   his course is set for the place of Life!

            Mandaean Prayer Book 139; cf. CPM pp.125–26

The summit of the Mount (Carmel) ... is the high estate of
perfection, which we here call union of the soul with God.

            St John of the Cross, Ascent of Mount Carmel, CWJC1 p.9

"Your head is like Mount Carmel," the Beloved tells the soul.
"The eternity of God lies hidden within you." The head is the
highest part of a human being, and it is from here that the
spiritual journey starts. Just as the feet have been used to symbolize the physical form and the physical realm, so too is the
head being used as a symbol for God.

"Your head is adorned with royal purple," the Beloved
continues, 'a king is held captive in your tresses'. Within your
head, beneath the 'tresses' of your hair, you can find God, the
true King of all creation. The divine King is held captive within
yourself."

In Stature like the Palm Tree

    BELOVED: How beautiful you are, how charming,
       my love, O daughter of delights!
       In stature like the palm tree,
       its fruit-clusters your breasts.
    "I will climb the palm tree," I resolved,
       I will seize its clusters of dates."

Your beauty is inexpressible.
At the highest point, within your head,
lies the fruit of spirituality.
I will conquer your heart.
I will harvest your spiritual treasure.

The Beloved encourages the soul by reminding her once again of her innate beauty and divinity. He compares the Lover to a palm tree, for human beings stand upright, "in stature like the palm tree". At the top lie the fruits, the "clusters of dates", the spiritual treasure. God and the entire inner creation are to be found within the head, behind the veil of ego. Dates are also a treasured and life-sustaining food of desert people, who symbolize the soul's wanderings in creation. The palm tree and its fruits are perhaps intended as an allusion to the Tree of Life:

> I (Wisdom) have grown tall as a palm in Engedi.
>> *Wisdom of Jesus Ben Sirach, 24:14, JB*

Or possibly the palm and its fruits signify the Lord himself:

> Praised be the great First Wellspring and Date Palm,
>   for the Date Palm is the Father.
>> *Mandaean Psalms, Thousand and Twelve Questions I:4, TTQ p.110*

"I will climb this human tree of life," says the Beloved, "I will reveal the soul's treasure." For it is only through him that the soul can be brought to fruition. Her spiritual harvest is a divine gift, bestowed by him. Though the treasure is in reality her own, the Beloved is the one who reveals it to the soul.

Your Breath Sweet-Scented as Apples

> BELOVED: May your breasts be clusters of grapes,
>   your breath sweet-scented as apples,
>   your speaking, superlative wine.
>
> *May your heart be full of divine love;*
> *may you breathe the fragrance of the Breath of God;*
> *may you be rapt in the ecstasy of the mystic Word.*

"Breasts" symbolize the spiritual heart. The warm heart of the soul is her inner capacity for divine love, her innate quality of giving rather than receiving. The Beloved prays that the innermost heart or being of his devotee may become full of the fruit of the vine, full of divine wine, full of love. Mystically, the spiritual heart of a human being is at the eye centre or single eye, where the soul becomes concentrated, leaving the body and ascending to higher regions.

"Your breath" refers to the divine Breath of Life, the Spirit, the divine Melody – may the soul experience the sweetness of that Sound, says the Beloved. May the soul become pure and "sweet-scented":

> She (Wisdom) is so pure, she pervades
>   and permeates all things.
> She is a Breath of the Power of God,
>   pure emanation of the glory of the Almighty.
> Hence, nothing impure can find a way into her.
>   *Wisdom of Solomon 7:24–25, JB*

And with the Beloved himself as a personification of that Melody, there can be but one response to such a prayer:

> My ears have heard the Voice of Life,
>   my nostrils have breathed the Perfume of Life.
>   *Mandaean Prayer Book, 104, CPM p.103*

"Speaking" or speech refer to the Word as the divine 'Utterance'. Using a very common mystic metaphor, it is described here as "superlative wine", the ecstasy of inner communion with the divine wine.

The soul now responds to the love of the divine Beloved:

Wine Flowing Straight to my Beloved

LOVER: Wine flowing straight to my Beloved,
as it runs on the lips of those who sleep.

The wine of my love flows back to its source – my Beloved.
His love awakens sleeping souls.

"I am filled with the 'superlative wine' of love," says the soul,
"that comes from my Beloved and returns from me to him." He
is love personified. Love begins and ends with him. The essence
of God, the Word and the Saviour is only love. "Those who
sleep" are the souls lost in the world. The wine of love "runs on
their lips" while they sleep – it touches their inner beings – and
awakens them.[13] The "wine" of the Beloved awakens sleeping
souls:

> And I drank and was intoxicated
>   with the Living Water that does not die.
> And my intoxication caused no heedlessness:
> Rather, I abandoned selfhood,
>   and turned towards the Most High, my God,
>   and was enriched by his gift.
>
> *Odes of Solomon 11:7–9, OSD p.50*

The wine of the world also lifts natural restraints and sets the
tongue wagging. Likewise, divine wine unlocks the gateway of
the heart, causing it to overflow with love and gratitude:

> On the gateway of my heart I wrote, "No thoroughfare".
> Love came laughing by and cried, "I enter everywhere".
>
> *Jami* [14]

I am my Beloved's

> LOVER: I am my Beloved's,
> and his desire is for me.

My love for him reflects his love for me.

It is the Beloved's love for the soul that draws the soul into the orbit of divine love:

> Herein is love, not that we loved God,
>   but that he loved us....
> We love him because he first loved us.
> > *1 John 4:10, 19, KJV*

> For I should not have known how to love the Lord
>   if he had not loved me.
> For who is able to know love,
>   except he who is loved?
> I love the Beloved, and my soul loves him,
>   and where his rest is, there too am I.
> > *Odes of Solomon 3:3–5, OSD p.16*

In this state of divine intoxication, the soul desires nothing more than to live in the atmosphere of the Beloved's love:

> Your Name, your memory, are all my soul desires.
> > *Isaiah 26:8, JB*

The soul then continues:

Let us Go to the Fields

> LOVER: Come, my Beloved,
> let us go to the fields.

> *Take me, my Lord.*
> *Let us travel together through the heavenly realms.*

The "fields" are the inner regions, the spiritual meadows or gardens where the Beloved "pastures his flock among the lilies". They are the:

> Habitation of the blessed,
>   fountain that gushes greatness;
> Trees of Fragrance,
>   fountains filled with Life;
> All the holy mountains,
>   fields that are green with Life,
>   dew of ambrosia (food of immortality).
> *Manichaean Psalm Book, MPB p.136*

The soul is expressing her desire to be in the heavenly mansions with her Beloved.

We will Go to the Vineyards

> LOVER: We will spend the night in the villages,
> and in the morning we will go to the vineyards.
> We will see if the vines are budding,
>   if their blossoms are opening,
> if the pomegranate trees are in flower.

> *After the dark night of spiritual struggle,*
> *we will awaken to a springtime of spiritual consciousness.*
> *We will burst out in blossom,*
> *giving off the perfume of love.*

"Night" symbolizes passage through an ordeal – the struggles and tribulations of a soul in its upward ascent, the 'dark night of the soul'. At night in the "villages", the inhabitants – the souls of this world – sleep the sleep of unconsciousness.

The soul sleeps in this world, in the realm of "night" and darkness. But "in the morning" – when awakening comes and the sun dispels the gloom, the soul says that she and her Beloved will enjoy the sweet fragrance of divine love. The "vines" in the "vineyards" are the souls on the Tree of Life, the True Vine. The "budding" and the "opening" of their "blossoms" herald their spiritual springtime, their awakening to a new life, a return to consciousness of the inward treasure:

> Listen to me, devout children,
>> and blossom like the rose
>> that grows on the bank of a watercourse.
> Give off a sweet smell like incense,
>> flower like the lily, spread your fragrance abroad.
> Sing a song of praise, blessing the Lord for all his works.
>> *Wisdom of Jesus Ben Sirach 39:13–14, JB*

> The Lord is upon my head like a crown of flowers,
>> and I shall never be without him.
> A crown of truth has been plaited for me,
>> and it has caused Thy shoots to grow within me.
> For it is not like a withered crown, which blossoms not:
>> but Thou art alive upon my head,
>> and Thou hast blossomed upon me.
> Thy fruits are full and perfect:
>> they are full of Thy salvation.
>> *Odes of Solomon 1:1–5, OSD p.12*

> The devout man receives the Lord's blessing as his reward,
>> in a moment God brings his blessing to flower.
>> *Wisdom of Jesus Ben Sirach 11:22, JB*

The Lover continues in a similar vein:

The Gift of my Love

> LOVER: Then I shall give you the gift of my love.
> The mandrakes yield their fragrance,
> the rarest fruits are at our doors;
> The new as well as the old,
> I have stored them for you my Beloved.

> *Then I can truly and unconditionally give my love to you.*
> *Then the rare fragrance of divine love will be ours.*
> *Old yearnings and new longings will merge into one,*
> *as my love reaches up to you.*

When the "vines" grow and blossom, then the love of the lover and the Beloved will be merged into one:

> The human heart is drawn to God by a natural tendency, even though a man has no clear knowledge of who God is. When we discover him at the well of faith, however, when we see how good he is, how beautiful, how kind, how gracious towards everyone, how ready to give himself as the supreme good to all who want him – heaven knows the gratification we (then) feel, the inspirations we have to unite ourselves forever with a goodness so supremely lovable! "I have found him at last," cries a soul moved in this way. "I have found the One I have been looking for, and now I am satisfied." ... The human heart melts with love when it has found God, when it has received from him the first kiss of faith – it has had its first sight of the infinite treasures of supreme beauty.
>
> *St Francis de Sales, Love of God 2:15, LG p.89*

This is the "gift of my love", the divine event full of the "fragrance of mandrakes", a plant whose purplish flowers were thought to possess magical qualities, and were said to induce love in the heart.[15] The gifts of love are the "rarest fruits at our doors". The divine treasure is close at hand. It lies just behind the single eye, the inner window through which the soul must look.

The "old" fruits are the heartaches of the soul as she passes through birth after birth in search of the divine Beloved, often unaware of what she is seeking. The "new" fruits are her longing for the Beloved and her union with him. "The new as well as the old, I have stored them for you," says the soul. Now these previously submerged and pent up yearnings will find fulfilment.

Why are you not my Brother?

> LOVER: Ah, why are you not my brother,
> nursed at my mother's breast!
> Then if I met you out of doors, I could kiss you
> without people thinking ill of me.

> *Would that people understood*
> *the true nature of my love for you.*
> *Then they would no longer think me mad or obsessed.*

"Out of doors" means in the outer, physical world. The physical form of a Master is indescribably beautiful, and many a loving disciple has wished to embrace him as the dearest of friends, or simply to lay their head at his feet in love and gratitude. But as the soul advances in love, she sees the spiritual form of the Master in the physical form. To the divine lover, they become identical, though this may be invisible to the eyes of others. The love of the soul for the Beloved, therefore, has no bounds, for the real union takes place inside, beyond the confines of this world. At first, it is a union of mind to mind, and later that of soul to soul. But this is all in secret – no one in the world knows what is taking place.

In the poem, the Lover says that people would misunderstand the nature of her love if they saw her embracing her Beloved in his physical form. In the physical world, her love is pure, like

that of a brother and sister. But people generally cannot understand this. We always draw things down to our own level, and
"think ill" of the devotees of a Master. We impute to others the
motives and desires of our own minds. We do not understand
that the devotees of a Master are not in love with a human being.
It is the creative Power, present within both the Master and the
disciple, that draws them. They are indeed "brother" and sister,
children of the same "mother", "nursed" at the same "breast".
Their "mother" is Wisdom, the Holy Spirit.

Into my Mother's House

> LOVER: I should lead you, I should take you
> into my mother's house, and you would teach me!
> I should give you spiced wine to drink,
> juice of my pomegranates.

> *Then we would go into the house of Wisdom,*
> *where you would teach me the ways of spiritual love,*
> *and my love would be yours.*

Her "mother's house" refers to the inner regions of the soul's
"mother", the Wisdom of God, the Spirit of Holiness. In that
house of the Spirit, says the soul, "you would teach me". In the
Hebrew, the "you" can also mean 'she' – Wisdom. In the heavenly
realms, the Master – whose essence is Wisdom – teaches the soul
many things that cannot be expressed in human language, that
are altogether transcendent and above the physical domain. This
is the 'secret' teaching, so frequently mentioned by esoteric
schools, and yet so little understood:

> These things have I spoken to you in proverbs. But the time
> comes, when I shall no more speak to you in proverbs, but I
> shall show you plainly of the Father.
>
> *John 16:25; cf. KJV*

For (now) we know in part, and we prophesy in part. But when that which is perfect is come, then that which is in part shall be done away.... For now we see through a glass, darkly, but then face to face.

1 Corinthians 13:9–10, 12, KJV

The giving of "spiced wine" and "juice of my pomegranates" once again represents the interplay and ecstasy of the divine love affair. Spices mingled with wine to make it more potent and pomegranate juice mixed with sherbet were favourite Oriental drinks. But the Lover emphasizes "*my* pomegranates" – it is the love of her soul that she is giving to her Beloved. The flowering of her "pomegranate trees" has now borne fruit, which she gives to him:

Pomegranate wine is my hearing (of) your voice:
  I live because I hear.

Egyptian Love Songs, PH500 14:10, LLSS p.177

His Right Arm Embraces me

LOVER: His left arm is under my head
and his right embraces me.

He guides me without.
He cradles me within.
I am safe in the enfolding arms of his loving Power.

As before, the soul says that she is supported in this world by the presence and guidance of the physical form of the Beloved. Inside, she is cocooned and comforted by his radiant spiritual form, a projection of God's Right Hand, his creative Power. This is the beginning and end of everything for a devotee, who completely merges into the Beloved at every level.

Until it Please to Awake

> BELOVED: I charge you,
> daughters of Jerusalem,
> not to stir my love, nor rouse it,
> until it please to awake.

Do not try to force the flow of love.
Let it awaken naturally from within.

Everything has to happen and will only happen at its own appointed time. There is no room for impatience of the mind – only for the longing soul to respond fully to the divine call of love.

FINALE

Who is this Coming Up from the Desert?

In the final scene of this mystic drama, the soul is granted her heart's desire: the consummation of her love. She is drawn up out of the physical body by the love, grace and power of her Beloved, and meets with him in the heavenly realms. The 'chorus' states the theme and the Beloved completes the story.

CHORUS: Who is this coming up from the desert,
        leaning on her Beloved?

BELOVED: I awakened you under the apple tree,
        there where your mother conceived you,
there where she who gave birth to you conceived you.

Set me like a seal on your heart,
        like a seal on your arm.
For love is strong as death,
jealousy relentless as Sheol.
The flash of it (love) is a flash of fire,
        a flame of Yahweh himself.
Love no flood can quench,
        no torrents drown.

Leaning on her Beloved

> CHORUS: Who is this coming up from the desert,
> leaning on her Beloved?

> *Who is this rising up from the material world*
> *with the help of her Beloved?*

The "desert" is the physical world, devoid of life-giving water –
the Living Water of the Creative Word. The soul is taken up out
of the physical body, "leaning on her Beloved". He is

> the Shepherd of the sheep that wanders
> in the desert (wilderness) of this world.
> *Psalms of Heracleides, Manichaean Psalm Book, MPB p.193*

"Leaning" implies that it is only with the help and support of a
Saviour that a soul can be "resurrected", can "rise from the dead",
can be awakened, can escape from exile and slavery, can come to
the single eye, can pass through the narrow gateway, and can be
filled with divine light and heavenly sound.

Under the Apple Tree

> BELOVED: I awakened you under the apple tree,
> there where your mother conceived you,
> there where she who gave birth to you conceived you.

> *Asleep beneath the Tree of Life, I awakened you.*
> *There, where the divine Spirit*
> *gave you being and existence.*

"I was the one who awakened you," says the Beloved, "while you
slept beneath the apple tree." As before, the "mother" is Wisdom
or the Holy Spirit, she who "conceives" or gives birth to all

souls. In the case of human beings, they also come to birth at the foot of the Tree of Life – the material world. Here, lost in illusion, they remain fast asleep until the Beloved finds and awakens them.

Perhaps the poet is also indicating that a soul has to take birth in this world – and fall asleep – before she can be awakened by the Beloved. A soul has to be in human form before initiation into the Word can be received from a Saviour. She has to take birth from her mother, meaning both a physical mother as well as the Holy Spirit. Without the power of the Holy Spirit, there is no creation and no human conception; and without human birth, there can be no initiation, and no salvation.

In the East, childbirth in the open air was not uncommon. The soul has to be born 'outside', in this world, before she can awaken to the beauties of the Spirit within.

Like a Seal on your Heart

> BELOVED: Set me like a seal on your heart,
>   like a seal on your arm.

> *Love me with all your being.*
> *Dedicate yourself to me.*

In the ancient world, a seal bore witness to the owner. It was the equivalent of a signature, worn either on a chain around the neck ("on your heart") or on a finger of the right hand ("on your arm").[1] The Hebrew term used here implies both arm and finger. So the Beloved, out of pure, selfless and divine love, requests and insists that the devotee becomes entirely his, both in her "heart" – her innermost being, her mind and soul – as well as in physical life, symbolized as the "arm":

> Love the Lord your God with all your heart, with all your soul and with all your might.... Let these words of mine

remain in your heart and in your soul. Fasten them on your
hand as a sign, and on your forehead as a circlet.

Teach them to your children, and say them over to them,
whether at rest in your house or walking abroad, at your
lying down or at your rising.   •

Write them on the doorposts of your house and on your
gates, so that you and your children may live long in the
(promised) land that Yahweh swore to your fathers he
would give them, for as long as there is a sky above the
earth.

Deuteronomy 6:5 (cf. KJV), 11:16–21 (JB);
cf. Deuteronomy 6:4–9; Matthew 22:37

Echoing the meaning of the previous stanza, the "seal" also refers
to initiation or baptism:[2]

I bind up this testimony,
    I seal this revelation in the heart of my disciples.

Isaiah 8:16, JB

Deep within them I (Yahweh) will plant my Law (Word),
    writing it on their hearts.
Then I will be their God,
    and they shall be my people.

Jeremiah 31:33–34, JB

Those who receive this seal are destined for it:

I turn not my face away from those that are mine,
    because I know them.
Before they came into being,
    I knew them;
And on their foreheads,
    I set my seal.

Odes of Solomon 8:14–15, OSD p.40

Love is Strong as Death

> BELOVED: For love is strong as death,
> jealousy relentless as Sheol.

One-pointed love of God overcomes death;
human desire leads to death.

Divine love has the power to conquer death. It can take the soul through the gateway of death while still living in the physical body. It can release the soul from the necessity of returning to the realm of birth and its inevitable partner, death. It also confers upon the soul the ability to undergo the process of physical death in full consciousness, going forward like a bride to meet her Beloved when physical existence ends.

"Jealousy relentless as Sheol" has a double meaning. Firstly, the Saviour or God is a 'jealous' lover. The essence of every soul is God. Nothing else but God exists. But from the point of view of the struggling soul, striving to reach him, attraction to anything other than God himself must be overcome. Therefore, many mystics have said that God is a jealous lover. The soul cannot attain union with him until everything else has been left aside:

> Death separates soul from body, but love separates all things from the soul – it will not tolerate what is not God or God's.
>
> Meister Eckhart, Sermon 4, MEST1 p.47

> Death separates the soul of a dying person from the body, from all worldly things. Love also separates from the body, from all worldly things, the soul of the individual who possesses it.
>
> St Francis de Sales, Love of God 7:9, LG p.295

"Jealousy" also epitomizes all the negative qualities of the mind, the human desire for material living that keeps the soul imprisoned here. Other translators have rendered the word as "passion", of an intense and human kind. Either way, it is the antithesis of divine love. "Sheol" is the hell of this world, "relentless" because it goes on and on in the same old way. The negative qualities of the mind, epitomized by the selfishness of "jealousy" or human passion are as relentless as the world of which they are a part, leading the soul through birth after birth, and death after death.

The law of the mind, of cause and effect, is also "jealous". It is an intricately woven fabric; everything is accounted for in the tiniest detail. There is absolutely no room for manoeuvre. Similarly with divine love: when the lover loses her individuality, her small self, and merges into the greater self of the Beloved, where is the room for manoeuvre? Who is left to do the manoeuvring?

So, ingeniously and characteristically, the poet works into the last stanzas a double meaning that includes the condition of the soul both before and after her salvation, for this is the essence of the entire affair. Love is the nature of God; "jealousy" or passion is the character of the mind. Death is the creation of the mind; love is the power that can conquer all.

Therefore, the Beloved concludes:

Love no Flood can Quench

> BELOVED: The flash of it (love) is a flash of fire,
> a flame of Yahweh himself.
> Love no flood can quench,
> no torrents drown.

The touch of divine love is the touch of God.
No power is greater than this love.

The Lord is an ocean of love, a sea of light, an all-consuming fire. The soul is a drop of this ocean, a flash or ray of this light, a flame or spark from his fire. The common ground in these images is that of unity between the source and its derivative. A drop cannot be distinguished from the ocean in which it dwells; a ray of light cannot be separated from its source; a flame cannot exist independent of its fire.

Such is the unifying power of divine love. A flame of this kind of love is a "flame of Yahweh himself":

> This flame is a flame of divine life. It wounds the soul with the tenderness of the life of God; and so deeply and profoundly does it wound it and fill it with tenderness that it causes it to melt in love.
>
> *St John of the Cross, Living Flame of Love I:7, CWJC3 p.20*

Love is the essence of the soul. Love is the essence of a Saviour. Love is the essence of the Word. There is nothing but love.

"Love no flood can quench, no torrents drown." Love for the world keeps the soul in slavery and exile for aeons upon aeons. But love for the Lord and the Saviour, the divine Beloved, is a flood that sweeps the soul up and into itself, carrying her back to God. The creation is a play of nothing but love; it is all a question of how the soul's love is directed. No flood or torrent of this, or any other world, can extinguish the fire of divine love.

Epilogue

You who Dwell in the Gardens

The Song of Songs *has a number of short 'appendices',
probably added by some of the poem's many scribes or
readers. Not all are of interest from a spiritual point of
view, but there is one that seems to have come from the pen
of a devotee who was moved by the poem's mystical import.*

Devotee: You who dwell in the gardens,
the companions listen for your voice;
Deign to let me hear it.

Haste away, my Beloved.
Be like a gazelle,
a young stag,
on the spicy mountains.

251

Deign to let Me Hear It

> DEVOTEE: You who dwell in the gardens,
> the companions listen for your voice;
> Deign to let me hear it.

> *You who make your home in the heavenly realms,*
> *your disciples yearn to hear*
> *the music of the divine Symphony.*
> *Open my soul, too, to hear it.*

The unknown devotee makes a plea to the one "who dwells in the gardens", in the 'fields of lilies' – to the light form of the Beloved who dwells in the heavenly regions. The "you" addresses the spiritual form, the expression of the divine Wisdom, the Word or *Logos*. The devotee says, "your disciples long to hear the divine Voice of God. Out of your compassion and kindness, permit me, too, to hear it."

> DEVOTEE: Haste away, my Beloved.
> Be like a gazelle,
> a young stag,
> on the spicy mountains.

> *You are free, my Beloved.*
> *By the power of the Name of God,*
> *you travel at will among the higher heavens.*

The devotee concludes: "But everything is in your hands, my Beloved. You are free. For you can leave this world at will to travel fleetly through the spiritual mountains of the soul, to scent the precious fragrances of the divine."

NOTES AND REFERENCES

Introduction

1. The earliest known manuscript traditions to assign verses to particular speakers are some versions of the *Septuagint* from the fourth and fifth centuries AD. That is about a thousand years after the *Song* was written.
2. *Mishnah, Abodah Zarah* 2:5, in *e.g. TM* p.439. The *Mishnah* is a compilation of several centuries worth of Jewish oral tradition, collated and written down in the late second century AD.

PART I – ORIGINS AND BACKGROUND

1. The Setting of the Song

1. Josephus, *Against Apion* 1:8.
2. *Song of Songs* 3:11.
3. *Song of Songs* 3:5, 5:8.
4. *Song of Songs* 1:14.
5. There are six uses of the term *nefesh*. See *Song of Songs* 1:7, 3:1–4, 5:6.
6. The *Wisdom of Solomon* and the *Wisdom of Jesus ben Sirach* belong to the *Apocrypha,* a collection of fourteen books printed as an appendix to the Old Testament in the *Septuagint* and the *Vulgate,* but not included in the Jewish canon. Protestant versions of the Bible do not include them, but they are a part of Catholic Bibles such as the *Jerusalem Bible.*
7. See *e.g. The Gospel of Jesus, GJ* pp.1004*ff.*
8. See Josephus, *Antiquities* XVIII:14 (1.3), *Jewish War* II:163 (8.14); in *e.g. The Gospel of Jesus, GJ* p.416.
9. See *e.g.* "Did Jesus Really Teach Reincarnation?", in *The Gospel of Jesus, GJ* pp.406–60.

10. *Wisdom of Solomon* 7:25, *JB*. See p.16.
11. *John* 9:5.
12. *Cf.* "The light of the body is the eye: if therefore your eye be single, your whole body will be full of light" *(Matthew* 6:22; *cf. KJV)*
13. See *The Gospel of Jesus, GJ* index: door (to the inner realms), gate(s).
14. *Nestorian Liturgy,* in *NR2* p.196.
15. *Pistis Sophia* 125, 135, *PS* pp.316, 350.
16. See *The Gospel of Jesus, GJ* pp.821–30.
17. See *The Gospel of Jesus, GJ* pp.830–50.
18. *Cf. John* 10:7.
19. *John* 10:1–18. See also *The Gospel of Jesus, GJ* index: parables: good Shepherd, Shepherd.
20. *Matthew* 25:1–13. See *The Bridegroom,* in *The Divine Romance, DR* pp.25–33; see also *The Gospel of Jesus, GJ* index: Bridegroom.

2. The Symbolism of the Song

1. *Song of Songs* 2:16, 6:3, *JB.*
2. *Psalms* 23:2; *cf. KJV.*
3. *Matthew* 13:2–9, 18–30. See also *The Gospel of Jesus, GJ* index: parables and similes: sower and the seed, tares; Seed.
4. *Cf. Genesis* 2:8.
5. *Psalms* 23:4, *KJV.*
6. *E.g.* see *The Robe of Glory,* in *PSW* pp.206–9.
7. *Exodus* 16:15*ff.*
8. *E.g. Matthew* 24:45*ff.,* 25:14*ff.*
9. *E.g. Psalms* 86, 90, 119, 143.
10. *Wisdom of Solomon* 7:27. See p.16.
11. *E.g.* see *The Gospel of Jesus, GJ* index: pearls; *The Pearl Merchant,* in *PSW* pp.56–70; *The Pearl Borer,* in *PSW* pp.71–73; *The Two Snakes,* in *PSW* pp.76–79; *The Robe of Glory,* in *PSW* pp.185–244.
12. *Exodus* 3:8, 17, 13:5, 33:3.
13. See *The Robe of Glory,* in *PSW* pp.188–288.
14. See *A Treasury of Mystic Terms,* where many of these metaphors are explained in detail.
15. *E.g. Isaiah* 6:10*ff.; Jeremiah* 17:14, 30:12*ff.*
16. See *The Gospel of Jesus, GJ* index: miracles: healing.
17. Zarathushtra, *Yasna* 31:6, 45:3, 50:6, 51:8; in *e.g. DSZ* pp.190, 540, 747, 784; in *e.g.* "*Manthra*", *A Treasury of Mystic Terms* 3, *TMT3* pp.201–2.
18. Zarathushtra, *Yasna* 29:1–3, 6, 31:9–10; in *e.g. DSZ*.

19. *Luke* 8:8, 14:35; *Mark* 4:9, 23, 7:16; *Matthew* 11:15, 13:9, 43.
20. *E.g. Psalms* 78:23–24.
21. *Cf. Exodus* 32:32–33, *Psalms* 69:28.
22. *Genesis* 28:12–13.
23. *Proverbs* 7:6–21.
24. Moses Maimonides, *The Guide of the Perplexed* II:45, II:47, III:33, III:51, *GP2* pp.393, 407, 532, 623.
25. *Zohar* III:71b, *WZ2* p.863.
26. *Book of Revelation* 13:17.
27. *E.g. The Guide of the Perplexed* II:45, *GP2* pp.392–93.
28. See *Tobit* 5:22, 7:16, 8:4, 7, 21; *cf. Tobit* 6:18, 7:10*ff.*, 10:6, 13.
29. *Cf. Isaiah* 17:10*ff.*, *Ezekiel* 8:14, *Zechariah* 12:11.
30. *E.g.* Rabbi Abraham ben Isaac ha-Levi Tamakh: *Commentary on the Song of Songs*, L.A. Feldman.
31. *Song of Songs* 3:11.
32. *Mishnah* 2, *Taanith* 4:8; in *e.g. TM* p.201.
33. *Hosea* 7:11, 11:11, 14:5; *4 Ezra* 5:25–26.
34. Josephus, *Against Apion* 1:8, *J1* p.179.
35. *Song of Songs* 2:5.
36. *Deuteronomy* 6:5.
37. *Song of Songs* 5:8.
38. Abraham Maimonides, *Kifayat al-'Abidin*, *HWP2* p.290.
39. *Song of Songs* 2:2.
40. See 'Obadayah Maimonides, *The Treatise of the Pool* I, II, III, *TP* pp.77, 79. See also pp.115, 193, 209.
41. *Song of Songs* 5:2.
42. Ibn 'Aknin, *IAHS* pp.128, in *TP* p.55.
43. See quote, p.195.
44. *Song of Songs* 7:12, *JB*.
45. *Song of Songs* 8:6. The accounts of Thomas Aquinas and Jean Gerson are both mentioned by St Francis de Sales (*Love of God* 7:9, in *e.g. LG* p.297).
46. *Song of Songs* 5:16, *JB*.
47. See p.259 (n.4).
48. *Exodus* 13:21–22, 14:19, 24, 33:9–10. See p.154–55.
49. See p.262 (n.6).

PART II – THE SONG

Title and Prologue – Your Love is more Delightful than Wine

1. The *JB* actually reads, "the king has brought me into his rooms". As the Jewish Publication Society translation of 1985 observes, emendation yields, "Take me, O king, into your chambers". This seems more likely, since it parallels the meaning of the previous line, and is in keeping with the opening of the poem.
2. *1 Kings* 4:32; *Proverbs* 1:1, 10:1, 25:1; *Wisdom of Jesus Ben Sirach* 47:18. See also p.18.
3. *Babylonian Talmud, Baba Bathra* 172.
4. *Deuteronomy* 54:5.
5. *Numbers* 33:38.
6. *Zohar* II:97a.
7. *I.e.* he has control over his mind.
8. See *The Gospel of Jesus, GJ* index: Name.
9. *E.g. King James Version.*
10. St Francis is quoting Jerome's fourth-century Latin *Vulgate*.
11. See pp.30–33. See also *The Gospel of Jesus, GJ* index: Bride-chambers.

First Poem – I am Black but Lovely

1. See pp.146, 216.
2. See also *The Gospel of Jesus, GJ* index: Mother.
3. *E.g.* see *The Gospel of Jesus, GJ* index: light, Sound.
4. See *e.g.* "vines", in *A Treasury of Mystic Terms* 5, *TMT5* pp.274–77.
5. See also *The Gospel of Jesus, GJ* index: dove.
6. *Isaiah* 60:8.
7. See *1 Kings* 5:6–10, 6:9–20, 34–36, 7:2–3, 7, 11–12.
8. There is some doubt concerning the identification of the "rose of Sharon and the "lily of the valleys". The "rose of Sharon" could indeed be a rose, or perhaps a lily. For the "lily of the valleys", the lily, the narcissus, the iris and the lotus have also been suggested. All, of course, are flowers of beauty.
9. The Hebrew is *tappuach,* meaning 'apple' in modern times. When the *Song* was written, it may have meant quince, apricot or orange. Likewise, the other references to apples and apple trees in the *Song.*
10. *Psalms* 34:8; *cf. Psalms* 119:103.
11. See comment concerning the Sufi use of such metaphors on p.37.
12. *Psalms* 23:5; *cf. KJV.*

13. *Isaiah* 49:2.
14. See *Joseph and Aseneth,* in *DR* pp.88–89, 90, 100–2, 157–58; *Odes of Solomon* 8:6, 20, 14:4, 18:7, 19:5, 22:7–9, 25:2, 9, 28:15, 38b:16, 20, *OSD* pp.38, 42, 64, 82, 86, 98, 114, 116, 128, 162; *Adam Gets a Letter,* in *PSW* pp.176–77; *The Robe of Glory,* in *PSW* pp.191, 223, 234–35.

Second Poem – I Hear my Beloved

1. See note 4.
2. See note 6.
3. *Mark* 4:39.
4. This stanza is usually attributed to the Beloved, attached to the preceding sentence which likens the soul to a dove hiding in crevices of the rock face. Now the Beloved continues, "Show me your face...." This may be, but it also makes considerable sense as the Lover's response, as interpreted here. But I am in two minds. Perhaps the poet was being intentionally ambiguous. The various commentaries also diverge at this point.
5. See note 7.
6. "Before the dawn wind rises." *Lit.* 'until the day blow'. Other interpretations take the "dawn wind" as the evening breeze. The Lover is waiting for the night when she can be with her Beloved. The essential meaning is the same.
7. The meaning of the Hebrew phrase emended and translated as "spicy mountains" is one that has been translated in many ways. The line is echoed in the epilogue (*Song of Songs* 8:14, see p.252), from which the present rendering is drawn. The extant Hebrew is almost certainly corrupt at this point, leaving the field wide open for speculation. The word translated as "spicy" is *'bether'*, hence some renderings have the "mountain of Bether", which is in Judah. But there is no immediately obvious meaning to this suggestion. The *JB* emends the word to mean, 'mountain of the victims cut in half' and thus, the "mountains of the covenant", recalling the biblical scene where God gave his promise to the prophet Abraham that his descendants would one day inherit the promised land (see *Genesis* 15:16*ff.*, also *Exodus* 3:8, 17, 13:5, 33:3). This is the "covenant" or agreement, the means, the law of nature or the path by which souls can be brought back to God. But a simpler rendering seems more appropriate here, and the echo of the line in the epilogue makes the "spicy mountains" a likely candidate.
8. See pp.197–98.
9. Bar Hebraeus, *Ethikon* I:V.8, *BHBD* p.131.

Third Poem – Who is this Coming Up from the Desert?

1. See note 17.
2. A departure from the *JB*. Emendation gives "lairs of leopards", which makes more sense than "mountains of leopards" as the *JB* has it, based on the literal Hebrew.
3. A departure from the *JB*, following the *NJB* and *JPS*.
4. See also *Exodus* 14:19, 24, 33:9–10. *cf. Deuteronomy* 31:15; *Numbers* 9:15–22, 10:11–12, 34, 11:25, 12:5, 10, 14:14, 16:42.
5. *Cf. Babylonian Talmud, Kethuboth 16b.*
6. *Cf.* Shakespeare, *Love's Labour's Lost V:2.826*, "Behold the window of my heart, mine eye."
7. Descriptions of the various parts of the human body, male or female, are still common in modern Arabic poetry. The term used for a eulogy of this nature is a *wasf*, meaning 'description'. In ancient Hebrew literature, *wasfs* are found only in the *Song of Songs*, where there are several. How the writer came to use this poetic form is a mystery, but it must be presumed that the poet was familiar with the tradition, either from his own or neighbouring cultures.
8. St John of the Cross, *Spiritual Canticle* XXXI:4; *cf. CWJC2* p.340.
9. See also *Psalms* 61:3, 144:1.
10. See note 17.
11. See note 2.
12. *E.g. 1 Enoch.*
14. *E.g. 3 Baruch, 2 and 3 Enoch,* the *Zohar* and various other Kabbalistic works, all speak of a hierarchy of heavenly realms.
15. *E.g. Ascension of Isaiah,* and throughout the Nag Hammadi library and other gnostic texts.
16. *Song of Songs* 3:9, 4:8, 11, 15, 5:15, 7:5, pp.72, 112–13, 158–60, 171–73, 176–77, 201, 204, 229–30.
17. "Come from Lebanon," as the *JB* has it, has been the cause of some debate among translators and commentators. It may be better translated as "come away to Lebanon" or "come away with me to", as it has been rendered here. "Come from Lebanon" has probably become an accepted reading since the children of Israel would have come *from* Lebanon on their return *to* Israel from Babylon, a meaning only to be preferred if the *Song of Songs* is to be taken as a poem concerning the traditionally believed relationship between Yahweh and Israel. This rendering receives some support from the Hebrew. The *JPS* translates the line as "come with me from", the meaning being one of 'going with' rather than being 'beckoned from'.
18. *Deuteronomy* 3:9; *cf. Deuteronomy* 4:48.

19. See *The Gospel of Jesus, GJ* index: beasts, wild or savage; enemies; robbers or thieves.

20. See also *Joseph and Aseneth,* in *DR* pp.118–22.

21. There is a quality about this passage which suggests that it may originally have been a response of the Lover to the Beloved. However, we will treat it as the dialogue has traditionally been assigned, as an expression of the Beloved's love for the Lover. There are a number of other passages to which the same observation applies.

22. *Psalms* 34:9.

23. St Francis de Sales, *Love of God* 6:7, *LG* p.237.

24. Gregory is using the Greek *Septuagint,* which here reads, "the smell of your garments as the smell of frankincense."

25. The Hebrew actually reads, "a closed spring *(gal),* a sealed fountain", rather than "a garden *(gan)* enclosed, a sealed fountain". Some scholars emend the Hebrew, as here. Either way, the meaning is the same.

26. *Acts* 9:15.

27. *Proverbs* 12:23, *LXX.*

28. See note 3.

29. Literally, 'a fountain of gardens', a poetic expression.

30. The Persian *pardes* is linked to the Persian *pairidaiza,* and the earlier Avestan *pairidaeza,* meaning 'a walled area', 'an enclosed area'. The English 'paradise' is derived from the Persian through the Greek *paradeisos,* also meaning 'paradise'.

31. "Nard" is spikenard, an aromatic plant with a root yielding an aromatic oil or ointment. "Saffron", used as a condiment, is obtained from the Palestinian crocus, the word meaning 'yellow' in Arabic. "Calamus" is sweet flag, a plant with a reedlike stem and an aromatic root, imported into ancient Palestine from India. "Cinnamon", a well-known spice, comes from the aromatic bark of several related species of tree.

32. See *The Gospel of Jesus, GJ* index: Living Waters.

33. *I.e.* "with the sons of men". See *Proverbs* 8:31, p.15.

Fourth Poem – I Sleep, but my Heart is Awake

1. See note 11.

2. The original translation refers to the soul as "it". To fit the present context, this has been changed to "she" and "her".

3. *Cf. Judges* 6:38.

4. Translation from an unpublished lecture by Rabbi Jerry Steinberg, in *HN* p.115.

5. See pp.128–29.
6. In the original translation, 'Obadayah Maimonides refers to the soul as masculine ("he", "his"). These have been changed to fit the present context ("she", "her"). The archaic English of the translation has also been modernized.
7. *Matthew* 7:7. See *The Gospel of Jesus, GJ* index: door (to inner realms), knocking at.
8. *Zohar Hadash, Lekh Lekha* 24c, *WZ3* p.1523.
9. *The Song of Songs and Lamentations, SSL* pp.63, 91.
10. See pp.143–44.
11. Another of the obscure phrases. Variant renderings include, "fitly set" *(JPS* and *KJV)*, "perching on a fountain rim" *(NJB)*, and "mounted like jewels" *(NIV)*.
12. See *1 Kings* 6:20–35.
13. See *1 Kings* 6:20–35.
14. See *1 Kings* 6:29–35.
15. *1 Kings* 10:22.
16. See note 2.
17. See note 2.

Fifth Poem – I Went Down to the Nut Orchard

1. *Lamentations* 2:15.
2. A common expression, especially in Christianity. See also *Hebrews* 12:22, *Galatians* 4:26.
3. See pp.163–65.
4. Another of the difficult phrases in the *Song*, where variant interpretations and renderings abound. As it stands, the Hebrew is more or less incomprehensible. Variant emendations and translations include, "You have placed me in the chariots of Amminadab," and "You have made me fearful, O nobleman's daughter." See *The Song of Songs and Lamentations, SSL* p.95.
5. *Philippians* 4:7; *cf. KJV.*
6. Obscurity surrounding the meaning of the term "Shulamite" has given rise to various interpretations. Rabbi Abraham ben Isaac ha-Levi says that the term refers to her perfection (Hebrew, *shelemut*). See *Commentary on the Song of Songs* VII:1, *RAIL* p.161.
7. *Song of Songs* 1:9, 2:14, 4:12, 2:2, pp.105–6, 130–35, 174–76, 114-15).
8. *Exodus* 16:14–15, 31. See also, *e.g. Book of Revelation* 2:7 (in *GJ* p.414); *John* 6:32–35, 47–51 (in *GJ* p.248); *Nehemiah* 9:15; *Psalms* 105:40. See also *The Gospel of Jesus, GJ* index: manna; Bread.

9. *Cf. Exodus* 14:15.
10. *E.g. Odes of Solomon* 4:10, 8:16, 14:2, 19:1–6, in *e.g. OSD* pp.20, 40, 64, 86–89; Clement of Alexandria, *Instructor* I:6, in *e.g. WCA1* pp.143–44, 142.
11. Rabbi Abraham ben Isaac ha-Levi, *Commentary on the Song of Songs* VII:5, *RAIL* p.169.
12. Rashi (*c.*1040–1105, French and Jewish, Bible and Talmud commentator), in *FM* p.26 (n.5).
13. Another difficult verse. Other renderings suggest "stirring" or "moving" the "lips of those that are asleep" (*JPS*), or "causing the lips of the sleepers to speak" (Rabbi Abraham ben Isaac ha-Levi, *Commentary on the Song of Songs* VII:10, *RAIL* p.175). The interpretation, however, remains the same.
14. Jami was a Sufi – but the primary source reference to this quote has proved elusive!
15. The mandrake *(Mandragora officinarum)* is a Eurasian plant with purplish flowers and a forked root from which a narcotic was once prepared; a member of the same family as the potato, tobacco, henbane and several of the nightshades.

Finale – Who is this Coming Up from the Desert?

1. *Cf. Genesis* 38:18, 41:42; *Jeremiah* 22:24; *Proverbs* 3:3.
2. See *The Gospel of Jesus, GJ* index: seal.

ABBREVIATIONS

The following abbreviations have been used (see *Bibliography* for full details). The use of cf. in the reference to a quotation indicates that the rendering is based on the reference given. This may entail minor editing, a collation of two or more sources or, more usually, simply the modernization of archaic English.

AAA	*Apocryphal Acts of the Apostles,* W.R. Wright
AB	*Archaeology and the Bible,* George A. Barton
ANT	*The Apocryphal New Testament,* M.R. James
BC	*The Books of Jeu and the Untitled Text in the Bruce Codex,* tr. V. MacDermot
BCB	*Breviarium Chaldaicum,* 3 vols., P. Bedjan
BHBD	*The Book of the Dove,* with some chapters from the *Ethikon,* Bar Hebraeus, tr. A.J. Wensinck
BPS	*The Book of the Poor in Spirit,* A Friend of God, ed. and tr. C.F. Kelley
CAG	"Coptic Apocryphal Gospels", tr. F. Robinson
CDSS	*The Complete Dead Sea Scrolls in English,* tr. G. Vermes
CH	*Clementine Homilies,* tr. T. Smith *et al.*
CPM	*The Canonical Prayerbook of the Mandaeans,* tr. E.S. Drower
CWJC1–3	*Complete Works of St John of the Cross,* 3 vols., tr. E.A. Peers
DR	*The Divine Romance: Tales of an Unearthly Love,* John Davidson
DSZ	*The Divine Songs of Zarathustra,* I.J.S. Taraporewala
FL	*The Fire of Love,* Richard Rolle, tr. C. Wolters
FM	*The Five Megilloth: Hebrew Text, English Translation (JPS) and Commentary,* Rabbi Dr S.M. Lehrman, ed. A. Cohen
GGGN	*From Glory to Glory: Texts From Gregory of Nyssa's Mystical Writings,* tr. and ed. H. Musurillo

GIP   *The Graces of Interior Prayer,* A. Poulain, tr. L.L.Y. Smith
GJ   *The Gospel of Jesus: In Search of His Original Teachings,* John
           Davidson
GMU   "Geburt und Entsendung des manichäischen Urmenschen",
           W.B. Henning
GP1–2   *The Guide of the Perplexed,* 2 vols., Moses Maimonides, tr.
           Shlomo Pines
GS   *The Gnostic Scriptures,* B. Layton
GSR   *Gnosis on the Silk Road: Gnostic Texts from Central Asia,*
           H.-J. Klimkeit
HEDA   *The Hymns and Homilies of Ephraim the Syrian and the
           Demonstrations of Aphrahat the Persian Sage,* tr. J. Gwynn
HN   *The Holy Name: Mysticism in Judaism,* Miriam Caravella
HWP1–2   *The High Ways to Perfection of Abraham Maimonides,*
           2 vols., Abraham Maimonides, tr. S. Rosenblatt
IADS1–2   *Isaaci Antiochi, Doctoris Syrorum: Opera Omnia,* 2 vols.,
           G.S. Bickell
IAHS   "Classical and Arabic Material in ibn 'Aknin's Hygiene of
           the Soul", A.S. Halkin
IDL   *Introduction to the Devout Life,* St Francis de Sales, tr.
           Michael Day
J1–10   *Josephus,* 10 vols., tr. H.StJ. Thackeray *et al.*
JB   *Jerusalem Bible* (1966)
JPS   *The Holy Scriptures,* 2 vols., Jewish Publications Society
           (1955)
JR   *John of Ruysbroeck: The Adornment of the Spiritual Marriage,
           The Sparkling Stone, The Book of Supreme Truth,* tr. C.A.
           Wynschenk, ed. Evelyn Underhill
KJV   *Authorized King James Version*
KRPH   *The Kabbalah or the Religious Philosophy of the Hebrews,*
           Adolphe Franck, tr. I. Sussnitz
LG   *The Love of God: A Treatise by Saint Francis de Sales,* tr.
           Vincent Kerns
LLSS   *A Study of the Language of Love in the Song of Songs and
           Ancient Egyptian Poetry,* J.B. White
LP   *The Ladder of Perfection,* Walter Hilton, tr. L. Sherley-Price
LSMH   "Lower (Second?) Section of the Manichaean Hymns", tr.
           Tsui Chi
LXX   *Septuagint* (C3rd BC Greek translation of the Bible)
MEM   "Mesopotamian Elements in Manichaeism", G. Widengren
MEST1–3   *Meister Eckhart: Sermons and Treatises,* 3 vols., tr. and ed.
           M.O.C. Walshe

MHCP	*The Manichaean Hymn-Cycles in Parthian*, M. Boyce
ML	*Manichaean Literature*, J.P. Asmussen
MM1–3	*Mitteriranische Manichaica aus Chinesisch-Turkestan*, 3 vols., F.C. Andreas and W.B. Henning
MPB	*A Manichaean Psalm-Book*, Part II, ed. & tr. C.R.C. Allberry
NHS11	*Nag Hammadi Studies* XI: *Nag Hammadi Codices V,2–5 and VI*, ed. Douglas M. Parrot
NHS20	*Nag Hammadi Studies* XX: *Nag Hammadi Codex II,2–7*, vol. 1, ed. Bentley Layton
NHS21	*Nag Hammadi Studies* XXI: *Nag Hammadi Codex II,2–7*, vol. 2, ed. Bentley Layton
NHS30	*Nag Hammadi Studies* XXX: *Nag Hammadi Codex VII, XIII*, ed. Birger A. Pearson
NIV	*The New International Version* (1973)
NJB	*New Jerusalem Bible* (1985)
NR1–2	*The Nestorians and Their Rituals*, 2 vols., G.P. Badger
OCB	*The Oxford Companion to the Bible*, ed. B.M. Metzger and M.D. Coogan
OPJG	*The Origin of the Prologue to St John's Gospel*, J.R. Harris
OSD	*The Odes of Solomon: Mystical Songs from the Time of Jesus*, John Davidson
OSS	*Origen: The Song of Songs, Commentary and Homilies*, tr. R.P. Lawson
P1–4	*The Philokalia*, 4 vols., tr. and ed. G.E.H. Palmer, P. Sherrard, Kallistos Ware
PCW1–10	*Philo*, 10 vols., tr. F.H. Colson and G.H. Whitaker
PH500	*Papyrus Harris* 500
PS	*Pistis Sophia*, tr. V. MacDermot
PSGG	*Pistis Sophia: A Gnostic Gospel*, G.R.S. Mead
PSW	*The Prodigal Soul: The Wisdom of Ancient Parables*, John Davidson
RAIL	*Rabbi Abraham ben Isaac ha-Levi Tamakh: Commentary on the Song of Songs*, L.A. Feldman
RMP	*A Reader in Manichaean Middle Persian and Parthian*, M. Boyce
SPZ	*Syrische Poesian*, P.P. Zingerle
SSFC	"The Song of Songs and the Fertility Cult", T.J. Meek
SSHS	*The Song of Songs: Translated from the Original Hebrew with an Introduction and Explanation*, H.J. Schonfield
SSL	*The Song of Songs and Lamentations: A Study, Modern Translation and Commentary*, Robert Gordis
TGH1–3	*Thrice-Greatest Hermes*, 3 vols., G.R.S. Mead

TM	*The Mishnah,* tr. H. Danby
TMT1–6	*A Treasury of Mystic Terms,* Part I, 6 vols., ed. John Davidson
TP	*The Treatise of the Pool,* 'Obadayah Maimonides, tr. Paul Fenton
TTQ	*The Thousand and Twelve Questions (Alf Trisar Shuialia),* tr. E.S. Drower
VME1–2	*Vida (Life) and Other Works,* 2 vols., Marina de Escobar
WBC1–4	*The Works of Bernard of Clairvaux, On the Song of Songs,* 4 vols., tr. K. Walsh and I.M. Edmonds
WCA1–2	*The Writings of Clement of Alexandria,* 2 vols., tr. W. Wilson
WFA	*The Writings of St Francis of Assisi,* Constance, Countess de la Warr
WZ1–3	*The Wisdom of the Zohar,* 3 vols., D. Goldstein, F.Lachower and Isaiah Tishby
ZBS	*The Zohar: Book of Splendour,* Gershom Scholem

BIBLIOGRAPHY

All texts referenced in the present book are listed, plus a few others of general interest. Subsections include both primary sources as well as studies, commentaries and so on. Editions referenced in the text are the ones listed below. Dates of first publication have been added in square brackets where significant. Books and articles are listed by their title, rather than by author or translator – in a selection such as this, it makes them easier to find. For a more complete bibliography, see *The Gospel of Jesus* (John Davidson, 1995, rev. edn. 2004).

Bibles

The Authorized King James Version [1611]; Oxford University Press, Oxford.

The Holy Scriptures, 2 vols.; Jewish Publication Society, Philadelphia, 1955.

The Jerusalem Bible; Darton, Longman and Todd, London, 1966.

The New English Bible; Oxford University Press, Oxford, 1961.

The New International Version; Hodder and Stoughton, London, 1973.

The New Jerusalem Bible; Darton, Longman and Todd, London, 1985.

The Revised Standard Version; Cambridge University Press, Cambridge, 1952.

Tanakh: The Holy Scriptures, The New Jewish Publication Society translation; Jewish Publication, Philadelphia, 1988.

Christianity (Apocryphal Literature)

The Apocryphal Acts of the Apostles, tr. W.R. Wright; Williams and Norgate, Edinburgh, 1871.

The Apocryphal New Testament, tr. M.R. James; Oxford University Press, Oxford, 1989 [1924].

The Apocryphal New Testament: A Collection of Apocryphal Christian Literature in an English Translation based on M.R. James, ed. J.K. Elliott; Oxford University Press, Oxford, 1993.

The Apocryphal Old Testament, ed. H.E.D. Sparks; Oxford University Press, Oxford, 1985.

The Clementine Homilies, tr. T. Smith *et al.;* T. & T. Clark, Edinburgh, 1870.

The Clementine Recognitions, tr. T. Smith; T. & T. Clark, Edinburgh, 1867.

"Coptic Apocryphal Gospels", tr. F. Robinson; in *Texts and Studies* IV, No. 2 (1896), Cambridge University Press, Cambridge.

New Testament Apocrypha, 2 vols., E. Hennecke, ed. W. Schneemelcher, tr. R.McL. Wilson; Westminster, Philadelphia, Pennsylvania, 1963–64.

The Odes and Psalms of Solomon, 2 vols., J.R. Harris and A. Mingana; Longmans, Green and Company, London, 1920.

The Odes of Solomon, tr. J.H. Bernard; Cambridge University Press, Cambridge, 1912.

The Odes of Solomon, tr. J.H. Charlesworth; Oxford University Press, Oxford, 1973.

"The Odes of Solomon", tr. J.A. Emerton, in *The Apocryphal Old Testament,* ed. H.E.D. Sparks; Oxford University Press, Oxford, 1985.

The Odes of Solomon: Mystical Songs from the Time of Jesus, John Davidson; Clear Books, 2004.

Christian Mysticism

The Ascent of Mount Carmel, St John of the Cross, tr. D. Lewis, ed. B. Zimmerman; Thomas Baker, London, 1906.

The Book of the Dove, together with some chapters from his Ethikon, Bar Hebraeus, tr. A.J. Wensinck; E.J. Brill, Leiden, 1919.

The Book of the Poor in Spirit, A Friend of God, ed. and tr. C.F. Kelley; Longmans, Green and Co., London, 1954.

The Book of Saint Bernard on the Love of God, ed. and tr. E.G. Gardner; J.M. Dent, London, 1916.

The Collected Works of St John of the Cross, tr. K. Kavanaugh and O. Rodriguez; Thomas Nelson, London, 1966.

The Complete Works of Dionysius the Areopagite, tr. John Parker; James Parker, London, 1897.

Complete Works of St John of the Cross, 2 vols., tr. D. Lewis; London, 1864–1906.

Complete Works of St John of the Cross, 3 vols., tr. E.A. Peers; Burns and Oates, London, 1964 (three vols. in one edn.) [1935, 1953].

The Complete Works of St Teresa of Jesus, tr. E.A. Peers; Sheed and Ward, London, 1946.

The Fire of Love, Richard Rolle, tr. C. Wolters; Penguin, London, 1982 [1972].

The Fire of Love and the Mending of Life or the Rule of Living, Richard Rolle, tr. R. Misyn, ed. R. Harvey; Kegan Paul, Trench, Trübner, London, 1896 [1434–1435].

From Glory to Glory: Texts From Gregory of Nyssa's Mystical Writings, tr. and ed. H. Musurillo; John Murray, London, 1962.

The Graces of Interior Prayer, A. Poulain, tr. L.L.Y. Smith; Routledge and Kegan Paul, London, 1950.

Introduction to the Devout Life, St Francis de Sales, tr. Michael Day; Burns and Oates, London, 1961 [1956].

John of Ruysbroeck: The Adornment of the Spiritual Marriage, The Sparkling Stone, The Book of Supreme Truth, John of Ruysbroeck, tr. C.A. Wynschenk, ed. Evelyn Underhill; J.M. Watkins, London, 1951.

The Ladder of Perfection, Walter Hilton, tr. L. Sherley-Price; Penguin, London, 1988.

The Love of God: A Treatise by Saint Francis de Sales, tr. Vincent Kerns; Burns and Oates, London, 1962.

Meister Eckhart: Sermons and Treatises, 3 vols., tr. and ed. M.O.C. Walshe; Element, Shaftesbury, UK, 1987 [1979].

Mysticism: A Study in the Nature and Development of Man's Spiritual Consciousness, E. Underhill; Methuen, London, 1948 [1911].

The Philokalia, 4 vols., tr. and ed. G.E.H. Palmer, P. Sherrard, Kallistos Ware; Faber and Faber, London, 1979–1995.

The Seven Steps of the Ladder of Spiritual Love, The Blessed Jan van Ruysbroeck, tr. F.S. Taylor; S.J., Dacre Press, London, 1944.

The Spiritual Espousals, Blessed Jan van Ruysbroeck, tr. E. Colledge; Faber and Faber, London, 1952.

Vida (Life) and Other Works, 2 vols., Marina de Escobar; compiled from her writings, Madrid, 1665–1673.

The Writings of St Francis of Assisi, Constance, Countess de la Warr; Burns and Oates, London, 1907.

Christianity (Miscellaneous)

Breviaricum Chaldaicum, 3 vols., P. Bedjan; Leipzig, 1886–87.

The Hymns and Homilies of Ephraim the Syrian and the Demonstrations of Aphrahat the Persian Sage, tr. J. Gwynn; James Parker, Oxford, 1898.

Isaaci Antiochi, Doctoris Syrorum: Opera Omnia, 2 vols., G.S. Bickell; Glessae, 1873, 1877.

The Gospel of Jesus: In Search of His Original Teachings, rev. edn. John Davidson; Science of the Soul Research Centre, New Delhi, and Clear Books, Bath, UK, 2004 [1995].

Light on Saint John, Maharaj Charan Singh; Radha Soami Satsang Beas, Punjab, India, 1985.

Light on Saint Matthew, Maharaj Charan Singh; Radha Soami Satsang Beas, Punjab, India, 1978.

The Nestorians and Their Rituals, 2 vols., G.P. Badger; Joseph Masters, London, 1852.

The Origin of the Prologue to St John's Gospel, J.R. Harris; Cambridge University Press, Cambridge, 1917.

The Oxford Companion to the Bible, ed. B.M. Metzger and M.D. Coogan; Oxford University Press, Oxford, 1993.

The Oxford Dictionary of the Christian Church, rev. edn. F.L. Cross and E.A. Livingstone; Oxford University Press, Oxford, 1983.

The Writings of Clement of Alexandria, 2 vols., tr. W. Wilson; T. & T. Clark, Edinburgh, 1867, 1869.

Gnosticism

The Books of Jeu and the Untitled Text in the Bruce Codex, tr. V. MacDermot; E.J. Brill, Leiden, 1978.

The Divine Romance: Tales of an Unearthly Love, John Davidson; Clear Books, Bath, 2004.

Fragments of a Faith Forgotten, G.R.S. Mead; Health Research, Mokelumne Hill, California, 1976 [1906].

The Gnostic Gospels, E. Pagels; Random House, New York, 1979.

The Gnostic Scriptures, B. Layton; SCM, London, 1987.

The Nag Hammadi Library in English, ed. J.M. Robinson; E.J. Brill, Leiden, 1988.

Nag Hammadi Studies XI: *Nag Hammadi Codices V,2–5 and VI,* ed. Douglas M. Parrott; E.J. Brill, Leiden, 1979.

Nag Hammadi Studies XX: *Nag Hammadi Codex II,2–7,* vol. 1, ed. Bentley Layton; E.J. Brill, Leiden, 1989.

Nag Hammadi Studies XXI: *Nag Hammadi Codex II,2–7,* vol. 2, ed. Bentley Layton; E.J. Brill, Leiden, 1989.

Nag Hammadi Studies XXX: *Nag Hammadi Codex VII, XIII,* ed. Birger A. Pearson; E.J. Brill, Leiden, 1996.

Pistis Sophia, tr. G. Horner; SPCK, London, 1924.

Pistis Sophia, tr. V. MacDermot; E.J. Brill, Leiden, 1978.

Pistis Sophia: A Gnostic Gospel, G.R.S. Mead; Garber Communications, New York, 1984 [1921].

The Prodigal Soul: The Wisdom of Ancient Parables, John Davidson; Clear Books, Bath, 2004.

Refutation of All Heresies, Hippolytus, tr. S.D.F. Salmond; T. & T. Clark, Edinburgh, 1868.

The Robe of Glory: An Ancient Parable of the Soul, John Davidson; Element, Shaftesbury, UK, 1992.

The Teachings of Silvanus, J. Zandee; Nederlands Instituut voor het Nabije Oosten, Leiden, 1991.

Judaism

"Abraham Maimonides and his Pietist Circle", S.D. Goitein; in *Jewish Medieval and Renaissance Studies,* ed. A.Altmann, Harvard University Press, Cambridge, Massachusetts, 1967.

"The Arabic Portion of the Cairo Genizah", I. Goldziher; in *Jewish Quarterly Review* XV (1903), Macmillan, London.

"Classical and Arabic Material in ibn Aknin's Hygiene of the Soul", A.S. Halkin; in *Proceedings of the American Academy for Jewish Research* XIV (1944), Jewish Publication Society, New York.

The Complete Dead Sea Scrolls in English, tr. G. Vermes; Penguin, London, 1998.

The Guide for the Perplexed (Dalalat al-ha'irin), 3 vols., Moses Maimonides, ed. and tr. Y. Qafih; Jerusalem, 1972.

The Guide of the Perplexed, 2 vols., Moses Maimonides, tr. Shlomo Pines; University of Chicago Press, Chicago, 1963.

The High Ways to Perfection of Abraham Maimonides, 2 vols., Abraham Maimonides, tr. S. Rosenblatt; Columbia University Press; New York, Jerusalem [New York, Baltimore], 1966, 1970 [1927, 1938].

The Holy Name: Mysticism in Judaism, M.B. Caravella; Radha Soami Satsang Beas, Dera Baba Jaimal Singh, Punjab, 2000.

The Jewish War, Josephus, tr. G.A. Williamson, rev. E.M. Smallwood; Penguin, London, 1981.

Josephus, 10 vols., tr. H.StJ. Thackeray *et al.;* William Heinemann, London, 1966–81 [1926–65].

Josephus: His Complete Works, tr. W. Whiston; Pickering and Inglis, London, 1963 [1867].

The Kabbalah or the Religious Philosophy of the Hebrews, Adolphe Franck, tr. I. Sussnitz; University Books, New York, 1967.

Major Trends in Jewish Mysticism, Gershom Scholem; Schocken Books, New York, 1946.

The Mishnah, tr. H. Danby; Oxford University Press, Oxford, 1992 [1933].

"The Mystical Doctrine of Rabbi 'Obadyah, Grandson of Moses Maimonides", G. Vajda; in *Journal of Jewish Studies* VI (1955), London.

The Old Testament Pseudoepigrapha, 2 vols., ed. J.H. Charlesworth; Darton, Longman and Todd, London, 1983.

Philo, 10 vols., tr. F.H. Colson and G.H. Whitaker; William Heinemann, London, 1941.

"Some Judaeo-Arabic Fragments of Rabbi Abraham he-Hasid, the Jewish Sufi", P. Fenton; in *Journal of Jewish Studies* XXVI (1981) London.

The Treatise of the Pool, 'Obadyah Maimonides, tr. P. Fenton; Octagon, London, 1981.

Who Wrote the Bible? R.E. Friedman; Jonathan Cape, London, 1988.

The Wisdom of the Zohar, 3 vols., D. Goldstein, F. Lachower and Isaiah Tishby; Oxford University Press, Oxford, 1989.

The Works of Philo Judaeus, 4 vols., tr. C.D. Yonge; H.G. Bohn, London, 1855.

The Zohar, 5 vols., tr. M. Simon and H. Spelling; Soncino Press; London, 1934.

The Zohar: The Book of Splendour, sel. and ed. Gershom Scholem; Rider, 1977 [1949].

Mandaeanism

The Canonical Prayerbook of the Mandaeans, tr. E.S. Drower; E.J. Brill, Leiden, 1959.

The Mandaeans of Iran and Iraq, E.S. Drower; Oxford University Press, Oxford, 1937.

The Secret Adam, E.S. Drower; Oxford University Press, Oxford, 1960.

The Thousand and Twelve Questions (Alf Trisar Shuialia), tr. E.S. Drower; Akademie-Verlag, Berlin, 1960.

Manichaeism

"Geburt und Entsendung des manichäischen Urmenschen", W.B. Henning; in *Nachrichten von der Gesellschaft der Wissenschaften zu Göttingen,* 1933, p.306ff.

Gnosis on the Silk Road: Gnostic Texts from Central Asia, H.-J. Klimkeit; Harper, San Francisco, 1993.

"Lower (Second?) Section of the Manichaean Hymns", tr. Tsui Chi; in *Bulletin of the School of Oriental and African Studies* XI (1943–46), University of London.

The Manichaean Hymn-Cycles in Parthian, tr. M. Boyce; Oxford University Press, London, 1954.

Manichaean Literature, J.P. Asmussen; Scholars' Facsimiles and Reprints, Delmar, New York, 1975.

A Manichaean Psalm-Book, Part II, ed. & tr. C.R.C. Allberry; Kohlhammer, Stuttgart, 1938.

"Mesopotamian Elements in Manichaeism", G. Widengren; in *Uppsala Universitets Arsskrift* 3 (1946), University of Uppsala, Uppsala, Sweden.

"Mitteriranische Manichaica aus Chinesisch-Turkestan", 3 vols., F.C. Andreas and W.B. Henning; in *Sitzungsberichte der Königlich Preussischen Akademie der Wissenschaften,* (1932, 1933, 1934), Berlin.

A Reader in Manichaean Middle Persian and Parthian, M. Boyce; E.J. Brill, Leiden, 1975.

"Syrische Poesian", P.P. Zingerle; in *Zeitschrift der Deutschen Morgenländischen Gesellschaft* 17 (1863).

Miscellaneous

Ancient Near Eastern Texts Relating to the Old Testament, ed. J.B. Pritchard; Princeton University Press, Princeton, New Jersey, 1969.

Archaeology and the Bible, George A. Barton; American Sunday School Union, Philadelphia, 1937 [1916].

"Babylonian and Hebrew Musical Terms", S. Langdon; in *Journal of the Royal Asiatic Society* (1921), London.

The Divine Songs of Zarathustra, I.J.S. Taraporewala; Hukhta Foundation, Bombay, 1993 [1951].

The Literature of the Ancient Egyptians, A. Erman, tr. A.M. Blackman; Methuen, London, 1927.

The Path of the Masters, Dr Julian Johnson; Radha Soami Satsang Beas, Punjab, India, 1993 [1939].

Thrice-Greatest Hermes, 3 vols., G.R.S. Mead; Theosophical Publishing Society, London, 1906.

A Treasury of Mystic Terms, Part I, 6 vols., ed. John Davidson; Science of the Soul Research Centre, New Delhi, 2003.

The Song of Songs (Studies, Commentaries, Translations)

"Babylonian Parallels to the Song of Songs", T.J. Meek; in *Journal of Biblical Literature* 43 (1924), Society of Biblical Literature, Boston.

The Books of Ruth, Esther, Ecclesiastes, The Song of Songs, Lamentations, W.J. Fürst; Cambridge University Press, Cambridge, 1975.

"The Canticle of Canticles in Mystical Theology", P.P. Parente; in *Catholic Biblical Quarterly* 6 (1944), pp.142–58, Catholic Biblical Quarterly, Washington D.C.

"Canticles and the Tammuz Cult", T.J. Meek; in *American Journal of Semitic Languages* 39 (1922), University of Chicago Press, Chicago.

The Commentary of Rabbi Solomon ben Isaac (Rashi) on the Song of Songs, ed. J.M. Rosenthal; New York, 1958.

Commentary on Song of Songs, Levi ben Gershom (Gersonides), tr. from Hebrew with an introduction and annotations, Menachem Kellner; Yale University Press, New Haven, 1998.

Commentary on the Canticles, Abraham ibn Ezra, ed. H.J. Matthews; Trübner, London, 1874.

A Commentary on the Song of Solomon, G. Burrowes; Banner of Truth Trust, London, 1973 [1853].

Commentary on the Song of Songs, Abraham ibn Ezra, ed. Mikraoth Gedoloth; Warsaw, 1874.

"The Commentary on the Song of Songs", Nahmanides, ed. C.B. Chavel; in *The Writings of Rabbi Moshe ben Nahman,* Jerusalem, 1964.

Commentary on the Song of Songs, Saadia, ed. J. Kapah; in *Hamesh Megilloth,* Jerusalem, 1961.

"The Commentary on the Song of Songs", Saadia, ed. S.A. Wertheimer; in *Sefer Geon ha-Geonim,* 1925.

Ecclesiastes and the Song of Solomon, Robert Davidson; Westminster John Knox Press, Philadelphia, 1986.

Ecclesiastes, Song of Songs, Iain Provan; Zondervan, Grand Rapids, Michigan, 2001.

The Embrace of the Soul: Reflections on the Song of Songs, Charles Rich, ed., with an introduction by Rhonda Chervin; St Bede's Publications, Still River, Massachusetts, 1984.

"En Marge du Commentaire sur la Cantique des Cantiques de Joseph ibn Aqnin'", G. Vajda; in *Revue des Etudes Juivres* IV (1965), Paris.

Esther, Song of Songs, Lamentations, G.A.F. Knight; SCM, London, 1955.

The Ethiopic Version of the Song of Songs, ed. H.C. Gleave; Taylor's Foreign Press, London, 1951.

Exquisite Desire: Religion, the Erotic, and the Song of Songs, Carey Ellen Walsh; Fortress Press, Minneapolis, 2000.

The Five Megilloth: Hebrew Text and English Translation, with Introduction and Commentary, ed. A. Cohen, revised and expanded by A.J. Rosenberg; Soncino, London, 1984.

The Five Megilloth and Jonah: A New Translation, H.L. Ginsberg; Jewish Publication Society of America, Philadelphia, 1969.

The Five Megilloth: Hebrew Text, English Translation (JPS) and Commentary, Rabbi Dr S.M. Lehrman, ed. A. Cohen; Soncino Press, Hindhead, UK, 1946.

The Genesis of Secrecy: On the Interpretation of Narrative, F. Kermode; Harvard University Press, Cambridge, Massachusetts, 1979.

The Great Code: The Bible and Literature, N. Frye; Harcourt Brace Jovanovich, New York, 1982.

A Handbook on Song of Songs, Graham S. Ogden and Lynell Zogbo; United Bible Societies, New York, 1998.

"Ibn 'Aknin's Commentary on the Song of Songs", A.S. Halkin; in *Alexander Marx Jubilee Volume,* Jewish Theological Seminary of America, New York, 1950.

"The Interpretation of the Song of Songs", in *The Servant of the Lord and other Essays on the Old Testament,* H.H. Rowley; Blackwell, Oxford, 1965.

Le Commentaire d'Ezra de Gérone sur la Cantique des Cantiques, tr. G.Vajda; Aubier Montagne, Paris, 1969.

Love and Politics: A New Commentary on the Song of Songs, Luis I.J. Stadelmann; Paulist Press, New York, 1992.

Love Lyrics from the Bible: A Translation and Literary Study of the Song of Songs, Marcia Falk; Almond Press, Sheffield, 1982.

The Message of the Song of Songs: The Lyrics of Love, Tom Gledhill; Inter-Varsity Press, 1994.

Midrash Zuta (on the *Song of Songs, Ruth, Lamentations* and *Ecclesiastes*), ed. S. Buber; Berlin, 1894.

The New Century Bible Commentary: The Song of Songs, J.G. Snaith; HarperCollins, London, 1993.

Origen: The Song of Songs, Commentary and Homilies, Ancient Christian Writers, no. 26, tr. and annotated R.P. Lawson; Newman Press, Westminster, Maryland / Mahwah, New Jersey, 1957.

"Paradisal Love: Johann Gottfried Herder and the Song of Songs", John D. Baildam, in *Journal for the Study of the Old Testament,* supplement 298, Sheffield Academic Press, Sheffield, 1999.

Paradoxes of Paradise: Identity and Difference in the Song of Songs, F. Landy; Almond Press, Sheffield, 1983.

Proverbs, Ecclesiastes, and the Song of Songs, Ellen F. Davis; Westminster John Knox Press, Louisville, 2000.

Proverbs, Ecclesiastes, Song of Songs, Duane A. Garrett; Broadman Holman, Nashville, 1993.

Rabbi Abraham ben Isaac ha-Levi Tamakh: Commentary on the Song of Songs, L.A. Feldman; van Gorcum, Assen, The Netherlands, 1970.

Revelation of God: A Commentary on the Books of the Song of Songs: G.A.F. Knight; Wm.B Eerdmans, Michigan, 1988.

Romance, She Wrote: A Hermeneutical Essay on Song of Songs, André LaCocque; Trinity Press International, Harrisburg, Pennsylvania, 1998.

Sermons on the Final Verses of the Song of Songs, 7 vols., John of Ford; Cistercian Publications, Michigan, 1977.

Sermons on the Song of Songs, Rev. J.M. Neale; J.T. Hayes, London, 1857.

"The Song of Fourteen Songs", Michael D. Goulder, in *Journal for the Study of the Old Testament,* supplement 36; Sheffield Academic Press, Sheffield, 1986.

The Song of Songs, A. Brenner; Sheffield Academic Press, Sheffield, 1989.

"The Song of Songs and Ancient Tamil Love Poems: Poetry and Symbolism", Abraham Mariaselvam, in *Analecta Biblica* 118; Editrice Pontificio Istituto Biblico, Rome, 1988.

The Song of Songs and Coheleth, C.D. Ginsburg, ed S.H. Blank; KTAV, New York, 1970 [1857, 1861].

The Song of Songs and Lamentations: A Study, Modern Translation and Commentary, rev. edn., Robert Gordis; KTAV, New York, 1974.

The Song of Songs and Other Poems, by S. Fowler Wright; Merton, London, 1925.

"The Song of Songs and Tamil Poetry", C. Rabin; in *Studies in Religion* 3:3 (1973–74), pp.206–19, University of Toronto Press, Toronto.

The Song of Songs and the Ancient Egyptian Love Songs, Michael V. Fox; University of Wisconsin Press, Madison, Wisconsin, 1985.

"The Song of Songs and the Fertility Cult", T.J. Meek; in *The Song of Songs: A Symposium,* ed. W.H. Schoff, Commercial Museum, Philadelphia, 1924.

"The Song of Songs as Wisdom Literature", M. Sadgrove; in *Studia Biblica* I, ed. L.A. Livingstone, Sixth International Congress on Biblical Studies; in *Journal for the Study of the Old Testament,* Academic Press, Sheffield, 1978.

The Song of Songs, Dianne Bergant; Liturgical Press, Collegeville, Minnesota, 2001.

"The Song of Songs" in *The Great Texts of the Bible,* ed. James Hastings; T. & T. Clark, Edinburgh, 1914.

The Song of Songs in the Middle Ages, Ann W. Astell; Cornell University Press, New York, 1990.

The Song of Songs in the Targumic Tradition, Isaac Jerusalmi; Ladino Books, Cincinnati, 1993.

Song of Songs, Lamentations, Duane Garrett and Paul R. House; Thomas Nelson, Nashville, 2004.

The Song of Songs, P. Jay; Anvil Press Poetry, London, 1975.

The Song of Songs, R. van Rossem; Folio Society, London, 1967.

The Song of Songs Rabbah, 2 vols., Jacob Neusner; Scholars Press, Georgia, 1989.

The Song of Songs, Tremper Longman III; William B. Eerdmans, Grand Rapids, Michigan, 2001.

The Song of Songs: Based on the Revised Standard Version, John G. Snaith; William B. Eerdmans, Grand Rapids, Michigan, 1993.

The Song of Songs: A Continental Commentary, Othmar Keel, tr. Frederick J. Gaiser; Fortress Press, Minneapolis, 1994.

The Song of Songs: Interpreted by early Christian and Medieval Commentators, tr. and ed. Richard A. Norris Jr; William B. Eerdmans, Grand Rapids, Michigan, 2003.

The Song of Songs: A New Translation with Introduction and Commentary, Ariel Bloch and Chana Bloch; Random House, New York, 1995.

The Song of Songs: A New Translation with Introduction and Commentary, Marvin H. Pope; Doubleday, Garden City, New York, 1977.

The Song of Songs: A Symposium, M.L. Margolis *et. al.,* ed. W.H. Schoff; Commercial Museum, Philadelphia, 1924.

The Song of Songs: Translated and Interpreted as a Dramatic Poem, L. Waterman; University of Michigan Press, Ann Arbor, 1948.

The Song of Songs: Translated from the Original Hebrew with an Introduction and Explanation, H.J. Schonfield; Elek Books, London, 1960.

"The Song of Songs", F. Landy; in *The Literary Guide to the Bible,* R. Alter and F. Kermode; Harvard University Press, Cambridge, Massachusetts, 1987.

"Spikenard and Saffron: The Imagery of the Song of Songs", Jill M. Munro, in *Journal for the Study of the Old Testament,* supplement 203; Sheffield Academic Press, Sheffield, 1995.

A Study of the Language of Love in the Song of Songs and Ancient Egyptian Poetry, J.B. White; Scholars Press, Montana, 1978.

Targum (Canticles), ed. Mikraoth Gedoloth, Warsaw, 1874.

"Targum (Canticles)", ed. J. Kapah; in *Hamesh Megilloth,* Jerusalem, 1961.

Targum de-Targum: An Old Neo-Aramaic Version of the Targum on Song of Songs, introduction, eclectic text, English tr., comparative notes, and glossary, Yona Sabar; Otto Harrassowitz, Wiesbaden, 1991.

"The Wasfs of the Song of Songs and Hermeneutic", R.N. Soulen; in *Journal of Biblical Literature* 86 (1967), Society of Biblical Literature, Boston.

Word of God, Song of Love: A Commentary on the Song of Songs, R.J. Tournay, tr. J.E. Crowley; Paulist Press, New York, 1988.

The Works of Bernard of Clairvaux, On the Song of Songs, 4 vols., tr. K. Walsh (vols. 1–3) and I.M. Edmonds (vols. 3–4); Irish University Press (vol. 1), Shannon, 1971; Cistercian Publications (vols. 2–4), Kalamazoo, Michigan, 1976, 1979, 1980.

The Works of Gilbert of Hoyland: Sermons on the Song of Songs, 4 vols., tr. L.C. Braceland; Cistercian Publications, Michigan, 1978–81.

The Works of William of St Thierry: Exposition on the Song of Songs, tr. Columba Hart; Irish University Press, Shannon, 1970.

The Zohar on the Song of Songs, Mantua, 1558.